Literary Theory

P9-CDG-320

Literary Theory
An Introduction

Terry Eagleton

With a New Preface

ANNIVERSARY EDITION

University of Minnesota Press
Minneapolis

For
Charles Swann
and
Raymond Williams

Copyright Terry Eagleton 1983, 1996, 2008

First published in this edition in Great Britain by
Blackwell Publishers Ltd.

First published in this edition in the United States in 2008 by
the University of Minnesota Press

All rights reserved. No part of this publication may be reproduced,
stored in a retrieval system, or transmitted, in any form or by any means,
electronic, mechanical, photocopying, recording, or otherwise, without
the prior written permission of the publisher.

Published in the United States by the University of Minnesota Press
111 Third Avenue South, Suite 290
Minneapolis, MN 55401-2520
http://www.upress.umn.edu

Library of Congress Cataloging-in-Publication Data

Eagleton, Terry, 1943–
Literary theory : an introduction / Terry Eagleton. — Anniversary ed.
p.   cm.
With a new preface.
Includes bibliographical references and index.
ISBN 978-0-8166-5447-5 (pb : alk. paper)
1. Criticism—History—20th century.   2. Literature—
History and criticism—Theory, etc.   I. Title.
PN94.E2 2008b
801'.95—dc22

2008006964

Printed in the United States of America on acid-free paper

The University of Minnesota is an equal-opportunity educator and employer.

20 19 18 17 16 15 14 13   10 9 8 7 6 5 4 3

Contents

Preface to the Anniversary Edition

This book is now a quarter of a century old, but if it seems somewhat longer in the tooth than that it is perhaps because so much has happened since it first appeared. One such development is that literary theory no longer occupies the commanding place that it seemed to have twenty-five years ago. When this book was first written, theory, like the latest Jean-Luc Godard movie, was new, foreign, subversive, enigmatic, and exciting. Some students still rightly find it all these things, but, just as the shock of modernist art was eventually absorbed until, as Fredric Jameson once remarked, Joyce's *Ulysses* came to seem really quite a conventional sort of story, so theory is no longer the outlandish affair that it once was. Indeed, as I note in the Afterword to this book, we have witnessed in recent times the growth of a kind of anti-theory—though one that is itself of theoretical interest. In this, it differs from the usual philistine objections to theory, which for the most part reflect more of an animus than an argument.

Has theory, then, become "institutionalized"? The question cannot be answered properly if the word "institutionalized" (a term that carries sinister connotations of syringes and straitjackets) is taken in a purely pejorative sense. That theory is now widely taught in academic institutions is to be commended, not condemned as some sort of squalid capitulation. Things have changed for the better since I taught Marxist theory every week at Oxford in the early 1970s in an informal session which was not even advertised on the university lecture list, which was widely disapproved of by my colleagues, and which operated less like an orthodox seminar than a kind of refuge for ideologically battered students. Most students of literature can now expect a theory course or two to be on offer, a fact that one naturally welcomes.

Yet perhaps this *is* a kind of capitulation, or at least a troubling compromise, since theory was never intended simply to take its place alongside Great Books courses as yet another product to attract the punters in the intellectual marketplace. To see it in this way is to misunderstand the kind of thing that it is. Theory at its best poses questions to these other pursuits, rather than meekly coexisting with them as one option among others. Rather than simply providing new methods for the study of literary works, it asks about the nature and function of literature and the literary institution. Rather than simply supplying us with yet more sophisticated ways of tackling canonical texts, it inquires into the very concept of canonicity. Its aim is not just to help us to see what literary works mean, or how valuable they are; instead, it queries our commonsense notions of what it is to "mean" in the first place, and poses questions about the criteria by which we evaluate literary art. To place a course of theory alongside a course on moon symbolism in D. H. Lawrence is to commit what the philosophers would call a category mistake. It would be like studying Marxism simply as one variant of sociology, rather than grasping the point that Marxism is a critique of the very concept of sociology. Academia, by its very structure, tends to encourage these sorts of conceptual mistakes. Like the marketplace, it juxtaposes sometimes incomparable things.

Properly understood, then, literary theory is a kind of metadiscourse. Rather than figuring as one way of speaking about literature among others, it adopts a critical stance to other forms of critical analysis. In particular, it tends to suspect that much of what is said is question-begging. Critics may ask whether a particular narrative twist is effective, but narratologists want to know what this strange animal called narrative is, and are reluctant to be fobbed off with our intuitive sense that everyone can recognize a story when they see one. If the critic discerns, say, Jungian patterns in a novel, the theorist is keen to know what "novel" actually means. Can it be defined? How does a short novel differ from a long short story? Critics may wrangle over whether Oscar Wilde is a major or minor writer, but theorists prefer to investigate the (often unconscious) norms and criteria by which we make such judgments. All reading involves interpretation, but hermeneutics inquires into what goes on when we interpret. A critic might speak of a literary character's unconscious; a theorist is more likely to ask what a "character" is, and whether the text can have an unconscious, too. What has happened over the past couple of decades is that what one might risk calling "pure" or "high" theory is no longer so much in fashion. There is less talk of semiotics, hermeneutics, poststructuralism, and phenomenology than in the 1970s and 1980s. Even psychoanalytic theory is somewhat less prominent than it used to be, despite its intellectual seductions and allures. Instead, postmodernism and postcolonialism have captured the commanding heights of the subject, along with a weakened yet surviving feminism. This is an interesting evolution, because it signals a shift from the rarefied peaks of pure theory to the troughs and plains of everyday culture. The same might be said of the so-called New Historicism that flourished in the 1980s and 1990s. Feminism, postmodernism, and postcolonialism are all much more than literary phenomena. This is true of "pure" theory as well, very little of which actually had its origin in the literary arena. Phenomenology, hermeneutics, and poststructuralism are philosophical currents; psychoanalysis is a curative practice; semiotics is a science of signs in general, not just literary ones. The New Historicism tried to erase the distinction between literary and nonliterary works, as structuralism had also done in its day. Even so, to speak in the same breath of, say, poststructuralism and postmodernism, or semiotics and postcolonialism, is to commit another category mistake. The first two items of these pairs are bodies of theory, while the second are cultural and political realities. To imagine that they are more or less the same would be like equating Heidegger's philosophy to global warming. This, too, is the kind of error that academia may tempt us to make.

This return to everyday cultural and political life is clearly to be welcomed. Yet there is, as usual, a price to be paid. Pure theory may have its problems, but its very distance from the everyday allows it to act from time to time as a powerful critique of it. There is, in fact, a concealed utopian dimension to much of this thought. Poststructuralism dreams of a time when rigid hierarchies and oppressive polarities will be prised open, to release a play of difference and diversity. Whatever the slippages involved in the act of interpretation, hermeneutics continues to pledge its faith in the possibility of human understanding. Reception theory (with its implicit slogan "More power to the reader!") seeks to liberate the reader from the passive, meekly conformist status he or she has so far been allotted by the critics, seeing readers instead as agents and cocreators. Behind this theoretical current the demands of the 1960s student movement can be dimly sensed.

This is not the case with much postmodernist theory. To be sure, there is a radical wing to it, but for the more complacent forms of postmodernist thought, pluralism, multiculturalism, and a respect for human difference are about as good as it gets. It is hard to see this as an adequate politics in a world where the mightiest capitalist power in history holds the rest of the world to ransom. It is characteristic of Marxism that it refuses a retreat from the social and political into "discourse" while also refusing a cynical or defeatist complicity with social existence as we know it. Other forms of political criticism, such as postcolonialism, can then be assessed according to this standard. Currents of postcolonial thought take for granted the global division of power and resources, and restrict themselves instead to questions of identity and ethnicity. But more promising varieties of postcolonial thought signal the persistence in the present of classical socialist critiques of Western imperialism, however revised such analyses need to be in light of what some optimistically call "late" capitalism.

I hope that the republication of this book on its twenty–fifth anniversary will help recapture the intense excitement theory was able to inspire at the time it was written. If the book's continuing popularity is anything to go by, that tide of excitement has by no means ebbed. I do not know whether to be delighted or outraged by the fact that *Literary Theory: An Introduction* was the subject of a study by a well-known U.S. business school, which was intrigued to discover how an academic text could become a best-seller.

T. E.

Preface

If one wanted to put a date on the beginnings of the transformation which
has overtaken literary theory in this century, one could do worse than settle
on 1917, the year in which the young Russian Formalist Viktor Shklovsky
published his pioneering essay 'Art as Device'. Since then, and especially
over the past two decades, there has been a striking proliferation of literary
theory: the very meaning of 'literature', 'reading' and 'criticism' has undergone deep alteration. But not much of this theoretical revolution has yet
spread beyond a circle of specialists and enthusiasts: it has still to make its
full impact on the student of literature and the general reader.

This book sets out to provide a reasonably comprehensive account of
modern literary theory for those with little or no previous knowledge of the
topic. Though such a project obviously involves omissions and oversim-
plifications, I have tried to popularize, rather than vulgarize, the subject.
Since there is in my opinion no 'neutral', value-free way of presenting it, I
have argued throughout a particular *case*, which I hope adds to the book's
interest.

The economist J. M. Keynes once remarked that those economists who
disliked theory, or claimed to get along better without it, were simply in the
grip of an older theory. This is also true of literary students and critics.
There are some who complain that literary theory is impossibly esoteric –
who suspect it as an arcane, elitist enclave somewhat akin to nuclear physics.
It is true that a 'literary education' does not exactly encourage analytical
thought; but literary theory is in fact no more difficult than many theoretical
enquiries, and a good deal easier than some. I hope the book may help to
demystify those who fear that the subject is beyond their reach. Some

students and critics also protest that literary theory 'gets in between the reader and the work'. The simple response to this is that without some kind of theory, however unreflective and implicit, we would not know what a 'literary work' was in the first place, or how we were to read it. Hostility to theory usually means an opposition to other people's theories and an oblivion of one's own. One purpose of this book is to lift that repression and allow us to remember.

T. E.

Introduction: What is Literature?

If there is such a thing as literary theory, then it would seem obvious that there is something called literature which it is the theory of. We can begin, then, by raising the question: what is literature?

There have been various attempts to define literature. You can define it, for example, as 'imaginative' writing in the sense of fiction – writing which is not literally true. But even the briefest reflection on what people commonly include under the heading of literature suggests that this will not do. Seventeenth-century English literature includes Shakespeare, Webster, Marvell and Milton; but it also stretches to the essays of Francis Bacon, the sermons of John Donne, Bunyan's spiritual autobiography and whatever it was that Sir Thomas Browne wrote. It might even at a pinch be taken to encompass Hobbes's *Leviathan* or Clarendon's *History of the Rebellion*. French seventeenth-century literature contains, along with Corneille and Racine, La Rochefoucauld's maxims, Bossuet's funeral speeches, Boileau's treatise on poetry, Madame de Sévigné's letters to her daughter and the philosophy of Descartes and Pascal. Nineteenth-century English literature usually includes Lamb (though not Bentham), Macaulay (but not Marx), Mill (but not Darwin or Herbert Spencer).

A distinction between 'fact' and 'fiction', then, seems unlikely to get us very far, not least because the distinction itself is often a questionable one. It has been argued, for instance, that out own opposition between 'historical' and 'artistic' truth does not apply at all to the early Icelandic sagas.[1] In the English late sixteenth and early seventeenth centuries, the word 'novel' seems to have been used about both true and fictional events, and even news reports were hardly to be considered factual. Novels and news reports were neither clearly factual nor clearly fictional: our own sharp discriminations between these categories simply did not apply.[2] Gibbon no doubt thought that he was writing the historical truth, and so perhaps did the authors of Genesis, but they are now read as 'fact' by some and 'fiction' by others; Newman certainly thought his theological meditations were true but they are now for many readers 'literature'. Moreover, if 'literature' includes much 'factual' writing, it also excludes quite a lot of fiction. *Superman* comic and Mills and Boon novels are fictional but not generally regarded as literature, and certainly not as Literature. If literature is 'creative' or 'imaginative' writing, does this imply that history, philosophy and natural science are uncreative and unimaginative?

Perhaps one needs a different kind of approach altogether. Perhaps literature is definable not according to whether it is fictional or 'imaginative', but because it uses language in peculiar ways. On this theory, literature is a kind of writing which, in the words of the Russian critic Roman Jakobson, represents an 'organized violence committed on ordinary speech'. Literature transforms and intensifies ordinary language, deviates systematically from everyday speech. If you approach me at a bus stop and murmur 'Thou still unravished bride of quietness,' then I am instantly aware that I am in the presence of the literary. I know this because the texture, rhythm and resonance of your words are in excess of their abstractable meaning – or, as the linguists might more technically put it, there is a disproportion between the signifiers and the signifieds. Your language draws attention to itself, flaunts its material being, as statements like 'Don't you know the drivers are on strike?' do not.

This, in effect, was the definition of the 'literary' advanced by the Russian formalists, who included in their ranks Viktor Shklovsky, Roman Jakobson, Osip Brik, Yury Tynyanov, Boris Eichenbaum and Boris Tomashevsky. The Formalists emerged in Russia in the years before the 1917 Bolshevik revolution, and flourished throughout the 1920s, until they were effectively silenced by Stalinism. A militant, polemical group of critics, they rejected the quasi-mystical symbolist doctrines which had influenced literary criticism before them, and in a practical, scientific spirit shifted attention to the material reality of the literary text itself. Criticism should dissociate art from mystery and concern itself with how literary texts actually worked: literature was not pseudo-religion or psychology or sociology but a particular organization of language. It had its own specific laws, structures and devices, which were to be studied in themselves rather than reduced to something else. The literary work was neither a vehicle for ideas, a reflection of social reality nor the incarnation of some transcendental truth: it was a material fact, whose functioning could be analysed rather as one could examine a machine. It was made of words, not of objects or feelings, and it was a mistake to see it as the expression of an author's mind. Pushkin's *Eugene Onegin*, Osip Brik once airily remarked, would have been written even if Pushkin had not lived.

Formalism was essentially the application of linguistics to the study of literature; and because the linguistics in question were of a formal kind, concerned with the structures of language rather than with what one might actually say, the Formalists passed over the analysis of literary 'content' (where one might always be tempted into psychology or sociology) for the study of literary form. Far from seeing form as the expression of content, they stood the relationship on its head: content was merely the 'motivation' of form, an occasion or convenience for a particular kind of formal exercise. *Don Quixote* is not 'about' the character of that name: the character is just a device for holding together different kinds of narrative technique. *Animal Farm* for the Formalists would not be an allegory of Stalinism; on the contrary, Stalinism would simply provide a useful opportunity for the construction of an allegory. It was this perverse insistence which won for the Formalists their derogatory name from their antagonists; and though they did not deny that art had a relation to social reality – indeed some of them were closely associated with the Bolsheviks – they provocatively claimed that this relation was not the critic's business.

The Formalists started out by seeing the literary work as a more or less arbitrary assemblage of 'devices', and only later came to see these devices as interrelated elements or 'functions' within a total textual system. 'Devices' included sound, imagery, rhythm, syntax, metre, rhyme, narrative techniques, in fact the whole stock of formal literary elements; and what all of these elements had in common was their 'estranging' or 'defamiliarizing' effect. What was specific to literary language, what distinguished it from other forms of discourse, was that it 'deformed' ordinary language in various ways. Under the pressure of literary devices, ordinary language was intensified, condensed, twisted, telescoped, drawn out, turned on its head. It was language 'made strange'; and because of this estrangement, the everyday world was also suddenly made unfamiliar. In the routines of everyday speech, our perceptions of and responses to reality become stale, blunted, or, as the Formalists would say, 'automatized'. Literature, by forcing us into a dramatic awareness of language, refreshes these habitual responses and renders objects more 'perceptible'. By having to grapple with language in a more strenuous, self-conscious way than usual, the world which that language contains is vividly renewed. The poetry of Gerard Manley Hopkins might provide a particularly graphic example of this. Literary discourse estranges or alienates ordinary speech, but in doing so, paradoxically, brings us into a fuller, more intimate possession of experience. Most of the time we breathe in air without being conscious of it: like language, it is the very medium in which we move. But if the air is suddenly thickened or infected we are forced to attend to our breathing with new vigilance, and the effect of this may be a heightened experience of our bodily life. We read a scribbled note from a friend without paying much attention to its narrative structure; but if a story breaks off and begins again, switches constantly from one narrative level to another and delays its climax to keep us in suspense, we become freshly conscious of how it is constructed at the same time as our engagement with it may be intensified. The story, as the Formalists would argue, uses 'impeding' or 'retarding' devices to hold our attention; and in literary language, these devices are 'laid bare'. It was this which moved Viktor Shklovsky to remark mischievously of Laurence Sterne's *Tristram Shandy*, a novel which impedes its own story-line so much that it hardly gets off the ground, that it was 'the most typical novel in world literature'.

The Formalists, then, saw literary language as a set of deviations from a norm, a kind of linguistic violence: literature is a 'special' kind of language, in contrast to the 'ordinary' language we commonly use. But to spot a deviation implies being able to identify the norm from which it swerves. Though 'ordinary language' is a concept beloved of some Oxford philosophers, the ordinary language of Oxford philosophers has little in common with the ordinary language of Glaswegian dockers. The language both social groups use to write love letters usually differs from the way they talk to the local vicar. The idea that there is a single 'normal' language, a common currency shared equally by all members of society, is an illusion. Any actual language consists of a highly complex range of discourses, differentiated according to class, region, gender, status and so on, which can by no means be neatly unified into a single homogeneous linguistic community. One person's norm may be another's deviation: 'ginnel' for 'alleyway' may be poetic in Brighton but ordinary language in Barnsley. Even the most 'prosaic' text of the fifteenth century may sound 'poetic' to us today because of its archaism. If we were to stumble across an isolated scrap of writing from some long-vanished civilization, we could not tell whether it was 'poetry' or not merely by inspecting it, since we might have no access to that society's 'ordinary' discourses; and even if further research were to reveal that it was 'deviatory', this would still not prove that it was poetry as not all linguistic deviations are poetic. Slang, for example. We would not be able to tell just by looking at it that it was not a piece of 'realist' literature, without much more information about the way it actually functioned as a piece of writing within the society in question.

It is not that the Russian Formalists did not realize all this. They recognized that norms and deviations shifted around from one social or historical context to another – that 'poetry' in this sense depends on where you happen to be standing at the time. The fact that a piece of language was 'estranging' did not guarantee that it was always and everywhere so: it was estranging only against a certain normative linguistic background, and if this altered then the writing might cease to be perceptible as literary. If everyone used phrases like 'unravished bride of quietness' in ordinary pub conversation, this kind of language might cease to be poetic. For the Formalists, in other words, 'literariness' was a function of the *differential* relations between one sort of discourse and another; it was not an eternally given property. They were not out to define 'literature', but 'literariness' – special uses of language, which could be found in 'literary' texts but also in many places outside them. Anyone who believes that 'literature' can be defined by such special uses of language has to face the fact that there is more metaphor in Manchester than there is in Marvell. There is no 'literary' device – metonymy, synecdoche, litotes, chiasmus and so on – which is not quite intensively used in daily discourse.

Nevertheless, the Formalists still presumed that 'making strange' was the essence of the literary. It was just that they relativized this use of language, saw it as a matter of contrast between one type of speech and another. But what if I were to hear someone at the next pub table remark 'This is awfully squiggly handwriting!' Is this 'literary' or 'non-literary' language? As a matter of fact it is 'literary' language, because it comes from Knut Hamsun's novel *Hunger*. But how do I know that it is literary? It doesn't, after all, focus any particular attention on itself as a verbal performance. One answer to the question of how I know that this is literary is that it comes from Knut Hamsun's novel *Hunger*. It is part of a text which I read as 'fictional', which announces itself as a 'novel', which may be put on university literature syllabuses and so on. The *context* tells me that it is literary; but the language itself has no inherent properties or qualities which might distinguish it from other kinds of discourse, and someone might well say this in a pub without being admired for their literary dexterity. To think of literature as the Formalists do is really to think of all literature as *poetry*. Significantly, when the Formalists came to consider prose writing, they often simply extended to it the kinds of technique they had used with poetry. But literature is usually judged to contain much besides poetry – to include, for example, realist or naturalistic writing which is not linguistically self-conscious or self-exhibiting in any striking way. People sometimes call writing 'fine' precisely because it *doesn't* draw undue attention to itself: they admire its laconic plainness or low-keyed sobriety. And what about jokes, football chants and slogans, newspaper headlines, advertisements, which are often verbally flamboyant but not generally classified as literature?

Another problem with the 'estrangement' case is that there is no kind of writing which cannot, given sufficient ingenuity, be read as estranging. Consider a prosaic, quite unambiguous statement like the one sometimes seen in the London Underground system: 'Dogs must be carried on the escalator.' This is not perhaps quite as unambiguous as it seems at first sight: does it mean that you *must* carry a dog on the escalator? Are you likely to be banned from the escalator unless you can find some stray mongrel to clutch in your arms on the way up? Many apparently straightforward notices contain such ambiguities: 'Refuse to be put in this basket,' for instance, or the British road-sign 'Way Out' as read by a Californian. But even leaving such troubling ambiguities aside, it is surely obvious that the underground notice could be read as literature. One could let oneself be arrested by the abrupt, minatory *staccato* of the first ponderous monosyllables; find one's mind drifting, by the time it had reached the rich allusiveness of 'carried', to suggestive resonances of helping lame dogs through life; and perhaps even detect in the very lilt and inflection of the word 'escalator' a miming of the rolling, up-and-down motion of the thing itself. This may well be a fruitless sort of pursuit, but it is not significantly more fruitless than claiming to hear the cut and thrust of the rapiers in some poetic description of a duel, and it at least has the advantage of suggesting that 'literature' may be at least as much a question of what people do to writing as of what writing does to them.

But even if someone were to read the notice in this way, it would still be a matter of reading it as *poetry*, which is only part of what is usually included in literature. Let us therefore consider another way of 'misreading' the sign which might move us a little beyond this. Imagine a late-night drunk dou-bled over the escalator handrail who reads the notice with laborious atten-tiveness for several minutes and then mutters to himself 'How true!' What kind of mistake is occurring here? What the drunk is doing, in fact, is taking the sign as some statement of general, even cosmic significance. By applying certain conventions of reading to its words, he prises them loose from their immediate context and generalizes them beyond their pragmatic purpose to something of wider and probably deeper import. This would certainly seem to be one operation involved in what people call literature. When the poet tells us that his love is like a red rose, we know by the very fact that he puts this statement in metre that we are not supposed to ask whether he actually had a lover who for some bizarre reason seemed to him to resemble a rose. He is telling us something about women and love in general. Literature, then, we might say, is 'non-pragmatic' discourse: unlike biology textbooks and notes to the milkman it serves no immediate practical purpose, but is to be taken as referring to a general state of affairs. Sometimes, though not always, it may employ peculiar language as though to make this fact obvious – to signal that what is at stake is a *way of talking* about a woman, rather than any particular real-life woman. This focusing on the way of talking, rather than on the reality of what is talked about, is sometimes taken to indicate that we mean by literature a kind of *self-referential* language, a language which talks about itself.

There are, however, problems with this way of defining literature too. For one thing, it would probably have come as a surprise to George Orwell to hear that his essays were to be read as though the topics he discussed were less important than the way he discussed them. In much that is classified as literature, the truth-value and practical relevance of what is said *is* considered important to the overall effect. But even if treating discourse 'non-pragmatically' is part of what is meant by 'literature', then it follows from this 'definition' that literature cannot in fact be 'objectively' defined. It leaves the definition of literature up to how somebody decides to *read*, not to the nature of what is written. There are certain kinds of writing – poems, plays, novels – which are fairly obviously intended to be 'non-pragmatic' in this sense, but this does not guarantee that they will actually be read in this way. I might well read Gibbon's account of the Roman empire not because I am misguided enough to believe that it will be reliably informative about ancient Rome but because I enjoy Gibbon's prose style, or revel in images of human corruption whatever their historical source. But I might read Robert Burns's poem because it is not clear to me, as a Japanese horticulturalist, whether or not the red rose flourished in eighteenth-century Britain. This, it will be said, is not reading it 'as literature'; but am I reading Orwell's essays as literature only if I generalize what he says about the Spanish civil war to some cosmic utterance about human life? It is true that many of the works studied as literature in academic institutions were 'constructed' to be read as literature, but it is also true that many of them were not. A piece of writing may start off life as history or philosophy and then come to be ranked as literature; or it may start off as literature and then come to be valued for its archaeological significance. Some texts are born literary, some achieve literariness, and some have literariness thrust upon them. Breeding in this respect may count for a good deal more than birth. What matters may not be where you came from but how people treat you. If they decide that you are literature then it seems that you are, irrespective of what you thought you were.

In this sense, one can think of literature less as some inherent quality or set of qualities displayed by certain kinds of writing all the way from *Beowulf* to Virginia Woolf, than as a number of ways in which people *relate themselves* to writing. It would not be easy to isolate, from all that has been variously called 'literature', some constant set of inherent features. In fact it would be as impossible as trying to identify the single distinguishing feature which all games have in common. There is no 'essence' of literature whatsoever. Any bit of writing may be read 'non-pragmatically', if that is what reading a text as literature means, just as any writing may be read 'poetically'. If I pore over the railway timetable not to discover a train connection but to stimulate in myself general reflections on the speed and complexity of modern existence, then I might be said to be reading it as literature. John M. Ellis has argued that the term 'literature' operates rather like the word 'weed': weeds are not particular kinds of plant, but just any kind of plant which for some reason or another a gardener does not what around.[3] Perhaps 'literature' means something like the opposite: any kind of writing which for some reason or another somebody values highly. As the philosophers might say, 'literature' and 'weed' are *functional* rather than *ontological* terms: they tell us about what we do, not about the fixed being of things. They tell us about the role of a text or a thistle in a social context, its relations with and differences from its surroundings, the ways it behaves, the purposes it may be put to and the human practices clustered around it. 'Literature' is in this sense a purely formal, empty sort of definition. Even if we claim that it is a non-pragmatic treatment of language, we have still not arrived at an 'essence' of literature because this is also so of other linguistic practices such as jokes. In any case, it is far from clear that we can discriminate neatly between 'practical' and 'non-practical' ways of relating ourselves to language. Reading a novel for pleasure obviously differs from reading a road sign for information, but how about reading a biology textbook to improve your mind? Is that a 'pragmatic' treatment of language or not? In many societies, 'literature' has served highly practical functions such as religious ones; distinguishing sharply between 'practical' and 'non-practical' may only be possible in a society like ours, where literature has ceased to have much practical function at all. We may be offering as a general definition a sense of the 'literary' which is in fact historically specific.

We have still not discovered the secret, then, of why Lamb, Macaulay and Mill are literature but not, generally speaking, Bentham, Marx and Darwin.

Perhaps the simple answer is that the first three are examples of 'fine writing', whereas the last three are not. This answer has the disadvantage of being largely untrue, at least in my judgement, but it has the advantage of suggesting that by and large people term 'literature' writing which they think is *good*. An obvious objection to this is that if it were entirely true there would be no such thing as 'bad literature'. I may consider Lamb and Macaulay overrated, but that does not necessarily mean that I stop regarding them as literature. You may consider Raymond Chandler 'good of his kind', but not exactly literature. On the other hand, if Macaulay were a *really* bad writer – if he had no grasp at all of grammar and seemed interested in nothing but white mice – then people might well not call his work literature at all, even bad literature. Value-judgements would certainly seem to have a lot to do with what is judged literature and what isn't – not necessarily in the sense that writing has to be 'fine' to be literary, but that it has to be *of the kind* that is judged fine: it may be an inferior example of a generally valued mode. Nobody would bother to say that a bus ticket was an example of inferior literature, but someone might well say that the poetry of Ernest Dowson was. The term 'fine writing', or *belles lettres*, is in this sense ambiguous: it denotes a sort of writing which is generally highly regarded, while not necessarily committing you to the opinion that a particular specimen of it is 'good'.

With this reservation, the suggestion that 'literature' is a highly valued kind of writing is an illuminating one. But it has one fairly devastating consequence. It means that we can drop once and for all the illusion that the category 'literature' is 'objective', in the sense of being eternally given and immutable. Anything can be literature, and anything which is regarded as unalterably and unquestionably literature – Shakespeare, for example – can cease to be literature. Any belief that the study of literature is the study of a stable, well-definable entity, as entomology is the study of insects, can be abandoned as a chimera. Some kinds of fiction are literature and some are not; some literature is fictional and some is not; some literature is verbally self-regarding, while some highly-wrought rhetoric is not literature. Literature, in the sense of a set of works of assured and unalterable value, distinguished by certain shared inherent properties, does not exist. When I use the words 'literary' and 'literature' from here on in this book, then, I place them under an invisible crossing-out mark, to indicate that these terms will not really do but that we have no better ones at the moment.

The reason why it follows from the definition of literature as highly valued writing that it is not a stable entity is that value-judgements are notoriously variable. 'Times change, values don't,' announces an advertisement for a daily newspaper, as though we still believed in killing off infirm infants or putting the mentally ill on public show. Just as people may treat a work as philosophy in one century and as literature in the next, or vice versa, so they may change their minds about what writing they consider valuable. They may even change their minds about the grounds they use for judging what is valuable and what is not. This, as I have suggested, does not necessarily mean that they will refuse the title of literature to a work which they have come to deem inferior: they may still call it literature, meaning roughly that it belongs to the *type* of writing which they generally value. But it does mean that the so-called 'literary canon', the unquestioned 'great tradition' of the 'national literature', has to be recognized as a *construct*, fashioned by particular people for particular reasons at a certain time. There is no such thing as a literary work or tradition which is valuable *in itself*, regardless of what anyone might have said or come to say about it. 'Value' is a transitive term: it means whatever is valued by certain people in specific situations, according to particular criteria and in the light of given purposes. It is thus quite possible that, given a deep enough transformation of our history, we may in the future produce a society which is unable to get anything at all out of Shakespeare. His works might simply seem desperately alien, full of styles of thought and feeling which such a society found limited or irrelevant. In such a situation, Shakespeare would be no more valuable than much present-day graffiti. And though many people would consider such a social condition tragically impoverished, it seems to me dogmatic not to entertain the possibility that it might arise rather from a general human enrichment. Karl Marx was troubled by the question of why ancient Greek art retained an 'eternal charm', even though the social conditions which produced it had long passed; but how do we know that it will remain 'eternally' charming, since history has not yet ended? Let us imagine that by dint of some deft archaeological research we discovered a great deal more about what ancient Greek tragedy actually meant to its original audiences, recognized that these concerns were utterly remote from out own, and began to read the plays again in the light of this deepened knowledge. One result might be that we stopped enjoying them. We might come to see that we had enjoyed them previously because we were unwittingly reading them in the light of our own preoccupations; once this became less possible, the drama might cease to speak at all significantly to us.

The fact that we always interpret literary works to some extent in the light of our own concerns – indeed that in one sense of 'our own concerns' we are incapable of doing anything else – might be one reason why certain works of literature seem to retain their value across the centuries. It may be, of course, that we still share many preoccupations with the work itself; but it may also be that people have not actually been valuing the 'same' work at all, even though they may think they have. 'Our' Homer is not identical with the Homer of the Middle Ages, nor 'our' Shakespeare with that of his contemporaries; it is rather that different historical periods have constructed a 'different' Homer and Shakespeare for their own purposes, and found in these texts elements to value or devalue, though not necessarily the same ones. All literary works, in other words, are 'rewritten', if only unconsciously, by the societies which read them; indeed there is no reading of a work which is not also a 're-writing'. No work, and no current evaluation of it, can simply be extended to new groups of people without being changed, perhaps almost unrecognizably, in the process; and this is one reason why what counts as literature is a notably unstable affair.

I do not mean that it is unstable because value-judgements are 'subjective'. According to this view, the world is divided between solid facts 'out there' like Grand Central station, and arbitrary value-judgements 'in here' such as liking bananas or feeling that the tone of a Yeats poem veers from defensive hectoring to grimly resilient resignation. Facts are public and unimpeachable, values are private and gratuitous. There is an obvious difference between recounting a fact, such as 'This cathedral was built in 1612,' and registering a value-judgement, such as 'This cathedral is a magnificent specimen of baroque architecture.' But suppose I made the first kind of statement while showing an overseas visitor around England, and found that it puzzled her considerably. Why, she might ask, do you keep telling me the dates of the foundation of all these buildings? Why this obsession with origins? In the society I live in, she might go on, we keep no record at all of such events: we classify our buildings instead according to whether they face north-west or south-east. What this might do would be to demonstrate part of the unconscious system of value-judgements which underlies my own descriptive statements. Such value-judgements are not necessarily of the same kind as 'This cathedral is a magnificent specimen of baroque architecture,' but they are value-judgements none the less, and no factual pronouncement I make can escape them. Statements of fact are after all *statements*, which presumes a number of questionable judgements: that those statements are worth making, perhaps more worth making than certain others, that I am the sort of person entitled to make them and perhaps able to guarantee their truth, that you are the kind of person worth making them to, that something useful is accomplished by making them, and so on. A pub conversation may well transmit information, but what also bulks large in such dialogue is a strong element of what linguists would call the 'phatic', a concern with the act of communication itself. In chatting to you about the weather I am also signalling that I regard conversation with you as valuable, that I consider you a worthwhile person to talk to, that I am not myself anti-social or about to embark on a detailed critique of your personal appearance.

In this sense, there is no possibility of a wholly disinterested statement. Of course stating when a cathedral was built is reckoned to be more disinterested in our own culture than passing an opinion about its architecture, but one could also imagine situations in which the former statement would be more 'value-laden' than the latter. Perhaps 'baroque' and 'magnificent' have come to be more or less synonymous, whereas only a stubborn rump of us cling to the belief that the date when a building was founded is significant, and my statement is taken as a coded way of signalling this partisanship. All of our descriptive statements move within an often invisible network of value-categories, and indeed without such categories we would have nothing to say to each other at all. It is not just as though we have something called factual knowledge which may then be distorted by particular interests and judgements, although this is certainly possible; it is also that without particular interests we would have no knowledge at all, because we would not see the point of bothering to get to know anything. Interests are *constitutive* of our knowledge, not merely prejudices which imperil it. The claim that knowledge should be 'value-free' is itself a value-judgement.

It may well be that a liking for bananas is a merely private matter, though this is in fact questionable. A thorough analysis of my tastes in food would probably reveal how deeply relevant they are to certain formative experiences in early childhood, to my relations with my parents and siblings and to a good many other cultural factors which are quite as social and 'non-subjective' as railway stations. This is even more true of that fundamental structure of beliefs and interests which I am born into as a member of a particular society, such as the belief that I should try to keep in good health, that differences of sexual role are rooted in human biology or that human beings are more important than crocodiles. We may disagree on this or that, but we can only do so because we share certain 'deep' ways of seeing and valuing which are bound up with our social life, and which could not be changed without transforming that life. Nobody will penalize me heavily if I dislike a particular Donne poem, but if I argue that Donne is not literature at all then in certain circumstances I might risk losing my job. I am free to vote Labour or Conservative, but if I try to act on the belief that this choice itself merely masks a deeper prejudice – the prejudice that the meaning of

democracy is confined to putting a cross on a ballot paper every few years –
then in certain unusual circumstances I might end up in prison.

The largely concealed structure of values which informs and underlies
our factual statements is part of what is meant by 'ideology'. By 'ideology' I
mean, roughly, the ways in which what we say and believe connects with the
power-structure and power-relations of the society we live in. It follows
from such a rough definition of ideology that not all of our underlying
judgements and categories can usefully be said to be ideological. It is deeply
ingrained in us to imagine ourselves moving forwards into the future (at least
one other society sees itself as moving backwards into it), but though this
way of seeing *may* connect significantly with the power-structure of our
society, it need not always and everywhere do so. I do not mean by 'ideology'
simply the deeply entrenched, often unconscious beliefs which people hold;
I mean more particularly those modes of feeling, valuing, perceiving and
believing which have some kind of relation to the maintenance and reproduction of social power. The fact that such beliefs are by no means merely
private quirks may be illustrated by a literary example.

In his famous study *Practical Criticism* (1929), the Cambridge critic I. A.
Richards sought to demonstrate just how whimsical and subjective literary
value-judgements could actually be by giving his undergraduates a set of
poems, withholding from them the titles and authors' names, and asking
them to evaluate them. The resulting judgements, notoriously, were highly
variable: time-honoured poets were marked down and obscure authors celebrated. To my mind, however, much the most interesting aspect of this
project, and one apparently quite invisible to Richards himself, is just how
tight a consensus of unconscious valuations underlies these particular differences of opinion. Reading Richards' undergraduates' accounts of literary
works, one is struck by the habits of perception and interpretation which
they spontaneously share – what they expect literature to be, what assumptions they bring to a poem and what fulfilments they anticipate they will
derive from it. None of this is really surprising: for all the participants in this
experiment were, presumably, young, white, upper- or upper-middle-class,
privately educated English people of the 1920s, and how they responded to
a poem depended on a good deal more than purely 'literary' factors. Their
critical responses were deeply entwined with their broader prejudices and
beliefs. This is not a matter of *blame*: there is no critical response which is
not so entwined, and thus no such thing as a 'pure' literary critical judgement or interpretation. If anybody is to be blamed it is I. A. Richards
himself, who as a young, white, upper-middle-class male Cambridge don
was unable to objectify a context of interests which he himself largely shared,

and was thus unable to recognize fully that local, 'subjective' differences of evaluation work within a particular, socially structured way of perceiving the world.

If it will not do to see literature as an 'objective', descriptive category, neither will it do to say that literature is just what people whimsically choose to call literature. For there is nothing at all whimsical about such kinds of value-judgement: they have their roots in deeper structures of belief which are as apparently unshakeable as the Empire State building. What we have uncovered so far, then, is not only that literature does not exist in the sense that insects do, and that the value-judgements by which it is constituted are historically variable, but that these value-judgements themselves have a close relation to social ideologies. They refer in the end not simply to private taste, but to the assumptions by which certain social groups exercise and maintain power over others. If this seems a far-fetched assertion, a matter of private prejudice, we may test it out by an account of the rise of 'literature' in England.

1

The Rise of English

In eighteenth-century England, the concept of literature was not confined as it sometimes is today to 'creative' or 'imaginative' writing. It meant the whole body of valued writing in society: philosophy, history, essays and letters as well as poems. What made a text 'literary' was not whether it was fictional – the eighteenth century was in grave doubt about whether the new upstart form of the novel was literature at all – but whether it conformed to certain standards of 'polite letters'. The criteria of what counted as literature, in other words, were frankly ideological: writing which embodied the values and 'tastes' of a particular social class qualified as literature, whereas a street ballad, a popular romance and perhaps even the drama did not. At this historical point, then, the 'value-ladenness' of the concept of literature was reasonably self-evident.

In the eighteenth century, however, literature did more than 'embody' certain social values: it was a vital instrument for their deeper entrenchment and wider dissemination. Eighteenth-century England had emerged, battered but intact, from a bloody civil war in the previous century which had set the social classes at each other's throats; and in the drive to reconsolidate a shaken social order, the neo-classical notions of Reason, Nature, order and propriety, epitomized in art, were key concepts. With the need to incorporate the increasingly powerful but spiritually rather raw middle classes into unity with the ruling aristocracy, to diffuse polite social manners, habits of 'correct' taste and common cultural standards, literature gained a new importance. It included a whole set of ideological institutions: periodicals, coffee houses, social and aesthetic treatises, sermons, classical translations, guidebooks to manners and morals. Literature was not a matter of 'felt experience', 'personal response' or 'imaginative uniqueness': such terms, indissociable for us today from the whole idea of the 'literary', would not have counted for much with Henry Fielding.

It was, in fact, only with what we now call the 'Romantic period' that our own definitions of literature began to develop. The modern sense of the word 'literature' only really gets under way in the nineteenth century. Literature in this sense of the word is an historically recent phenomenon: it was invented sometime around the turn of the eighteenth century, and would have been thought extremely strange by Chaucer or even Pope. What happened first was a narrowing of the category of literature to so-called 'creative' or 'imaginative' work. The final decades of the eighteenth century witness a new division and demarcation of discourses, a radical reorganizing of what we might call the 'discursive formation' of English society. 'Poetry' comes to mean a good deal more than verse: by the time of Shelley's *Defence of Poetry* (1821), it signifies a concept of human creativity which is radically at odds with the utilitarian ideology of early industrial capitalist England. Of course a distinction between 'factual' and 'imaginative' writing had long been recognized: the word 'poetry' or 'poesy' had traditionally singled out fiction, and Philip Sidney had entered an eloquent plea for it in his *Apology for Poetry*. But by the time of the Romantic period, literature was becoming virtually synonymous with the 'imaginative': to write about what did not exist was somehow more soul-stirring and valuable than to pen an account of Birmingham or the circulation of the blood. The word 'imaginative' contains an ambiguity suggestive of this attitude: it has a resonance of the descriptive term 'imaginary', meaning 'literally untrue', but is also of course an evaluative term, meaning 'visionary' or 'inventive'.

Since we ourselves are post-Romantics, in the sense of being products of that epoch rather than confidently posterior to it, it is hard for us to grasp just what a curious historically particular idea this is. It would certainly have seemed so to most of the English writers whose 'imaginative vision' we now reverently elevate above the merely 'prosaic' discourse of those who can find nothing more dramatic to write about than the Black Death or the Warsaw ghetto. Indeed it is in the Romantic period that the descriptive term 'prosaic' begins to acquire its negative sense of prosy, dull, uninspiring. If what does not exist is felt to be more attractive than what does, if poetry or the imagination is privileged over prose or 'hard fact', then it is a reasonable assumption that this says something significant about the kinds of society in which the Romantics lived.

The historical period in question is one of revolution: in America and France the old colonialist or feudalist regimes are overthrown by middle-class insurrection, while England achieves its point of economic 'take-off', arguably on the back of the enormous profits it has reaped from the eighteenth-century slave trade and its imperial control of the seas, to become the world's first industrial capitalist nation. But the visionary hopes and dynamic energies released by these revolutions, energies with which Romantic writing is alive, enter into potentially tragic contradiction with the harsh realities of the new bourgeois regimes. In England, a crassly philistine Utilitarianism is rapidly becoming the dominant ideology of the industrial middle class, fetishizing fact, reducing human relations to market exchanges and dismissing art as unprofitable ornamentation. The callous disciplines of early industrial capitalism uproot whole communities, convert human life into wage-slavery, enforce an alienating labour-process on the newly formed working class and understand nothing which cannot be transformed into a commodity on the open market. As the working class responds with militant protest to this oppression, and as troubling memories of revolution across the Channel still haunt their rulers, the English state reacts with a brutal political repressiveness which converts England, during part of the Romantic period, into what is in effect a police state.[1]

In the face of such forces, the privilege accorded by the Romantics to the 'creative imagination' can be seen as considerably more than idle escapism. On the contrary, 'literature' now appears as one of the few enclaves in which the creative values expunged from the face of English society by industrial capitalism can be celebrated and affirmed. 'Imaginative creation' can be offered as an image of non-alienated labour; the intuitive, transcendental scope of the poetic mind can provide a living criticism of those rationalist or empiricist ideologies enslaved to 'fact'. The literary work itself comes to be seen as a mysterious organic unity, in contrast to the fragmented individualism of the capitalist marketplace: it is 'spontaneous' rather than rationally calculated, creative rather than mechanical. The word 'poetry', then, no longer refers simply to a technical mode of writing: it has deep social, political and philosophical implications, and at the sound of it the ruling class might quite literally reach for its gun. Literature has become a whole alternative ideology, and the 'imagination' itself, as with Blake and Shelley, becomes a political force. Its task is to transform society in the name of those energies and values which art embodies. Most of the major Romantic poets were themselves political activists, perceiving continuity rather than conflict between their literary and social commitments.

Yet we can already begin to detect within this literary radicalism another, and to us more familiar, emphasis: a stress upon the sovereignty and autonomy of the imagination, its splendid remoteness from the merely prosaic

matters of feeding one's children or struggling for political justice. If the
'transcendental' nature of the imagination offered a challenge to an anaemic
rationalism, it could also offer the writer a comfortingly absolute alternative
to history itself. Indeed such a detachment from history reflected the Romantic writer's actual situation. Art was becoming a commodity like anything else, and the Romantic artist little more than a minor commodity
producer; for all his rhetorical claim to be 'representative' of humankind, to
speak with the voice of the people and utter eternal verities, he existed more
and more on the margins of a society which was not inclined to pay high
wages to prophets. The finely passionate idealism of the Romantics, then,
was also idealist in a more philosophical sense of the word. Deprived of any
proper place within the social movements which might actually have transformed industrial capitalism into a just society, the writer was increasingly
driven back into the solitariness of his own creative mind. The vision of a
just society was often enough inverted into an impotent nostalgia for the
old 'organic' England which had passed away. It was not until the time of
William Morris, who in the late nineteenth century harnessed this Romantic
humanism to the cause of the working-class movement, that the gap between
poetic vision and political practice was significantly narrowed.[2]

It is no accident that the period we are discussing sees the rise of modern
'aesthetics', or the philosophy of art. It is mainly from this era, in the work
of Kant, Hegel, Schiller, Coleridge and others, that we inherit our contemporary ideas of the 'symbol' and 'aesthetic experience', of 'aesthetic harmony' and the unique nature of the artefact. Previously men and women had
written poems, staged plays or painted pictures for a variety of purposes,
while others had read, watched or viewed them in a variety of ways. Now
these concrete, historically variable practices were being subsumed into
some special, mysterious faculty known as the 'aesthetic', and a new breed of
aestheticians sought to lay bare its inmost structures. It was not that such
questions had not been raised before, but now they began to assume a new
significance. The assumption that there was an unchanging object known as
'art', or an isolatable experience called 'beauty' or the 'aesthetic', was largely
a product of the very alienation of art from social life which we have already
touched on. If literature had ceased to have any obvious function – if the
writer was no longer a traditional figure in the pay of the court, the church
or an aristocratic patron – then it was possible to turn this fact to literature's
advantage. The whole point of 'creative' writing was that it was gloriously
useless, an 'end in itself' loftily removed from any sordid social purpose.
Having lost his patron, the writer discovered a substitute in the poetic.[3] It is,
in fact, somewhat improbable that the *Iliad* was art to the ancient Greeks in
the same sense that a cathedral was an artefact for the Middle Ages or Andy

Warhol's work is art for us; but the effect of aesthetics was to suppress these historical differences. Art was extricated from the material practices, social relations and ideological meanings in which it is always caught up, and raised to the status of a solitary fetish.

At the centre of aesthetic theory at the turn of the eighteenth century is the semi-mystical doctrine of the symbol.[4] For Romanticism, indeed, the symbol becomes the panacea for all problems. Within it, a whole set of conflicts which were felt to be insoluble in ordinary life – between subject and object, the universal and the particular, the sensuous and the conceptual, material and spiritual, order and spontaneity – could be magically resolved. It is not surprising that such conflicts were sorely felt in this period. Objects in a society which could see them as no more than commodities appeared lifeless and inert, divorced from the human subjects who produced or used them. The concrete and the universal seemed to have drifted apart: an aridly rationalist philosophy ignored the sensuous qualities of particular things, while a short-sighted empiricism (the 'official' philosophy of the English middle class, then as now) was unable to peer beyond particular bits and pieces of the world to any total picture which they might compose. The dynamic, spontaneous energies of social progress were to be fostered, but curbed of their potentially anarchic force by a restraining social order. The symbol fused together motion and stillness, turbulent content and organic form, mind and world. Its material body was the medium of an absolute spiritual truth, one perceived by direct intuition rather than by any laborious process of critical analysis. In this sense the symbol brought such truths to bear on the mind in a way which brooked no question: either you saw it or you didn't. It was the keystone of an irrationalism, a forestalling of reasoned critical enquiry, which has been rampant in literary theory ever since. It was a *unitary* thing, and to dissect it – to take it apart to see how it worked – was almost as blasphemous as seeking to analyse the Holy Trinity. All of its various parts worked spontaneously together for the common good, each in its subordinate place; and it is therefore hardly surprising to find the symbol, or the literary artefact as such, being regularly offered throughout the nineteenth and twentieth centuries as an ideal model of human society itself. If only the lower orders were to forget their grievances and pull together for the good of all, much tedious turmoil could be avoided.

To speak of 'literature and ideology' as two separate phenomena which can be interrelated is, as I hope to have shown, in one sense quite unnecessary. Literature, in the meaning of the word we have inherited, *is* an ideology. It has the most intimate relations to questions of social power. But if the reader is still unconvinced, the narrative of what happened to literature in the later nineteenth century might prove a little more persuasive.

If one were asked to provide a single explanation for the growth of English studies in the later nineteenth century, one could do worse than reply: 'the failure of religion'. By the mid-Victorian period, this traditionally reliable, immensely powerful ideological form was in deep trouble. It was no longer winning the hearts and minds of the masses, and under the twin impacts of scientific discovery and social change its previous unquestioned dominance was in danger of evaporating. This was particularly worrying for the Victorian ruling class, because religion is for all kinds of reasons an extremely effective form of ideological control. Like all successful ideologies, it works much less by explicit concepts or formulated doctrines than by image, symbol, habit, ritual and mythology. It is affective and experiential, entwining itself with the deepest unconscious roots of the human subject; and any social ideology which is unable to engage with such deepseated a-rational fears and needs, as T. S. Eliot knew, is unlikely to survive very long. Religion, moreover, is capable of operating at every social level: if there is a doctrinal inflection of it for the intellectual elite, there is also a pietistic brand of it for the masses. It provides an excellent social 'cement', encompassing pious peasant, enlightened middle-class liberal and theological intellectual in a single organization. Its ideological power lies in its capacity to 'materialize' beliefs as practices: religion is the sharing of the chalice and the blessing of the harvest, not just abstract argument about consubstantiation or hyperdulia. Its ultimate truths, like those mediated by the literary symbol, are conveniently closed to rational demonstration, and thus absolute in their claims. Finally religion, at least in its Victorian forms, is a *pacifying* influence, fostering meekness, self-sacrifice and the contemplative inner life. It is no wonder that the Victorian ruling class looked on the threatened dissolution of this ideological discourse with something less than equanimity.

Fortunately, however, another, remarkably similar discourse lay to hand: English literature. George Gordon, early Professor of English Literature at Oxford, commented in his inaugural lecture that 'England is sick, and . . . English literature must save it. The Churches (as I understand) having failed, and social remedies being slow, English literature has now a triple function: still, I suppose, to delight and instruct us, but also, and above all, to save our souls and heal the State.'[5] Gordon's words were spoken in our own century, but they find a resonance everywhere in Victorian England. It is a striking thought that had it not been for this dramatic crisis in mid-nineteenth-century ideology, we might not today have such a plentiful supply of Jane Austen casebooks and bluffer's guides to Pound. As religion progressively ceases to provide the social 'cement', affective values and basic mythologies by which a socially turbulent class-society can be welded together, 'English' is constructed as a subject to carry this ideological burden from the Victorian period onwards. The key figure here is Matthew Arnold, always preternaturally sensitive to the needs of his social class, and engagingly candid about being so. The urgent social need, as Arnold recognizes, is to 'Hellenize' or cultivate the philistine middle class, who have proved unable to underpin their political and economic power with a suitably rich and subtle ideology. This can be done by transfusing into them something of the traditional style of the aristocracy, who as Arnold shrewdly perceives are ceasing to be the dominant class in England, but who have something of the ideological wherewithal to lend a hand to their middle-class masters. State-established schools, by linking the middle class to 'the best culture of their nation', will confer on them 'a greatness and a noble spirit, which the tone of these classes is not of itself at present adequate to impart'.[6]

The true beauty of this manoeuvre, however, lies in the effect it will have in controlling and incorporating the working class:

> It is of itself a serious calamity for a nation that its tone of feeling and grandeur of spirit should be lowered or dulled. But the calamity appears far more serious still when we consider that the middle classes, remaining as they are now, with their narrow, harsh, unintelligent, and unattractive spirit and culture, will almost certainly fail to mould or assimilate the masses below them, whose sympathies are at the present moment actually wider and more liberal than theirs. They arrive, these masses, eager to enter into possession of the world, to gain a more vivid sense of their own life and activity. In this their irrepressible development, their natural educators and initiators are those immediately above them, the middle classes. If these classes cannot win their sympathy or give them their direction, society is in danger of falling into anarchy.[7]

Arnold is refreshingly unhypocritical: there is no feeble pretence that the education of the working class is to be conducted chiefly for their own benefit, or that his concern with their spiritual condition is, in one of his own most cherished terms, in the least 'disinterested'. In the even more disarmingly candid words of a twentieth-century proponent of this view: 'Deny to working-class children any common share in the immaterial, and presently they will grow into the men who demand with menaces a communism of the material.'[8] If the masses are not thrown a few novels, they may react by throwing up a few barricades.

Literature was in several ways a suitable candidate for this ideological enterprise. As a liberal, 'humanizing' pursuit, it could provide a potent antidote to political bigotry and ideological extremism. Since literature, as we know, deals in universal human values rather than in such historical trivia as civil wars, the oppression of women or the dispossession of the English peasantry, it could serve to place in cosmic perspective the petty demands of working people for decent living conditions or greater control over their own lives, and might even with luck come to render them oblivious of such issues in their high-minded contemplation of eternal truths and beauties. English, as a Victorian handbook for English teachers put it, helps to 'promote sympathy and fellow feeling among all classes'; another Victorian writer speaks of literature as opening a 'serene and luminous region of truth where all may meet and expatiate in common', above 'the smoke and stir, the din and turmoil of man's lower life of care and business and debate'.[9] Literature would rehearse the masses in the habits of pluralistic thought and feeling, persuading them to acknowledge that more than one viewpoint than theirs existed – namely, that of their masters. It would communicate to them the moral riches of bourgeois civilization, impress upon them a reverence for middle-class achievements, and, since reading is an essentially solitary, contemplative activity, curb in them any disruptive tendency to collective political action. It would give them a pride in their national language and literature: if scanty education and extensive hours of labour prevented them personally from producing a literary masterpiece, they could take pleasure in the thought that others of their own kind – English people – had done so. The people, according to a study of English literature written in 1891, 'need political culture, instruction, that is to say, in what pertains to their relation to the State, to their duties as citizens; and they need also to be impressed sentimentally by having the presentation in legend and history of heroic and patriotic examples brought vividly and attractively before them'.[10] All of this, moreover, could be achieved without the cost and labour of teaching them the Classics: English literature was written in their own language, and so was conveniently available to them.

Like religion, literature works primarily by emotion and experience, and so was admirably well-fitted to carry through the ideological task which religion left off. Indeed by our own time literature has become effectively identical with the opposite of analytical thought and conceptual enquiry: whereas scientists, philosophers and political theorists are saddled with these drably discursive pursuits, students of literature occupy the more prized territory of feeling and experience. Whose experience, and what kinds of feeling, is a different question. Literature from Arnold onwards is the enemy of 'ideological dogma', an attitude which might have come as a surprise to Dante, Milton and Pope; the truth or falsity of beliefs such as that blacks are inferior to whites is less important than what it feels like to experience them. Arnold himself had beliefs, of course, though like everybody else he regarded his own beliefs as reasoned positions rather than ideological dogmas. Even so, it was not the business of literature to communicate such beliefs directly – to argue openly, for example, that private property is the bulwark of liberty. Instead, literature should convey *timeless* truths, thus distracting the masses from their immediate commitments, nurturing in them a spirit of tolerance and generosity, and so ensuring the survival of private property. Just as Arnold attempted in *Literature and Dogma* and *God and the Bible* to dissolve away the embarrassingly doctrinal bits of Christianity into poetically suggestive sonorities, so the pill of middle-class ideology was to be sweetened by the sugar of literature.

There was another sense in which the 'experiential' nature of literature was ideologically convenient. For 'experience' is not only the homeland of ideology, the place where it takes root most effectively; it is also in its literary form a kind of vicarious self-fulfilment. If you do not have the money and leisure to visit the Far East, except perhaps as a soldier in the pay of British imperialism, then you can always 'experience' it at second hand by reading Conrad or Kipling. Indeed according to some literary theories this is even more real than strolling round Bangkok. The actually impoverished experience of the mass of people, an impoverishment bred by their social conditions, can be supplemented by literature: instead of working to change such conditions (which Arnold, to his credit, did more thoroughly than almost any of those who sought to inherit his mantle), you can vicariously fulfil someone's desire for a fuller life by handing them *Pride and Prejudice*.

It is significant, then, that 'English' as an academic subject was first institutionalized not in the Universities, but in the Mechanics' Institutes, working men's colleges and extension lecturing circuits.[11] English was literally the poor man's Classics – a way of providing a cheapish 'liberal' education for those beyond the charmed circles of public school and Oxbridge. From the outset, in the work of 'English' pioneers like F. D. Maurice and Charles Kingsley, the emphasis was on solidarity between the social classes, the cultivation of 'larger sympathies', the instillation of national pride and the transmission of 'moral' values. This last concern – still the distinctive hallmark of literary studies in England, and a frequent source of bemusement to intellectuals from other cultures – was an essential part of the ideological project; indeed the rise of 'English' is more or less concomitant with an historic shift in the very meaning of the term 'moral', of which

Arnold, Henry James and F. R. Leavis are the major critical exponents. Morality is no longer to be grasped as a formulated code or explicit ethical system: it is rather a sensitive preoccupation with the whole quality of life itself, with the oblique, nuanced particulars of human experience. Somewhat rephrased, this can be taken as meaning that the old religious ideologies have lost their force, and that a more subtle communication of moral values, one which works by 'dramatic enactment' rather than rebarbative abstraction, is thus in order. Since such values are nowhere more vividly dramatized than in literature, brought home to 'felt experience' with all the unquestionable reality of a blow on the head, literature becomes more than just a handmaiden of moral ideology: it *is* moral ideology for the modern age, as the work of F. R. Leavis was most graphically to evince.

The working class was not the only oppressed layer of Victorian society at whom 'English' was specifically beamed. English literature, reflected a Royal Commission witness in 1877, might be considered a suitable subject for 'women . . . and the second- and third-rate men who . . . become schoolmasters.'[12] The 'softening' and 'humanizing' effects of English, terms recurrently used by its early proponents, are within the existing ideological stereotypes of gender clearly feminine. The rise of English in England ran parallel to the gradual, grudging admission of women to the institutions of higher education; and since English was an untaxing sort of affair, concerned with the finer feelings rather than with the more virile topics of *bona fide* academic 'disciplines', it seemed a convenient sort of non-subject to palm off on the ladies, who were in any case excluded from science and the professions. Sir Arthur Quiller Couch, first Professor of English at Cambridge University, would open with the word 'Gentlemen' lectures addressed to a hall filled largely with women. Though modern male lecturers may have changed their manners, the ideological conditions which make English a popular University subject for women to read have not.

If English had its feminine aspect, however, it also acquired a masculine one as the century drew on. The era of the academic establishment of English is also the era of high imperialism in England. As British capitalism became threatened and progressively outstripped by its younger German and American rivals, the squalid, undignified scramble of too much capital chasing too few overseas territories, which was to culminate in 1914 in the first imperialist world war, created the urgent need for a sense of national mission and identity. What was at stake in English studies was less English *literature* than *English* literature: our great 'national poets' Shakespear and Milton, the sense of an 'organic' national tradition and identity to which new recruits could be admitted by the study of humane letters. The reports of educational bodies and official enquiries into the teaching of English, in this period and in the early twentieth century, are strewn with nostalgic back-references to the 'organic' community of Elizabethan England in which nobles and groundlings found a common meeting-place in the Shakespearian theatre, and which might still be reinvented today. It is no accident that the author of one of the most influential Government reports in this area, *The Teaching of English in England* (1921), was none other than Sir Henry Newbolt, minor jingoist poet and perpetrator of the immortal line 'Play up! play up! and play the game!' Chris Baldick has pointed to the importance of the admission of English literature to the Civil Service examinations in the Victorian period: armed with this conveniently packaged version of their own cultural treasures, the servants of British imperialism could sally forth overseas secure in a sense of their national identity, and able to display that cultural superiority to their envying colonial peoples.[13]

It took rather longer for English, a subject fit for women, workers and those wishing to impress the natives, to penetrate the bastions of ruling-class power in Oxford and Cambridge. English was an upstart, amateurish affair as academic subjects went, hardly able to compete on equal terms with the rigours of Greats or philology; since every English gentleman read his own literature in his spare time anyway, what was the point of submitting it to systematic study? Fierce rearguard actions were fought by both ancient Universities against this distressingly dilettante subject: the definition of an academic subject was what could be examined, and since English was no more than idle gossip about literary taste it was difficult to know how to make it unpleasant enough to qualify as a proper academic pursuit. This, it might be said, is one of the few problems associated with the study of English which have since been effectively resolved. The frivolous contempt for his subject displayed by the first really 'literary' Oxford professor, Sir Walter Raleigh, has to be read to be believed.[14] Raleigh held his post in the years leading up to the First World War; and his relief at the outbreak of the war, an event which allowed him to abandon the feminine vagaries of literature and put his pen to something more manly – war propaganda – is palpable in his writing. The only way in which English seemed likely to justify its existence in the ancient Universities was by systematically mistaking itself for the Classics; but the classicists were hardly keen to have this pathetic parody of themselves around.

If the first imperialist world war more or less put paid to Sir Walter Raleigh, providing him with an heroic identity more comfortingly in line with that of his Elizabethan namesake, it also signalled the final victory of English studies at Oxford and Cambridge. One of the most strenuous antagonists of English – philology – was closely bound up with Germanic influence; and since England happened to be passing through a major war with Germany, it was possible to smear classical philology as a form of ponderous Teutonic nonsense with which no self-respecting Englishman should be caught associating.[15] England's victory over Germany meant a renewal of national pride, an upsurge of patriotism which could only aid English's cause; but at the same time the deep trauma of the war, its almost intolerable questioning of every previously held cultural assumption, gave rise to a 'spiritual hungering', as one contemporary commentator described it, for which poetry seemed to provide an answer. It is a chastening thought that we owe the University study of English, in part at least, to a meaningless massacre. The Great War, with its carnage of ruling-class rhetoric, put paid to some of the more strident forms of chauvinism on which English had previously thrived: there could be few more Walter Raleighs after Wilfred Owen. English Literature rode to power on the back of wartime nationalism; but it also represented a search for spiritual solutions on the part of an English ruling class whose sense of identity had been profoundly shaken, whose psyche was ineradicably scarred by the horrors it had endured. Literature would be at once solace and reaffirmation, a familiar ground on which Englishmen could regroup both to explore, and to find some alternative to, the nightmare of history.

The architects of the new subject at Cambridge were on the whole individuals who could be absolved from the crime and guilt of having led working-class Englishmen over the top. F. R. Leavis had served as a medical orderly at the front; Queenie Dorothy Roth, later Q. D. Leavis, was as a woman exempt from such involvements, and was in any case still a child at the outbreak of war. I. A. Richards entered the army after graduation; the renowned pupils of these pioneers, William Empson and L. C. Knights, were also still children in 1914. The champions of English, moreover, stemmed on the whole from an alternative social class to that which had led Britain into war. F. R. Leavis was the son of a musical instruments dealer, Q. D. Roth the daughter of a draper and hosier, I. A. Richards the son of a works manager in Cheshire. English was to be fashioned not by the patrician dilettantes who occupied the early Chairs of Literature at the ancient universities, but by the offspring of the provincial petty bourgeoisie. They were members of a social class entering the traditional Universities for the first time, able to identify and challenge the social assumptions which informed its literary judgements in a way that the devotees of Sir Arthur Quiller

Couch were not. None of them had suffered the crippling disadvantages of a purely literary education of the Quiller Couch kind: F. R. Leavis had migrated to English from history, his pupil Q. D. Roth drew in her work on psychology and cultural anthropology. I. A. Richards had been trained in mental and moral sciences.

In fashioning English into a serious discipline, these men and women blasted apart the assumptions of the pre-war upper-class generation. No subsequent movement within English studies has come near to recapturing the courage and radicalism of their stand. In the early 1920s it was desperately unclear why English was worth studying at all; by the early 1930s it had become a question of why it was worth wasting your time on anything else. English was not only a subject worth studying, but *the* supremely civilizing pursuit, the spiritual essence of the social formation. Far from constituting some amateur or impressionistic enterprise, English was an arena in which the most fundamental questions of human existence – what it meant to be a person, to engage in significant relationship with others, to live from the vital centre of the most essential values – were thrown into vivid relief and made the object of the most intensive scrutiny. *Scrutiny* was the title of the critical journal launched in 1932 by the Leavises, which has yet to be surpassed in its tenacious devotion to the moral centrality of English studies, their crucial relevance to the quality of social life as a whole. Whatever the 'failure' or 'success' of *Scrutiny*, however, one might argue the toss between the anti-Leavisian prejudice of the literary establishment and the waspishness of the *Scrutiny* movement itself, the fact remains that English students in England today are 'Leavisites' whether they know it or not, irremediably altered by that historic intervention. There is no more need to be a card-carrying Leavisite today than there is to be a card-carrying Copernican: that current has entered the bloodstream of English studies in England as Copernicus reshaped our astronomical beliefs, has become a form of spontaneous critical wisdom as deep-seated as our conviction that the earth moves round the sun. That the 'Leavis debate' is effectively dead is perhaps the major sign of *Scrutiny*'s victory.

What the Leavises saw was that if the Sir Arthur Quiller Couches were allowed to win out, literary criticism would be shunted into an historical siding of no more inherent significance than the question of whether one preferred potatoes to tomatoes. In the face of such whimsical 'taste', they stressed the centrality of rigorous critical analysis, a disciplined attention to the 'words on the page'. They urged this not simply for technical or aesthetic reasons, but because it had the closest relevance to the spiritual crisis of modern civilization. Literature was important not only in itself, but because it encapsulated creative energies which were everywhere on the defensive in modern 'commercial' society. In literature, and perhaps in literature alone, a vital feel for the creative uses of language was still manifest, in contrast to the philistine devaluing of language and traditional culture blatantly apparent in 'mass society'. The quality of a society's language was the most telling index of the quality of its personal and social life: a society which had ceased to value literature was one lethally closed to the impulses which had created and sustained the best of human civilization. In the civilized manners of eighteenth-century England, or in the 'natural', 'organic' agrarian society of the seventeenth century, one could discern a form of living sensibility without which modern industrial society would atrophy and die.

To be a certain kind of English student in Cambridge in the late 1920s and 1930s was to be caught up in this buoyant, polemical onslaught against the most trivializing features of industrial capitalism. It was rewarding to know that being an English student was not only valuable but the most important way of life one could imagine – that one was contributing in one's own modest way to rolling back twentieth-century society in the direction of the 'organic' community of seventeenth-century England, that one moved at the most progressive tip of civilization itself. Those who came up to Cambridge humbly expecting to read a few poems and novels were quickly demystified: English was not just one discipline among many but the most central subject of all, immeasurably superior to law, science, politics, philosophy or history. These subjects, *Scrutiny* grudgingly conceded, had their place; but it was a place to be assessed by the touchstone of literature, which was less an academic subject than a spiritual exploration coterminous with the fate of civilization itself. With breathtaking boldness, *Scrutiny* redrew the map of English literature in ways from which criticism has never quite recovered. The main thoroughfares on this map ran through Chaucer, Shakespeare, Jonson, the Jacobeans and Metaphysicals, Bunyan, Pope, Samuel Johnson, Blake, Wordsworth, Keats, Austen, George Eliot, Hopkins, Henry James, Joseph Conrad, T. S. Eliot and D. H. Lawrence. This *was* 'English literature': Spencer, Dryden, Restoration drama, Defoe, Fielding, Richardson, Sterne, Shelley, Byron, Tennyson, Browning, most of the Victorian novelists, Joyce, Woolf and most writers after D. H. Lawrence constituted a network of 'B' roads interspersed with a good few cul-de-sacs. Dickens was first out and then in; 'English' included two and a half women, counting Emily Brontë as a marginal case; almost all of its authors were conservatives.

Dismissive of mere 'literary' values, *Scrutiny* insisted that how one evaluated literary works was deeply bound up with deeper judgements about the nature of history and society as a whole. Confronted with critical approaches which saw the dissection of literary texts as somehow discourteous, an equivalent in the literary realm to grievous bodily harm, it promoted the most scrupulous analysis of such sacrosanct objects. Appalled by the complacent assumption that any work written in elegant English was more or less as good as any other, it insisted on the most rigorous discrimination between different literary qualities: some works 'made for life', while others most assuredly did not. Restless with the cloistered aestheticism of conventional criticism, Leavis in his early years saw the need to address social and political questions: he even at one point guardedly entertained a form of economic communism. *Scrutiny* was not just a journal, but the focus of a moral and cultural crusade: its adherents would go out to the schools and universities to do battle there, nurturing through the study of literature the kind of rich, complex, mature, discriminating, morally serious responses (all key *Scrutiny* terms) which would equip individuals to survive in a mechanized society of trashy romances, alienated labour, banal advertisements and vulgarizing mass media.

I say 'survive', because apart from Leavis's brief toying with 'some form of economic communism', there was never any serious consideration of actually trying to *change* such a society. It was less a matter of seeking to transform the mechanized society which gave birth to this withered culture than of seeking to withstand it. In this sense, one might claim, *Scrutiny* had thrown in the towel from the start. The only form of change it contemplated was education: by implanting themselves in the educational institutions, the Scrutineers hoped to develop a rich, organic sensibility in selected individuals here and there, who might then transmit this sensibility to others. In this faith in education, Leavis was the true inheritor of Matthew Arnold. But since such individuals were bound to be few and far between, given the insidious effects of 'mass civilization', the only real hope was that an embattled cultivated minority might keep the torch of culture burning in the contemporary waste land and pass it on, via their pupils, to posterity. There are real grounds for doubting that education has the transformative power which Arnold and Leavis assigned to it. It is, after all, *part* of society rather than a solution to it; and who, as Marx once asked, will educate the educators? *Scrutiny* espoused this idealist 'solution', however, because it was loath to contemplate a political one. Spending your English lessons alerting schoolchildren to the manipulativeness of advertisements or the linguistic poverty of the popular press is an important task, and certainly more important than getting them to memorize *The Charge of the Light Brigade*. *Scrutiny* actually founded such 'cultural studies' in England, as one of its most enduring achievements. But it is also possible to point out to students that advertisements and the popular press only exist in their present form because of the profit motive. 'Mass' culture is not the inevitable product of 'industrial' society, but the offspring of a particular form of industrialism which organizes production for profit rather than for use, which concerns itself with what will sell rather than with what is valuable. There is no reason to assume that such a social order is unchangeable; but the changes necessary would go far beyond the sensitive reading of *King Lear*. The whole *Scrutiny* project was at once hair-raisingly radical and really rather absurd. As one commentator has shrewdly put it, the Decline of the West was felt to be avertible by close reading.[16] Was it really true that *literature* could roll back the deadening effects of industrial labour and the philistinism of the media? It was doubtless comforting to feel that by reading Henry James one belonged to the moral vanguard of civilization itself; but what of all those people who did not read Henry James, who had never even heard of James, and would no doubt go to their graves complacently ignorant that he had been and gone? These people certainly composed the overwhelming social majority; were they morally callous, humanly banal and imaginatively bankrupt? One was speaking perhaps of one's own parents and friends here, and so needed to be a little circumspect. Many of these people seemed morally serious and sensitive enough: they showed no particular tendency to go around murdering, looting and plundering, and even if they did it seemed implausible to attribute this to the fact that they had not read Henry James. The *Scrutiny* case was inescapably elitist: it betrayed a profound ignorance and distrust of the capacities of those not fortunate enough to have read English at Downing College. 'Ordinary' people seemed acceptable if they were seventeenth-century cowherds or 'vital' Australian bushmen.

But there was another problem, too, more or less the reverse of this. For if not all of those who could not recognize an enjambement were nasty and brutish, not all of those who could were morally pure. Many people were indeed deep in high culture, but it would transpire a decade or so after the birth of *Scrutiny* that this had not prevented some of them from engaging in such activities as superintending the murder of Jews in central Europe. The strength of Leavisian criticism was that it was able to provide an answer, as Sir Walter Raleigh was not, to the question, why read Literature? The answer, in a nutshell, was that it made you a better person. Few reasons could have been more persuasive than that. When the Allied troops moved into the concentration camps some years after the founding of *Scrutiny*, to arrest commandants who had whiled away their leisure hours with a volume of Goethe, it appeared that someone had some explaining to do. If reading literature did make you a better person, then it was hardly in the direct ways that this case at its most euphoric had imagined. It was possible to explore the 'great tradition' of the English novel and believe that in doing so you were addressing questions of fundamental value – questions which were of vital relevance to the lives of men and women wasted in fruitless labour in the factories of industrial capitalism. But it was also conceivable that you were destructively cutting yourself off from such men and women, who might be a little slow to recognize how a poetic enjambement enacted a movement of physical balancing.

The lower-middle-class origins of the architects of English are perhaps relevant here. Nonconformist, provincial, hard-working and morally conscientious, the Scrutineers had no difficulty in identifying for what it was the frivolous amateurism of the upper-class English gentlemen who filled the early Chairs of Literature at the ancient Universities. These men were not their kind of men: they were not what the son of a shopkeeper or daughter of a draper would be especially inclined to respect, as a social elite who had excluded their own people from the ancient Universities. But if the lower middle class has a deep animus against the effete aristocracy perched above it, it also works hard to discriminate itself from the working class set below it, a class into whose ranks it is always in danger of falling. *Scrutiny* arose out of this social ambivalence: radical in respect of the literary-academic Establishment, coterie-minded with regard to the mass of the people. Its fierce concern with 'standards' challenged the patrician dilettantes who felt that Walter Savage Landor was probably just as charming in his own way as John Milton, at the same time as it posed searching tests for anyone trying to muscle in on the game. The gain was a resolute singleness of purpose, uncontaminated by wine-tasting triviality on the one hand and 'mass' banality on the other. The loss was a profoundly ingrown isolationism: *Scrutiny* became a defensive elite which, like the Romantics, viewed itself as 'central' while being in fact peripheral, believed itself to be the 'real' Cambridge while the real Cambridge was busy denying it academic posts, and perceived itself as the vanguard of civilization while nostalgically lauding the organic wholeness of exploited seventeenth-century farm labourers.

The only sure fact about the organic society, as Raymond Williams has commented, is that it has always gone.[17] Organic societies are just convenient myths for belabouring the mechanized life of modern industrial capitalism. Unable to present a political alternative to this social order, the Scrutineers offered an 'historical' one instead, as the Romantics had done before them. They insisted, of course, that there was no literal returning to the golden age, as almost every English writer who has pressed the claims of some historical utopia has been careful to do. Where the organic society lingered on for the Leavisites was in certain uses of the English language. The language of commercial society was abstract and anaemic: it had lost touch with the living roots of sensuous experience. In really 'English' writing, however, language 'concretely enacted' such felt experience: true English literature was verbally rich, complex, sensuous and particular, and the best poem, to caricature the case a little, was one which read aloud sounded rather like chewing an apple. The 'health' and 'vitality' of such language was the product of a 'sane' civilization: it embodied a creative wholeness which had been historically lost, and to read literature was thus to regain vital touch with the roots of one's own being. Literature *was* in a sense an organic society all of its own: it was important because it was nothing less than a whole social ideology.

The Leavisian belief in 'essential Englishness' – its conviction that some kinds of English were more English than others – was a kind of petty-bourgeois version of the upper-class chauvinism which had helped to bring English to birth in the first place. Such rampant jingoism was less in evidence after 1918, as ex-servicemen and state-aided middle-class students began to infiltrate the public-school ethos of Oxbridge, and 'Englishness' was a more modest, home-spun alternative to it. English as a subject was in part the offshoot of a gradual shift in class tone within English culture: 'Englishness' was less a matter of imperialist flag-waving than of country dancing; rural, populist and provincial rather than metropolitan and aristocratic. Yet if it excoriated the bland assumptions of a Sir Walter Raleigh on one level, it was also in complicity with them on another. It was chauvinism modulated by a new social class, who with a little straining could see themselves as rooted in the 'English people' of John Bunyan rather than in a snobbish ruling caste. Their task was to safeguard the robust vitality of Shakespearian English from the *Daily Herald*, and from ill-starred languages such as French where words were not able concretely to enact their own meanings. This whole notion of language rested upon a naive mimeticism: the theory was that words are somehow healthiest when they approach the condition of things, and thus cease to be words at all. Language is alienated or degenerate unless it is crammed with the physical textures of actual experience, plumped with the rank juices of real life. Armed with this trust in essential Englishness, latinate or verbally disembodied writers (Milton, Shelley) could be shown the door, and pride of place assigned to the 'dramatically concrete' (Donne, Hopkins). There was no question of seeing such re-mapping of the literary terrain as simply one arguable *construction* of a tradition, informed by definite ideological preconceptions: such authors, it was felt, just did manifest the essence of Englishness.

The literary map was in fact already being drawn elsewhere, by a body of criticism which influenced Leavis greatly. In 1915 T. S. Eliot had come to London, son of an 'aristocratic' St Louis family whose traditional role of cultural leadership was being eroded by the industrial middle class of their own nation.[18] Repelled like *Scrutiny* by the spiritual barrenness of industrial capitalism, Eliot had glimpsed an alternative in the life of the old American South – yet another candidate for the elusive organic society, where blood and breeding still counted for something. Culturally displaced and spiritually disinherited, Eliot arrived in England, and in what has rightly been described as 'the most ambitious feat of cultural imperialism the century seems likely to produce',[19] began to carry out a wholesale salvage and demolition job on its literary traditions. The Metaphysical poets and Jacobean dramatists were suddenly upgraded; Milton and the Romantics were rudely toppled; selected European products, including the French Symbolists, were imported.

This, as with *Scrutiny*, was much more than a 'literary' revaluation: it reflected nothing less than a whole political reading of English history. In the early seventeenth century, when the absolute monarchy and the Anglican church still flourished, poets like John Donne and George Herbert (both conservative Anglicans) displayed a unity of sensibility, an easy fusion of thought and feeling. Language was in direct touch with sensory experience, the intellect was 'at the tip of the senses', and to have a thought was as physical as smelling a rose. By the end of the century, the English had fallen from this paradisal state. A turbulent civil war had beheaded the monarch, lower-class puritanism had disrupted the Church, and the forces which were to produce modern secular society – science, democracy, rationalism, economic individualism – were in the ascendant. From about Andrew Marvell onwards, then, it was downhill all the way. Somewhere in the seventeenth century, though Eliot is unsure of the precise date, a 'dissociation of sensibility' set in: thinking was no longer like smelling, language drifted loose from experience, and the upshot was the literary disaster of John Milton, who anaesthetized the English language into an arid ritual. Milton was also, of course, a puritan revolutionary, which may not have been entirely irrelevant to Eliot's distaste; indeed he was part of the great nonconformist radical tradition in England which produced F. R. Leavis, whose quickness to endorse Eliot's judgement of *Paradise Lost* is thus particularly ironic. After Milton, the English sensibility continued to dissociate itself into separate halves: some poets could think but not feel, while others could feel but not think. English literature degenerated into Romanticism and Victorianism: by now the heresies of 'poetic genius',

'personality' and the 'inner light' were firmly entrenched, all anarchic doctrines of a society which had lost collective belief and declined into an errant
individualism. It was not until the appearance of T. S. Eliot that English
literature began to recuperate.

What Eliot was in fact assaulting was the whole ideology of middle-class
liberalism, the official ruling ideology of industrial capitalist society. Liberalism, Romanticism, protestantism, economic individualism: all of these are
the perverted dogmas of those expelled from the happy garden of the
organic society, with nothing to fall back on but their own paltry individual
resources. Eliot's own solution is an extreme right-wing authoritarianism:
men and women must sacrifice their petty 'personalities' and opinions to an
impersonal order. In the sphere of literature, this impersonal order is the
Tradition.[20] Like any other literary tradition, Eliot's is in fact a highly
selective affair: indeed its governing principle seems to be not so much
which works of the past are eternally valuable, as which will help T. S. Eliot
to write his own poetry. This arbitrary construct, however, is then paradoxically imbued with the force of an absolute authority. The major works of
literature form between them an ideal order, occasionally redefined by the
entry of a new masterpiece. The existing classics within the cramped space
of the Tradition politely reshuffle their positions to make room for a newcomer, and look different in the light of it; but since this newcomer must
somehow have been in principle included in the Tradition all along to have
gained admission at all, its entry serves to confirm that Tradition's central
values. The Tradition, in other words, can never be caught napping: it has
somehow mysteriously foreseen the major works still unwritten, and though
these works, once produced, will occasion a revaluation of the Tradition
itself, they will be effortlessly absorbed into its maw. A literary work can be
valid only by existing in the Tradition, as a Christian can be saved only by
living in God; all poetry may be literature but only some poetry is Literature, depending on whether or not the Tradition happens to flow through it.
This, like divine grace, is an inscrutable affair: the Tradition, like the
Almighty or some whimsical absolute monarch, sometimes withholds its
favour from 'major' literary reputations and bestows it instead on some
humble little text buried in the historical backwoods. Membership of the
club is by invitation only: some writers, such as T. S. Eliot, just do discover
that the Tradition (or the 'European mind', as Eliot sometimes calls it) is
spontaneously welling up within them, but as with the recipients of divine
grace this is not a question of personal merit, and there is nothing much you
can do about it one way or the other. Membership of the Tradition thus
permits you to be at once authoritarian and self-abnegatingly humble, a

combination which Eliot was later to find even more possible through membership of the Christian Church.

In the political sphere, Eliot's advocacy of authority took various forms. He flirted with the quasi-fascistic French movement *Action Française*, and made a few rather negative references to Jews. After his conversion to Christianity in the mid-1920s he advocated a largely rural society run by a few 'great families' and a small elite of theological intellectuals much like himself. Most people in such a society would be Christian, though since Eliot had an extremely conservative estimate of most people's ability to believe anything at all, this religious faith would have to be largely unconscious, lived out in the rhythm of the seasons. This panacea for the redemption of modern society was being offered to the world roughly at the time when Hitler's troops were marching into Poland.

The advantage of a language closely wedded to experience, for Eliot, was that it enabled the poet to bypass the deadly abstractions of rationalist thought and seize his readers by the 'cerebral cortex, the nervous system, and the digestive tracts'.[21] Poetry was not to engage the reader's mind: it did not really matter what a poem actually *meant*, and Eliot professed himself to be quite unperturbed by apparently outlandish interpretations of his own work. Meaning was no more than a sop thrown to the reader to keep him distracted, while the poem went stealthily to work on him in more physical and unconscious ways. The erudite Eliot, author of intellectually difficult poems, in fact betrayed all the contempt for the intellect of any right-wing irrationalist. He shrewdly perceived that the languages of middle-class liberal rationalism were exhausted: nobody was much likely to be convinced by talk of 'progress' or 'reason' any more, not least when millions of corpses lay on the battlefields of Europe. Middle-class liberalism had failed; and the poet must delve behind these discredited notions by evolving a sensory language which would make 'direct communication with the nerves'. He must select words with 'a network of tentacular roots reaching down to the deepest terrors and desires',[22] suggestively enigmatic images which would penetrate to those 'primitive' levels at which all men and women experienced alike. Perhaps the organic society lived on after all, though only in the collective unconscious; perhaps there were certain deep symbols and rhythms in the psyche, archetypes immutable throughout history, which poetry might touch and revive. The crisis of European society – global war, severe class-conflict, failing capitalist economies – might be resolved by turning one's back on history altogether and putting mythology in its place. Deep below finance capitalism lay the Fisher King, potent images of birth, death and resurrection in which human beings might discover a common identity. Eliot accordingly published *The Waste Land* in 1922, a poem which intimates that fertility cults hold the clue to the salvation of the West. His scandalous avant-garde techniques were deployed for the most arrière-garde ends: they wrenched apart routine consciousness so as to revive in the reader a sense of common identity in the blood and guts.

Eliot's view that language had become stale and unprofitable in industrial society, unsuitable for poetry, had affinities with Russian Formalism; but it was also shared by Ezra Pound, T. E. Hulme and the Imagist movement. Poetry had fallen foul of the Romantics, become a mawkish, womanly affair full of gush and fine feeling. Language had gone soft and lost its virility: it needed to be stiffened up again, made hard and stone-like, reconnected with the physical world. The ideal Imagist poem would be a laconic three-line affair of gritty images, like an army officer's rapped-out command. Emotions were messy and suspect, part of a clapped-out epoch of high-flown liberal-individualist sentiment which must now yield to the dehumanized mechanical world of modern society. For D. H. Lawrence, emotions, 'personality' and the 'ego' were equally discredited, and must give way to the ruthlessly impersonal force of spontaneous-creative Life. Behind the critical stance, once again, was politics: middle-class liberalism was finished, and would be ousted by some version of that tougher, masculine discipline which Pound was to discover in fascism.

The *Scrutiny* case, at least at first, did not take the road of extreme right-wing reaction. On the contrary, it represented nothing less than the last-ditch stand of liberal humanism, concerned, as Eliot and Pound were not, with the unique value of the individual and the creative realm of the inter-personal. These values could be summarized as 'Life', a word which *Scrutiny* made a virtue out of not being able to define. If you asked for some reasoned theoretical statement of their case, you had thereby demonstrated that you were in the outer darkness: either you felt Life or you did not. Great literature was a literature reverently open to Life, and what Life was could be demonstrated by great literature. The case was circular, intuitive, and proof against all argument, reflecting the enclosed coterie of the Leavisites themselves. It was not clear what side Life put you on in the General Strike, or whether celebrating its vibrant presence in poetry was compatible with endorsing mass unemployment. If Life was creatively at work anywhere then it was in the writings of D. H. Lawrence, whom Leavis championed from an early date; yet 'spontaneous-creative life' in Lawrence seemed happily to co-exist with the most virulent sexism, racism and authoritarianism, and few of the Scrutineers seemed particularly disturbed by the contradiction. The extreme right-wing features which Lawrence shared with Eliot and Pound – a raging contempt for liberal and democratic values, a slavish submission to impersonal authority – were more or less edited out: Lawrence was effectively reconstructed as a liberal humanist, and slotted into place as the triumphant culmination of the 'great tradition' of English fiction from Jane Austen to George Eliot, Henry James and Joseph Conrad.

Leavis was right to discern in the acceptable face of D. H. Lawrence a powerful critique of the inhumanity of industrial capitalist England. Lawrence, like Leavis himself, was among other things an inheritor of the nineteenth-century lineage of Romantic protest against the mechanized wage-slavery of capitalism, its crippling social oppressiveness and cultural devastation. But since both Lawrence and Leavis refused a political analysis of the system they opposed, they were left with nothing but talk about spontaneous-creative life which grew more stridently abstract the more it insisted on the concrete. As it became less and less apparent how responding to Marvell around the seminar table was to transform the mechanized labour of factory workers, the liberal humanism of Leavis was pressed into the arms of the most banal political reaction. *Scrutiny* survived until 1953, and Leavis lived until 1978; but in these later stages Life evidently entailed a fierce hostility to popular education, an implacable opposition to the transistor radio and a dark suspicion that 'telly-addiction' had much to do with demands for student participation in higher education. Modern 'technologico-Benthamite' society was to be condemned unreservedly as 'cretinized and cretinizing': this, it seemed, was the final consequence of rigorous critical discrimination. The later Leavis was to regret the passing of the English gentleman; the wheel had come full circle.

Leavis's name is closely associated with 'practical criticism' and 'close reading', and some of his own published work ranks with the most subtle, pioneering English criticism that the century has seen. It is worth pondering this term 'practical criticism' a little further. Practical criticism meant a method which spurned belle-lettristic waffle and was properly unafraid to take the text apart; but it also assumed that you could judge literary 'greatness' and 'centrality' by bringing a focused attentiveness to bear on poems or pieces of prose isolated from their cultural and historical contexts. Given *Scrutiny*'s assumptions, there was really no problem here: if literature is 'healthy' when it manifests a concrete feel for immediate experience, then you can judge this from a scrap of prose as surely as a doctor can judge whether or not you are sick by registering your pulse-beat and skin-colour. There was no need to examine the work in its historical context, or even discuss the structure of ideas on which it drew. It was a matter of assessing the tone and sensibility of a particular passage, 'placing' it definitively and then moving on to the next. It is not clear how this procedure was more than just a more rigorous form of wine-tasting, given that what the literary impressionists might call 'blissful' you might call 'maturely robust'. If Life seemed altogether too broad and nebulous a term, the critical techniques for detecting it seemed correspondingly too narrow. Since practical criticism in itself threatened to become too pragmatic a pursuit for a movement concerned with nothing less than the fate of civilization, the Leavisites needed to underpin it with a 'metaphysic', and found one ready to hand in the work of D. H. Lawrence. Since Life was not a theoretical system but a matter of particular intuitions, you could always take your stand on these in order to attack other people's systems; but since Life was also as absolute a value as you could imagine, you could equally use it to lambaste those utilitarians and empiricists who could see no further than their noses. It was possible to spend quite a lot of time crossing from one of these fronts to another, depending on the direction of the enemy fire. Life was as remorseless and unquestionable a metaphysical principle as you could wish, dividing the literary sheep from the goats with evangelical certainty; but since it only ever manifested itself in concrete particularities, it constituted no systematic theory in itself and was consequently invulnerable to assault.

'Close reading' is also a phrase worth examining. Like 'practical criticism' it meant detailed analytic interpretation, providing a valuable antidote to aestheticist chit-chat; but it also seemed to imply that every previous school of criticism had read only an average of three words per line. To call for close reading, in fact, is to do more than insist on due attentiveness to the text. It inescapably suggests an attention to *this* rather than to something else: to the 'words on the page' rather than to the contexts which produced and surround them. It implies a limiting as well as a focusing of concern – a limiting badly needed by literary talk which would ramble comfortably from the texture of Tennyson's language to the length of his beard. But in dispelling such anecdotal irrelevancies, 'close reading' also held at bay a good deal else: it encouraged the illusion that any piece of language, 'literary' or not, can be adequately studied or even understood in isolation. It was the beginnings of a 'reification' of the literary work, the treatment of it as an object in itself, which was to be triumphantly consummated in the American New Criticism.

A major link between Cambridge English and the American New Criticism was the work of the Cambridge critic I. A. Richards. If Leavis sought to redeem criticism by converting it into something approximating a religion, thus carrying on the work of Matthew Arnold, Richards sought in his works of the 1920s to lend it a firm basis in the principles of a hard-nosed 'scientific' psychology. The brisk, bloodless quality of his prose contrasts suggestively with the tortuous intensity of a Leavis. Society is in crisis, Richards argues, because historical change, and scientific discovery in particular, has outstripped and devalued the traditional mythologies by which men and women have lived. The delicate equipoise of the human psyche has therefore been dangerously disturbed; and since religion will no longer serve to retrim it, poetry must do the job instead. Poetry, Richards remarks with stunning off-handedness, 'is capable of saving us; it is a perfectly possible means of overcoming chaos'.[23] Like Arnold, he advances literature as a conscious ideology for reconstructing social order, and does so in the socially disruptive, economically decaying, politically unstable years which followed the Great War.

Modern science, Richards claims, is the model of true knowledge, but emotionally it leaves something to be desired. It will not satisfy the mass of the people's demand for answers to the questions 'what?' and 'why?', contenting itself instead with answering the question 'how?'. Richards himself does not believe that 'what?' and 'why?' are genuine questions, but he generously concedes that most people do; and unless some pseudo-answers are supplied to such pseudo-questions society is likely to fall apart. The role of poetry is to supply such pseudo-answers. Poetry is an 'emotive' rather than 'referential' language, a kind of 'pseudo-statement' which appears to describe the world but in fact simply organizes our feelings about it in satisfying ways. The most efficient kind of poetry is that which organizes the maximum number of impulses with the minimum amount of conflict or frustration. Without such psychic therapy, standards of value are likely to collapse beneath the 'more sinister potentialities of the cinema and the loud-speaker'.[24]

Richards's quantifying, behaviourist model of the mind was in fact part of the social problem to which he was proposing a solution. Far from questioning the alienated view of science as a purely instrumental, neutrally 'referential' affair, he subscribes to this positivist fantasy and then lamely seeks to supplement it with something more cheering. Whereas Leavis waged war on the technologico-Benthamites, Richards tried to beat them at their own game. Linking a defective utilitarian theory of value to an essentially aestheticist view of human experience (art, Richards assumes, defines all the most excellent experiences), he offers poetry as a means of 'exquisitely reconciling' the anarchy of modern existence. If historical contradictions cannot be resolved in reality, they can be harmoniously conciliated as discrete psychological 'impulses' within the contemplative mind. Action is not

especially desirable, since it tends to impede any full equilibrium of impulses. 'No life,' Richards remarks, 'can be excellent in which the elemen-
tary responses are disorganized and confused.'[25] Organizing the lawless
lower impulses more effectively will ensure the survival of the higher, finer
ones; it is not far from the Victorian belief that organizing the lower classes
will ensure the survival of the upper ones, and indeed is significantly related
to it.

The American New Criticism, which flourished from the late 1930s to the
1950s, was deeply marked by these doctrines. New Criticism is generally
taken to encompass the work of Eliot, Richards and perhaps also Leavis and
William Empson, as well as a number of leading American literary critics,
among them John Crowe Ransom, W. K. Wimsatt, Cleanth Brooks, Allen
Tate, Monroe Beardsley and R. P. Blackmur. Significantly, the American
movement had its roots in the economically backward South – in the region
of traditional blood and breeding where the young T. S. Eliot had gained an
early glimpse of the organic society. In the period of American New Criticism, the South was in fact undergoing rapid industrialization, invaded by
Northern capitalist monopolies; but 'traditional' Southern intellectuals like
John Crowe Ransom, who gave New Criticism its name, could still discover
in it an 'aesthetic' alternative to the sterile scientific rationalism of the
industrial North. Spiritually displaced like T. S. Eliot by the industrial
invasion, Ransom found refuge first in the so-called Fugitives literary movement of the 1920s, and then in the right-wing Agrarian politics of the 1930s.
The ideology of New Criticism began to crystallize: scientific rationalism
was ravaging the 'aesthetic life' of the old South, human experience was
being stripped of its sensuous particularity, and poetry was a possible solution. The poetic response, unlike the scientific, respected the sensuous
integrity of its object: it was not a matter of rational cognition but an
affective affair which linked us to the 'world's body' in an essentially religious bond. Through art, an alienated world could be restored to us in all its
rich variousness. Poetry, as an essentially contemplative mode, would spur
us not to change the world but to reverence it for what it was, teach us to
approach it with a disinterested humility.

Like *Scrutiny*, in other words, New Criticism was the ideology of an
uprooted, defensive intelligentsia who reinvented in literature what they
could not locate in reality. Poetry was the new religion, a nostalgic haven
from the alienations of industrial capitalism. The poem itself was as opaque
to rational enquiry as the Almighty himself: it existed as a self-enclosed
object, mysteriously intact in its own unique being. The poem was that
which could not be paraphrased, expressed in any language other than itself:

each of its parts was folded in on the others in a complex organic unity which it would be a kind of blasphemy to violate. The literary text, for American New Criticism as for I. A. Richards, was therefore grasped in what might be called 'functionalist' terms: just as American functionalist sociology developed a 'conflict-free' model of society, in which every element 'adapted' to every other, so the poem abolished all friction, irregularity and contradiction in the symmetrical cooperation of its various features. 'Coherence' and 'integration' were the keynotes; but if the poem was also to induce in the reader a definite ideological attitude to the world – one, roughly, of contemplative acceptance – this emphasis on internal coherence could not be pushed to the point where the poem was cut off from reality altogether, splendidly revolving in its own autonomous being. It was therefore necessary to combine this stress on the text's internal unity with an insistence that, through such unity, the work 'corresponded' in some sense to reality itself. New Criticism, in other words, stopped short of a full-blooded formalism, awkwardly tempering it with a kind of empiricism – a belief that the poem's discourse somehow 'included' reality within itself.

If the poem was really to become an object in itself, New Criticism had to sever it from both author and reader. I. A. Richards had naively assumed that the poem was no more than a transparent medium through which we could observe the poet's psychological processes: reading was just a matter of recreating in our own mind the mental condition of the author. Indeed much traditional literary criticism had held this view in one form or another. Great literature is the product of Great Men, and its value lies chiefly in allowing us intimate access to their souls. There are several problems with such a position. To begin with, it reduces all literature to a covert form of autobiography: we are not reading literary works as literary works, simply as second-hand ways of getting to know somebody. For another thing, such a view entails that literary works are indeed 'expressions' of an author's mind, which does not seem a particularly helpful way of discussing *Little Red Riding Hood* or some highly stylized courtly love lyric. Even if I do have access to Shakespeare's mind when reading *Hamlet*, what is the point of putting it this way, since all of his mind that I have access to is the text of *Hamlet*? Why not just say instead that I am reading *Hamlet*, as he left no evidence of it other than the play itself? Was what he 'had in mind' different from what he wrote, and how can we know? Did he himself know what he had in mind? Are writers always in full possession of their own meanings?

The New Critics broke boldly with the Great Man theory of literature, insisting that the author's intentions in writing, even if they could be recovered, were of no relevance to the interpretation of his or her text. Neither were the emotional responses of particular readers to be confused with the poem's meaning: the poem meant what it meant, regardless of the poet's intentions or the subjective feelings the reader derived from it.[26] Meaning was public and objective, inscribed in the very language of the literary text, not a question of some putative ghostly impulse in a long-dead author's head, or the arbitrary private significances a reader might attach to his words. We shall be considering the pros and cons of this viewpoint in Chapter 2; meanwhile, it should be recognized that the New Critics' attitudes to these questions were closely bound up with their urge to convert the poem into a self-sufficient object, as solid and material as an urn or icon. The poem became a spatial figure rather than a temporal process. Rescuing the text from author and reader went hand in hand with disentangling it from any social or historical context. One needed, to be sure, to know what the poem's words would have meant to their original readers, but this fairly technical sort of historical knowledge was the only kind permitted. Literature was a solution to social problems, not part of them; the poem must be plucked free of the wreckage of history and hoisted into a sublime space above it.

What New Criticism did, in fact, was to convert the poem into a fetish. If I. A. Richards had 'dematerialized' the text, reducing it to a transparent window on to the poet's psyche, the American New Critics rematerialized it with a vengeance, making it seem less like a process of meaning than something with four corners and a pebbledash front. This is ironic, since the very social order against which such poetry was a protest was rife with such 'reifications', transforming people, processes and institutions into 'things'. The New Critical poem, like the Romantic symbol, was thus imbued with an absolute mystical authority which brooked no rational argument. Like most of the other literary theories we have examined so far, New Criticism was at root a full-blooded irrationalism, one closely associated with religious dogma (several of the leading American New Critics were Christians), and with the right-wing 'blood and soil' politics of the Agrarian movement. Yet this is not to suggest that New Criticism was hostile to critical analysis, any more than was *Scrutiny*. Whereas some earlier Romantics tended to bow low in reverent silence before the unfathomable mystery of the text, the New Critics deliberately cultivated the toughest, most hard-headed techniques of critical dissection. The same impulse which stirred them to insist on the 'objective' status of the work also led them to promote a strictly 'objective' way of analysing it. A typical New Critical account of a poem offers a stringent investigation of its various 'tensions', 'paradoxes' and 'ambivalences', showing how these are resolved and integrated by its solid structure. If poetry was

to be the new organic society in itself, the final solution to science, materialism, and the decline of the 'aesthetic' slave-owning South, it could hardly be
surrendered to critical impressionism or soggy subjectivism.

New Criticism, moreover, evolved in the years when literary criticism in
North America was struggling to become 'professionalized', acceptable as
a respectable academic discipline. Its battery of critical instruments was a
way of competing with the hard sciences on their own terms, in a society
where such science was the dominant criterion of knowledge. Having
begun life as a humanistic supplement or alternative to technocratic society,
the movement thus found itself reproducing such technocracy in its own
methods. The rebel merged into the image of his master, and as the
1940s and 1950s drew on was fairly quickly coopted by the academic
Establishment. Before long, New Criticism seemed the most natural thing in
the literary critical world; indeed it was difficult to imagine that there had
ever been anything else. The long trek from Nashville, Tennessee, home
of the Fugitives, to the East Coast Ivy League universities had been
accomplished.

There were at least two good reasons why New Criticism went down well
in the academies. First, it provided a convenient pedagogical method of
coping with a growing student population.[27] Distributing a brief poem for
students to be perceptive about was less cumbersome than launching a Great
Novels of the World course. Second, New Criticism's view of the poem as
a delicate equipoise of contending attitudes, a disinterested reconciliation of
opposing impulses, proved deeply attractive to sceptical liberal intellectuals
disoriented by the clashing dogmas of the Cold War. Reading poetry in the
New Critical way meant committing yourself to nothing: all that poetry
taught you was 'disinterestedness', a serene, speculative, impeccably even-
handed rejection of anything in particular. It drove you less to oppose
McCarthyism or further civil rights than to experience such pressures as
merely partial, no doubt harmoniously balanced somewhere else in the
world by their complementary opposites. It was, in other words, a recipe for
political inertia, and thus for submission to the political status quo. There
were, naturally, limits to this benign pluralism: the poem, in Cleanth
Brooks's words, was a 'unification of attitudes into a hierarchy subordinated
to a total and governing attitude'.[28] Pluralism was all very well, provided that
it did not violate hierarchical order; the varied contingencies of the poem's
texture could be pleasurably savoured, so long as its ruling structure remained intact. Oppositions were to be tolerated, as long as they could finally
be fused into harmony. The limits of New Criticism were essentially the
limits of liberal democracy: the poem, John Crowe Ransom wrote, was 'like

a democratic state, so to speak, which realizes the ends of a state without sacrificing the personal character of its citizens'.[29] It would be interesting to know what the Southern slaves would have made of this assertion.

The reader may have noticed that 'literature', in the work of the last few critics I have discussed, has imperceptibly slid over into 'poetry'. The New Critics and I. A. Richards are almost exclusively concerned with poems; T. S. Eliot stretches to the drama but not to the novel; F. R. Leavis deals with the novel but examines it under the rubric of 'dramatic poem' – that is, as anything but the novel. Most literary theories, in fact, unconsciously 'foreground' a particular literary genre, and derive their general pronouncements from this; it would be interesting to trace this process through the history of literary theory, identifying the particular literary form which is being taken as a paradigm. In the case of modern literary theory, the shift into poetry is of particular significance. For poetry is of all literary genres the one most apparently sealed from history, the one where 'sensibility' may play in its purest, least socially tainted form. It would be difficult to see *Tristram Shandy* or *War and Peace* as tightly organized structures of symbolic ambivalence. Even within poetry, however, the critics I have just reviewed are strikingly uninterested in what might rather simplistically be called 'thought'. The criticism of Eliot displays an extraordinary lack of interest in what literary works actually *say*: its attention is almost entirely confined to qualities of language, styles of feeling, the relations of image and experience. A 'classic' for Eliot is a work which springs from a structure of shared beliefs, but what these beliefs are is less important than the fact that they are commonly shared. For Richards, bothering with beliefs is a positive obstacle to literary appreciation: the strong emotion we feel on reading a poem may *feel* like a belief, but this is just another pseudo-condition. Only Leavis escapes this formalism, with his view that the complex formal unity of a work, and its 'reverent openness before life', are facets of a single process. In practice, however, his work tends to divide between 'formal' criticism of poetry and 'moral' criticism of fiction.

I have mentioned that the English critic William Empson is sometimes included in New Criticism; but he is in fact much more interestingly read as a remorseless opponent of their major doctrines. What makes Empson seem a New Critic is his lemon-squeezing style of analysis, the breathtaking offhand ingenuity with which he unravels ever finer nuances of literary meaning; but all this is in the service of an old-fashioned liberal rationalism deeply at odds with the symbolist esotericism of an Eliot or Brooks. In his major works *Seven Types of Ambiguity* (1930), *Some Versions of Pastoral* (1935), *The Structure of Complex Words* (1951) and *Milton's God* (1961), Empson turns a cold douche of very English common sense on such fervid pieties, evident in his deliberately flattened, low-keyed, airily colloquial prose style. Whereas New Criticism sunders the text from rational discourse and a social context, Empson impudently insists on treating poetry as a species of 'ordinary' language capable of being rationally paraphrased, a type of utterance in continuity with our usual ways of speaking and acting. He is an unabashed 'intentionalist', reckoning into account what the author probably meant and interpreting this in the most generous, decent, English sort of way. Far from existing as an opaquely enclosed object, the literary work for Empson is open-ended: understanding it involves grasping the general contexts in which words are socially used, rather than simply tracing patterns of internal verbal coherence, and such contexts are always likely to be indeterminate. It is interesting to contrast Empson's famous 'ambiguities' with New Criticism's 'paradox', 'irony' and 'ambivalence'. The latter terms suggest the economic fusion of two opposite but complementary meanings: the New Critical poem is a taut structure of such antitheses, but they never really threaten our need for coherence because they are always resolvable into a closed unity. Empsonian ambiguities, on the other hand, can never be finally pinned down: they indicate points where the poem's language falters, trails off or gestures beyond itself, pregnantly suggestive of some potentially inexhaustible context of meaning. Whereas the reader is shut out by a locked structure of ambivalences, reduced to admiring passivity, 'ambiguity' solicits his or her active participation: an ambiguity as Empson defined it is 'any verbal nuance, however slight, which gives room for alternative reactions to the same piece of language'.[30] It is the reader's response which makes for ambiguity, and this response depends on more than the poem alone. For I. A. Richards and the New Critics, the meaning of a poetic word is radically 'contextual', a function of the poem's internal verbal organization. For Empson, the reader inevitably brings to the work whole social contexts of discourse, tacit assumptions of sense-making which the text may challenge but with which it is also in continuity. Empson's poetics are liberal, social and democratic, appealing, for all their dazzling idiosyncrasy, to the likely sympathies and expectations of a common reader rather than to the technocratic techniques of the professional critic.

Like all English common sense, Empson's has its severe limitations. He is an old-style Enlightenment rationalist whose trust in decency, reasonableness, common human sympathies and a general human nature is as winning as it is suspect. Empson engages in constant self-critical questioning of the gap between his own intellectual subtlety and a simple common humanity: 'pastoral' is defined as the literary mode in which both can genially co-exist, though never without an uneasy ironic self-consciousness of the incongruity. But the irony of Empson, and of his favoured form of pastoral, are also signs of a deeper contradiction. They mark the dilemma of the liberal-minded literary intellectual of the 1920s and 1930s, aware of the gross disparity between a now highly specialized form of critical intelligence and the 'universal' preoccupations of the literature on which it goes to work. Such a baffled, ambiguous consciousness, aware of the clash between pursuing ever finer poetic nuances and the economic depression, is able to resolve those commitments only by faith in a 'common reason' which may in fact be less common and more socially particular than it looks. Pastoral is not exactly Empson's organic society: it is the looseness and incongruity of the form, rather than any 'vital unity', which attracts him, its ironic juxtapositions of lords and peasants, the sophisticated and the simple. But pastoral does none the less provide him with a kind of imaginary solution to a pressing historical problem: the problem of the intellectual's relation to 'common humanity', the relation between a tolerant intellectual scepticism and more taxing convictions, and the social relevance of a professionalized criticism to a crisis-ridden society.

Empson sees that the meanings of a literary text are always in some measure promiscuous, never reducible to a final interpretation; and in the opposition between his 'ambiguity' and New Critical 'ambivalence' we find a kind of early pre-run of the debate between structuralists and post-structuralists which we shall explore later. It has also been suggested that Empson's concern for authorial intentions is in some ways reminiscent of the work of the German philosopher Edmund Husserl.[31] Whether or not this is true, it provides a convenient transition to the next chapter.

2

Phenomenology, Hermeneutics, Reception Theory

In 1918 Europe lay in ruins, devastated by the worst war in history. In the wake of that catastrophe, a wave of social revolutions rolled across the continent: the years around 1920 were to witness the Berlin Spartacus uprising and the Vienna General Strike, the establishment of workers' soviets in Munich and Budapest, and mass factory occupations throughout Italy. All of this insurgency was violently crushed; but the social order of European capitalism had been shaken to its roots by the carnage of the war and its turbulent political aftermath. The ideologies on which that order had customarily depended, the cultural values by which it ruled, were also in deep turmoil. Science seemed to have dwindled to a sterile positivism, a myopic obsession with the categorizing of facts; philosophy appeared torn between such a positivism on the one hand, and an indefensible subjectivism on the other; forms of relativism and irrationalism were rampant, and art reflected this bewildering loss of bearings. It was in this context of wide-spread ideological crisis, one which long pre-dated the First World War itself, that the German philosopher Edmund Husserl sought to develop a new philosophical method which would lend absolute certainty to a disinte-grating civilization. It was a choice, Husserl was to write later in his *The Crisis of the European Sciences* (1935), between irrationalist barbarity on the one hand, and spiritual rebirth through an 'absolutely self-sufficient science of the spirit' on the other.

Husserl, like his philosopher predecessor René Descartes, started out on his hunt for certainty by provisionally rejecting what he called the 'natural attitude' – the commonsensical person-in-the-street belief that objects existed independently of ourselves in the external world, and that our information about them was generally reliable. Such an attitude merely took the possibility of knowledge for granted, whereas it was this, precisely, which was in question. What then *can* we be clear about and certain of? Although we cannot be sure of the independent existence of things, Husserl argues, we can be certain of how they appear to us immediately in consciousness, whether the actual thing we are experiencing is an illusion or not. Objects can be regarded not as things in themselves but as things posited, or 'intended', by consciousness. All consciousness is consciousness of something: in thinking, I am aware that my thought is 'pointing towards' some object. The act of thinking and the object of thought are internally related, mutually dependent. My consciousness is not just a passive registration of the world, but actively constitutes or 'intends' it. To establish certainty, then, we must first of all ignore, or 'put in brackets', anything which is beyond our immediate experience; we must reduce the external world to the contents of our consciousness alone. This, the so-called 'phenomenological reduction', is Husserl's first important move. Everything not 'immanent' to consciousness must be rigorously excluded; all realities must be treated as pure 'phenomena', in terms of their appearances in our mind, and this is the only absolute data from which we can begin. The name Husserl gave to his philosophical method – phenomenology – stems from this insistence. Phenomenology is a science of pure phenomena.

This, however, is not enough to resolve our problems. For perhaps all we find, when we inspect the contents of our minds, is no more than a random flux of phenomena, a chaotic stream of consciousness, and we can hardly found certainty upon this. The kind of 'pure' phenomena with which Husserl is concerned, however, are more than just random individual particulars. They are a system of universal *essences*, for phenomenology varies each object in imagination until it discovers what is invariable about it. What is presented to phenomenological knowledge is not just, say, the experience of jealousy or of the colour red, but the universal types or essences of these things, jealousy or redness as such. To grasp any phenomenon wholly and purely is to grasp what is essential and unchanging about it. The Greek word for type is *eidos*; and Husserl accordingly speaks of his method as effecting an 'eidetic' abstraction, along with its phenomenological reduction.

All of this may sound intolerably abstract and unreal, which indeed it is. But the aim of phenomenology was in fact the precise opposite of abstraction: it was a return to the concrete, to solid ground, as its famous slogan 'Back to the things themselves!' suggested. Philosophy had been too concerned with concepts and too little with hard data: it had thus built its precarious, top-heavy intellectual systems on the frailest of foundations.

Phenomenology, by seizing what we could be experientially sure of, could furnish the basis on which genuinely reliable knowledge could be constructed. It could be a 'science of sciences', providing a method for the study of anything whatsoever: memory, matchboxes, mathematics. If offered itself as nothing less than a science of human consciousness – human consciousness conceived not just as the empirical experience of particular people, but as the very 'deep structures' of the mind itself. Unlike the sciences, it asked not about this or that particular form of knowledge, but about the conditions which made any sort of knowledge possible in the first place. It was thus, like the philosophy of Kant before it, a 'transcendental' mode of enquiry; and the human subject, or individual consciousness, which preoccupied it was a 'transcendental' subject. Phenomenology examined not just what I happened to perceive when I looked at a particular rabbit, but the universal essence of rabbits and of the act of perceiving them. It was not, in other words, a form of empiricism, concerned with the random, fragmentary experience of particular individuals; neither was it a kind of 'psychologism', interested just in the observable mental processes of such individuals. It claimed to lay bare the very structures of consciousness itself, and in the same act to lay bare the very phenomena themselves.

It should be obvious even from this brief account of phenomenology that it is a form of methodological idealism, seeking to explore an abstraction called 'human consciousness' and a world of pure possibilities. But if Husserl rejected empiricism, psychologism and the positivism of the natural sciences, he also considered himself to be breaking with the classical idealism of a thinker like Kant. Kant had been unable to solve the problem of how the mind can really know objects outside it at all; phenomenology, in claiming that what is given in pure perception is the very essence of things, hoped to surmount this scepticism.

It all seems a far cry from Leavis and the organic society. But is it? After all, the return to 'things in themselves', the impatient dismissal of theories unrooted in 'concrete' life, is not so far from Leavis's naively mimetic theory of poetic language as embodying the very stuff of reality itself. Leavis and Husserl both turn to the consolations of the concrete, of what can be known on the pulses, in a period of major ideological crisis; and this recourse to 'things themselves' involves in both cases a thoroughgoing irrationalism. For Husserl, knowledge of phenomena is absolutely certain, or as he says 'apodictic', because it is intuitive: I can doubt such things no more than I can doubt a sharp tap on the skull. For Leavis, certain forms of language are 'intuitively' right, vital and creative, and however much he conceived of criticism as a collaborative argument there was in the end no gainsaying this.

For both men, moreover, what is intuited in the act of grasping the concrete phenomenon is something universal: the *eidos* for Husserl, Life for Leavis. They do not, in other words, have to move beyond the security of the immediate sensation in order to develop a 'global' theory: the phenomena come ready equipped with one. But it is bound to be an authoritarian theory, since it depends wholly on intuition. Phenomena for Husserl do not need to be *interpreted*, constructed this way or that in reasoned argument. Like certain literary judgements, they force themselves upon us 'irresistibly', to use a key Leavisian word. It is not difficult to see the relation between such dogmatism – one manifest throughout Leavis's own career – and a conservative contempt for rational analysis. Finally, we may note how Husserl's 'intentional' theory of consciousness suggests that 'being' and 'meaning' are always bound up with one another. There is no object without a subject, and no subject without an object. Object and subject, for Husserl as for the English philosopher F. H. Bradley, who influenced T. S. Eliot, are really two sides of the same coin. In a society where objects appear as alienated, cut off from human purposes, and human subjects are consequently plunged into anxious isolation, this is certainly a consoling doctrine. Mind and world have been put back together again – at least in the mind. Leavis, too, is concerned to heal the disabling rift between subjects and objects, 'men' and their 'natural human environments', which is the result of 'mass' civilization.

If phenomenology secured a knowable world with one hand, it established the centrality of the human subject with the other. Indeed it promised nothing less than a science of subjectivity itself. The world is what I posit or 'intend': it is to be grasped in relation to me, as a correlate of my consciousness, and that consciousness is not just fallibly empirical but transcendental. This was a reassuring sort of thing to learn about oneself. The crass positivism of nineteenth-century science had threatened to rob the world of subjectivity altogether, and neo-Kantian philosophy had tamely followed suit; the course of European history from the later nineteenth century onwards appeared to cast grave doubt on the traditional presumption that 'man' was in control of his destiny, that he was any longer the creative centre of his world. Phenomenology, in reaction, restored the transcendental subject to its rightful throne. The subject was to be seen as the source and origin of all meaning: it was not really itself part of the world, since it brought that world to be in the first place. In this sense, phenomenology recovered and refurbished the old dream of classical bourgeois ideology. For such ideology had pivoted on the belief that 'man' was somehow prior to his history and social conditions, which flowed from him as water shoots forth from a fountain.

How this 'man' had come to be in the first place – whether he might be the product of social conditions, as well as the producer of them – was not a question to be seriously contemplated. In recentring the world upon the human subject, then, phenomenology was providing an imaginary solution to a grievous historical problem.

In the realm of literary criticism, phenomenology had some influence on the Russian Formalists. Just as Husserl 'bracketed off' the real object so as to attend to the act of knowing it, so poetry for the Formalists bracketed the real object and focused instead on the way it was perceived.[1] But the main critical debt to phenomenology is evident in the so-called Geneva school of criticism, which flourished in particular in the 1940s and 1950s, and whose major luminaries were the Belgian Georges Poulet, the Swiss critics Jean Starobinski and Jean Rousset, and the Frenchman Jean-Pierre Richard. Also associated with the school were Emil Staiger, Professor of German at the University of Zürich, and the early work of the American critic J. Hillis Miller.

Phenomenological criticism is an attempt to apply the phenomenological method to literary works. As with Husserl's 'bracketing' of the real object, the actual historical context of the literary work, its author, conditions of production and readership are ignored; phenomenological criticism aims instead at a wholly 'immanent' reading of the text, totally unaffected by anything outside it. The text itself is reduced to a pure embodiment of the author's consciousness: all of its stylistic and semantic aspects are grasped as organic parts of a complex totality, of which the unifying essence is the author's mind. To know this mind, we must not refer to anything we actually know of the author – biographical criticism is banned – but only to those aspects of his or her consciousness which manifest themselves in the work itself. Moreover, we are concerned with the 'deep structures' of this mind, which can be found in recurrent themes and patterns of imagery; and in grasping these we are grasping the way the writer 'lived' his world, the phenomenological relations between himself as subject and the world as object. The 'world' of a literary work is not an objective reality, but what in German is called *Lebenswelt*, reality as actually organized and experienced by an individual subject. Phenomenological criticism will typically focus upon the way an author experiences time or space, on the relation between self and others or his perception of material objects. The methodological concerns of Husserlian philosophy, in other words, very often become the 'content' of literature for phenomenological criticism.

To seize these transcendental structures, to penetrate to the very interior of a writer's consciousness, phenomenological criticism tries to achieve complete objectivity and disinterestedness. It must purge itself of its own predilections, plunge itself empathetically into the 'world' of the work, and reproduce as exactly and unbiasedly as possible what it finds there. If it is tackling a Christian poem, it is not concerned to pass value-judgements on this particular world-view, but to demonstrate what it felt like for the author to 'live' it. It is, in other words, a wholly uncritical, non-evaluative mode of analysis. Criticism is not seen as a construction, an active interpretation of the work which will inevitably engage the critic's own interests and biases; it is a mere passive reception of the text, a pure transcription of its mental essences. A literary work is presumed to constitute an organic whole, and so indeed do all the works of a particular author; phenomenological criticism can thus move with aplomb between the most chronologically disparate, thematically different texts in its resolute hunt for unities. It is an idealist, essentialist, anti-historical, formalist and organicist type of criticism, a kind of pure distillation of the blind spots, prejudices and limitations of modern literary theory as a whole. The most impressive and remarkable fact about it is that it succeeded in producing some individual critical studies (not least those by Poulet, Richard and Starobinski) of considerable insight.

For phenomenological criticism, the language of a literary work is little more than an 'expression' of its inner meanings. This somewhat second-hand view of language runs back to Husserl himself. For there is really little place for language as such in Husserlian phenomenology. Husserl speaks of a purely private or internal sphere of experience; but such a sphere is in fact a fiction, since all experience involves language and language is ineradicably social. To claim that I am having a wholly private experience is meaningless: I would not be able to have an experience in the first place unless it took place in the terms of some language within which I could identify it. What supplies meaningfulness to my experience for Husserl is not language but the act of perceiving particular phenomena as universals – an act which is supposed to occur independently of language itself. For Husserl, in other words, meaning is something which pre-dates language: language is no more than a secondary activity which gives names to meanings I somehow already possess. How I can possibly come to possess meanings without already having a language is a question which Husserl's system is incapable of answering.

The hallmark of the 'linguistic revolution' of the twentieth century, from Saussure and Wittgenstein to contemporary literary theory, is the recognition that meaning is not simply something 'expressed' or 'reflected' in language: it is actually *produced* by it. It is not as though we have meanings, or experiences, which we then proceed to cloak with words; we can only have the meanings and experiences in the first place because we have a language to have them in. What this suggests, moreover, is that our experience as individuals is social to its roots; for there can be no such thing as a private language, and to imagine a language is to imagine a whole form of social life. Phenomenology, by contrast, wishes to keep certain 'pure' internal experiences free from the social contaminations of language – or alternatively to see language as no more than a convenient system for 'fixing' meanings which have been formed independently of it. Husserl himself, in a revealing phrase, writes of language as 'conform[ing] in a pure measure to what is seen in its full clarity'.[2] But how is one able to see something clearly at all, without the conceptual resources of a language at one's disposal? Aware that language poses a severe problem for his theory, Husserl tries to resolve the dilemma by imagining a language which would be purely expressive of consciousness – which would be freed from any burden of having to indicate meanings exterior to our minds at the time of speaking. The attempt is doomed to failure: the only imaginable such 'language' would be purely solitary, interior utterances which would signify nothing whatsoever.[3]

This idea of a meaningless solitary utterance untainted by the external world is a peculiarly fitting image of phenomenology as such. For all its claims to have retrieved the 'living world' of human action and experience from the arid clutches of traditional philosophy, phenomenology begins and ends as a head without a world. It promises to give a firm grounding for human knowledge, but can do so only at a massive cost: the sacrifice of human history itself. For surely human meanings are in a deep sense historical: they are not a question of intuiting the universal essence of what it is to be an onion, but a matter of changing, practical transactions between social individuals. Despite its focus on reality as actually experienced, as *Lebenswelt* rather than inert fact, its stance towards that world remains contemplative and unhistorical. Phenomenology sought to solve the nightmare of modern history by withdrawing into a speculative sphere where eternal certainty lay in wait; as such, it became a symptom, in its solitary, alienated brooding, of the very crisis it offered to overcome.

The recognition that meaning is historical was what led Husserl's most celebrated pupil, the German philosopher Martin Heidegger, to break with his system of thought. Husserl begins with the transcendental subject; Heidegger rejects this starting-point and sets out instead from a reflection on the irreducible 'givenness' of human existence, or *Dasein* as he calls it. It is for this reason that his work is often characterized as 'existentialist', in contrast to the remorseless 'essentialism' of his mentor. To move from

Husserl to Heidegger is to move from the terrain of pure intellect to a philosophy which meditates on what it feels like to be alive. Whereas English philosophy is usually modestly content to enquire into acts of promising or contrast the grammar of the phrases 'nothing matters' and 'nothing chatters', Heidegger's major work *Being and Time* (1927) addresses itself to nothing less than the question of Being itself – more particularly, to that mode of being which is specifically human. Such existence, Heidegger argues, is in the first place always being-in-the-world: we are human subjects only because we are practically bound up with others and the material world, and these relations are constitutive of our life rather than accidental to it. The world is not an object 'out there' to be rationally analysed, set over against a contemplative subject: it is never something we can get outside of and stand over against. We emerge as subjects from inside a reality which we can never fully objectify, which encompasses both 'subject' and 'object', which is inexhaustible in its meanings and which constitutes us quite as much as we constitute it. The world is not something to be dissolved *à la* Husserl to mental images: it has a brute, recalcitrant being of its own which resists our projects, and we exist simply as part of it. Husserl's enthroning of the transcendental ego is merely the latest phase of a rationalist Enlightenment philosophy for which 'man' imperiously stamps his own image on the world. Heidegger, by contrast, will partly decentre the human subject from this imaginary position of dominance. Human existence is a dialogue with the world, and the more reverent activity is to listen rather than to speak. Human knowledge always departs from and moves within what Heidegger calls 'pre-understanding'. Before we have come to think systematically at all, we already share a host of tacit assumptions gleaned from our practical bound-upness with the world, and science or theory are never more than partial abstractions from these concrete concerns, as a map is an abstraction of a real landscape. Understanding is not first of all a matter of isolatable 'cognition', a particular act I perform, but part of the very structure of human existence. For I live humanly only by constantly 'projecting' myself forwards, recognizing and realizing fresh possibilities of being; I am never purely identical with myself, so to speak, but a being always already thrown forwards in advance of myself. My existence is never something which I can grasp as a finished object, but always a question of fresh possibility, always problematic; and this is equivalent to saying that a human being is constituted by history, or time. Time is not a medium we move in as a bottle might move in a river: it is the very structure of human life itself, something I am made out of before it is something I measure. Understanding, then, before it is a question of understanding anything in particular, is a dimension of

Dasein, the inner dynamic of my constant self-transcendence. Understanding is radically historical: it is always caught up with the concrete situation I am in, and that I am trying to surpass.

If human existence is constituted by time, it is equally made up of language. Language for Heidegger is not a mere instrument of communication, a secondary device for expressing 'ideas': it is the very dimension in which human life moves, that which brings the world to be in the first place. Only where there is language is there 'world', in the distinctively human sense. Heidegger does not think of language primarily in terms of what you or I might say: it has an existence of its own in which human beings come to participate, and only by participating in it do they come to be human at all. Language always pre-exists the individual subject, as the very realm in which he or she unfolds; and it contains 'truth' less in the sense that it is an instrument for exchanging accurate information than in the sense that it is the place where reality 'un-conceals' itself, gives itself up to our contemplation. In this sense of language as a quasi-objective event, prior to all particular individuals, Heidegger's thinking closely parallels the theories of structuralism.

What is central to Heidegger's thought, then, is not the individual subject but Being itself. The mistake of the Western metaphysical tradition has been to see Being as some kind of objective entity, and to separate it sharply from the subject; Heidegger seeks rather to return to pre-Socratic thought, before the dualism between subject and object opened up, and to regard Being as somehow encompassing both. The result of this suggestive insight, in his later work particularly, is an astonishing cringing before the mystery of Being. Enlightenment rationality, with its ruthlessly dominative, instrumental attitude towards Nature, must be rejected for a humble listening to the stars, skies and forests, a listening which in the acid words of one English commentator bears all the marks of a 'stupefied peasant'. Man must 'make way' for Being by making himself wholly over to it: he must turn to the earth, the inexhaustible mother who is the primary fount of all meaning. Heidegger, the Black Forest philosopher, is yet another Romantic exponent of the 'organic society', though in his case the results of this doctrine were to be more sinister than in the case of Leavis. The exaltation of the peasant, the downgrading of reason for spontaneous 'pre-understanding', the celebration of wise passivity – all of these, combined with Heidegger's belief in an 'authentic' existence-towards-death superior to the life of the faceless masses, led him in 1933 into explicit support of Hitler. The support was short-lived; but it was implicit for all that in elements of the philosophy.

What is valuable in that philosophy, among other things, is its insistence that theoretical knowledge always emerges from a context of practical social interests. Heidegger's model of a knowable object is, significantly, a tool: we know the world not contemplatively, but as a system of interrelated things which, like a hammer, are 'to hand', elements in some practical project. Knowing is deeply related to doing. But the other side of that peasant-like practicality is a contemplative mysticism: when the hammer breaks, when we cease to take it for granted, its familiarity is stripped from it and it yields up to us its authentic being. A broken hammer is more of a hammer than an unbroken one. Heidegger shares with the Formalists the belief that art is such a defamiliarization: when van Gogh shows us a pair of peasant shoes he estranges them, allowing their profoundly authentic shoeness to shine forth. Indeed for the later Heidegger it is in art alone that such phenomenological truth is able to manifest itself, just as for Leavis literature comes to stand in for a mode of being which modern society has supposedly lost. Art, like language, is not to be seen as the expression of an individual subject: the subject is just the place or medium where the truth of the world speaks itself, and it is this truth which the reader of a poem must attentively *hear*. Literary interpretation for Heidegger is not grounded in human activity: it is not first of all something we *do*, but something we must let happen. We must open ourselves passively to the text, submitting ourselves to its mysteriously inexhaustible being, allowing ourselves to be interrogated by it. Our posture before art, in other words, must have something of the servility which Heidegger advocated for the German people before the Führer. The only alternative to the imperious reason of bourgeois industrial society, it would appear, is a slavish self-abnegation.

I have said that understanding for Heidegger is radically historical, but this now needs to be qualified somewhat. The title of his major work is *Being and Time* rather than *Being and History*; and there is a significant difference between the two concepts. 'Time' is in one sense a more abstract notion than history: it suggests the passing of the seasons, or the way I might experience the shape of my personal life, rather than the struggles of nations, the nurturing and slaughtering of populations or the making and toppling of states. 'Time' for Heidegger is still an essentially metaphysical category, in a way that 'history' for other thinkers is not. It is a derivation from what we actually do, which is what I am taking 'history' to mean. This kind of concrete history concerns Heidegger hardly at all: indeed he distinguishes between *Historie*, meaning roughly 'what happens', and *Geschichte*, which is 'what happens' experienced as authentically meaningful. My own personal history is authentically meaningful when I accept responsibility for my own existence, seize my own future possibilities and live in enduring awareness of my own future death. This may or may not be true; but it does not seem to have any immediate relevance to how I live 'historically' in the sense of being bound up with particular individuals, actual social relations and concrete institutions. All of this, from the Olympian heights of Heidegger's ponderously esoteric prose, looks very small beer indeed. 'True' history for Heidegger is an inward, 'authentic' or 'existential' history – a mastering of dread and nothingness, a resoluteness towards death, a 'gathering in' of my powers – which operates in effect as a substitute for history in its more common and practical senses. As the Hungarian critic Georg Lukács put it, Heidegger's famous 'historicity' is not really distinguishable from *a*historicity.

In the end, then, Heidegger fails to overturn the static, eternal truths of Husserl and the Western metaphysical tradition by historicizing them. All he does instead is set up a different kind of metaphysical entity – *Dasein* itself. His work represents a flight from history as much as an encounter with it; and the same can be said of the fascism with which he flirted. Fascism is a desperate, last-ditch attempt on the part of monopoly capitalism to abolish contradictions which have become intolerable; and it does so in part by offering a whole alternative history, a narrative of blood, soil, the 'authentic' race, the sublimity of death and self-abnegation, the Reich that will endure for a thousand years. This is not to suggest that Heidegger's philosophy as a whole is no more than a rationale for fascism; it *is* to suggest that it provided one imaginary solution to the crisis of modern history as fascism provided another, and that the two shared a number of features in common.

Heidegger describes his philosophical enterprise as a 'hermeneutic of Being'; and the word 'hermeneutic' means the science or art of interpretation. Heidegger's form of philosophy is generally referred to as 'hermeneutical phenomenology', to distinguish it from the 'transcendental phenomenology' of Husserl and his followers; it is called this because it bases itself upon questions of historical interpretation rather than on transcendental consciousness.[4] The word 'hermeneutics' was originally confined to the interpretation of sacred scripture; but during the nineteenth century it broadened its scope to encompass the problem of textual interpretation as a whole. Heidegger's two most famous predecessors as 'hermeneuticists' were the German thinkers Schleiermacher and Dilthey; his most celebrated successor is the modern German philosopher Hans-Georg Gadamer. With Gadamer's central study *Truth and Method* (1960), we are in the arena of problems which have never ceased to plague modern literary theory. What is the meaning of a literary text? How relevant to this meaning is the author's intention? Can we hope to understand works which are culturally and historically alien to us? Is 'objective' understanding possible, or is all understanding relative to our own historical situation? There is, as we shall see, a good deal more at stake in these issues than 'literary interpretation' alone.

For Husserl, meaning was an 'intentional object'. By this he meant that it was neither reducible to the psychological acts of a speaker or listener, nor completely independent of such mental processes. Meaning was not objective in the sense that an armchair is, but it was not simply subjective either. It was a kind of 'ideal' object, in the sense that it could be expressed in a number of different ways but still remain the same meaning. On this view, the meaning of a literary work is fixed once and for all: it is identical with whatever 'mental object' the author had in mind, or 'intended', at the time of writing.

This, in effect, is the position taken up by the American hermeneuticist E. D. Hirsch Jr, whose major work, *Validity in Interpretation* (1967), is considerably indebted to Husserlian phenomenology. It does not follow for Hirsch that because the meaning of a work is identical with what the author meant by it at the time of writing, only one interpretation of the text is possible. There may be a number of different valid interpretations, but all of them must move within the 'system of typical expectations and probabilities' which the author's meaning permits. Nor does Hirsch deny that a literary work may 'mean' different things to different people at different times. But this, he claims, is more properly a matter of the work's 'significance' rather than its 'meaning'. The fact that I may produce *Macbeth* in a way which makes it relevant to nuclear warfare does not alter the fact that this is not what *Macbeth*, from Shakespeare's own viewpoint, 'means'. Significances vary throughout history, whereas meanings remain constant; authors put in meanings, whereas readers assign significances.

In identifying the meaning of a text with what the author meant by it, Hirsch does not presume that we always have access to the author's intentions. He or she may be long dead, or may have forgotten what she intended altogether. It follows that we may sometimes hit on the 'right' interpretation of a text but never be in a position to know this. This does not worry Hirsch much, as long as his basic position – that literary meaning is absolute and immutable, wholly resistant to historical change – is maintained. Why Hirsch is able to maintain this position is essentially because his theory of meaning, like Husserl's, is pre-linguistic. Meaning is something which the author *wills*: it is a ghostly, wordless mental act which is then 'fixed' for all time in a particular set of material signs. It is an affair of consciousness, rather than of words. Quite what such a wordless consciousness consists in is not made plain. Perhaps the reader would care to experiment here by looking up from the book for a moment and 'meaning' something silently in his or her head. What did you 'mean'? And was it different from the words in which you have just formulated the response? To believe that meaning consists of words plus a wordless act of willing or intending is rather like believing that every time I open the door 'on purpose' I make a silent act of willing while opening it.

There are obvious problems with trying to determine what is going on in somebody's head and then claiming that this is the meaning of a piece of writing. For one thing, a great many things are likely to be going on in an author's head at the time of writing. Hirsch accepts this, but does not consider that these are to be confused with 'verbal meaning'; to sustain his theory, however, he is forced to make a fairly drastic reduction of all that the author might have meant to what he calls meaning 'types', manageable categories of meaning into which the text may be narrowed, simplified and sifted by the critic. Our interest in a text can thus only be in these broad typologies of meaning, from which all particularity has been carefully banished. The critic must seek to reconstruct what Hirsch calls the 'intrinsic genre' of a text, by which he means, roughly, the general conventions and ways of seeing which would have governed the author's meanings at the time of writing. Little more than this is likely to be available to us: it would doubtless be impossible to recover *exactly* what Shakespeare meant by 'cream-fac'd loon', so we have to settle for what he might generally have had in mind. All of the particular details of a work are presumed to be governed by such generalities. Whether this does justice to the detail, complexity and conflictive nature of literary works is another question. To secure the meaning of a work for all time, rescuing it from the ravages of history, criticism has to police its potentially anarchic details, hemming them back with the compound of 'typical' meaning. Its stance towards the text is authoritarian and juridical: anything which cannot be herded inside the enclosure of 'probable authorial meaning' is brusquely expelled, and everything remaining within that enclosure is strictly subordinated to this single governing intention. The unalterable meaning of the sacred scripture has been preserved; what one does with it, how one uses it, becomes a merely secondary matter of 'significance'.

The aim of all this policing is the protection of private property. For Hirsch an author's meaning is his own, and should not be stolen or trespassed upon by the reader. The meaning of the text is not to be socialized, made the public property of its various readers; it belongs solely to the author, who should have the exclusive rights over its disposal long after he or she is dead. Interestingly, Hirsch concedes that his own point of view is really quite arbitrary. There is nothing in the nature of the text itself which constrains a reader to construe it in accordance with authorial meaning; it is just that if we do not choose to respect the author's meaning then we have no 'norm' of interpretation, and risk opening the floodgates to critical anarchy. Like most authoritarian regimes, that is to say, Hirschian theory is quite unable rationally to justify its own ruling values. There is no more reason in principle why the author's meaning should be preferred than there is for preferring the reading offered by the critic with the shortest hair or the largest feet. Hirsch's defence of authorial meaning resembles those defences of landed titles which begin by tracing their process of legal inheritance over the centuries, and end up by admitting that if you push that process back far enough the titles were gained by fighting someone else for them.

Even if critics could obtain access to an author's intention, would this securely ground the literary text in a determinate meaning? What if we asked for an account of the meaning of the author's intentions, and then for an account of that, and so on? Security is possible here only if authorial meanings are what Hirsch takes them to be: pure, solid, 'self-identical' facts which can be unimpeachably used to anchor the work. But this is a highly dubious way of seeing any kind of meaning at all. Meanings are not as stable and determinate as Hirsch thinks, even authorial ones – and the reason they are not is because, as he will not recognize, they are the products of language, which always has something slippery about it. It is difficult to know what it could be to have a 'pure' intention or express a 'pure' meaning; it is only because Hirsch holds meaning apart from language that he is able to trust to such chimeras. An author's intention is itself a complex 'text', which can be debated, translated and variously interpreted just like any other.

Hirsch's distinction between 'meaning' and 'significance' is in one obvious sense valid. It is unlikely that Shakespeare thought that he was writing about nuclear warfare. When Gertrude describes Hamlet as 'fat' she probably does not mean that he is overweight, as modern readers might tend to suspect. But the absoluteness of Hirsch's distinction is surely untenable. It is just not possible to make such a complete distinction between 'what the text means' and 'what it means to me'. My account of what *Macbeth* might have meant in the cultural conditions of its time is still *my* account, inescapably influenced by my own language and frames of cultural reference. I can never pick myself up by my bootstraps out of all that and come to know in some absolutely objective way what it was Shakespeare actually had in mind. Any such notion of absolute objectivity is an illusion Hirsch does not himself seek such absolute certainty, largely because he knows he cannot have it: he must content himself instead with reconstructing the authors's 'probable' intention. But he pays no attention to the ways in which such reconstructing can only go on within his own historically conditioned frames of meaning and perception. Indeed such 'historicism' is the very target of his polemic. Like Husserl, then, he offers a form of knowledge which is timeless and sublimely disinterested. That his own work is far from disinterested – that he believes himself to be safeguarding the immutable meaning of literary works from certain contemporary ideologies – is only one factor which might lead us to view such claims with suspicion.

The target which Hirsch has firmly in his sights is the hermeneutics of Heidegger, Gadamer and others. For him, the insistence of these thinkers that meaning is always historical opens the door to complete relativism. On this argument, a literary work can mean one thing on Monday and another on Friday. It is interesting to speculate why Hirsch should find this possibility so fearful; but to stop the relativist rot he returns to Husserl and argues that meaning is unchangeable because it is always the intentional act of an individual at some particular point in time. There is one fairly obvious sense in which this is false. If I say to you in certain circumstances, 'Close the door!' and when you have done so impatiently add, 'I meant of course open the window', you would be quite entitled to point out that the English words 'Close the door' mean what they mean whatever I might have intended them to mean. This is not to say that one could not imagine contexts in which 'Close the door' meant something entirely different from its usual meaning: it could be a metaphorical way of saying, 'Don't negotiate any further'. The meaning of the sentence, like any other, is by no means immutably fixed: with enough ingenuity one could probably invent contexts in which it could mean a thousand different things. But if a gale is ripping through the room and I am wearing only a swimming costume, the meaning of the words would probably be situationally clear; and unless I had made a slip of the tongue or suffered some unaccountable lapse of attention it would be futile for me to claim that I had 'really' meant 'Open the window'. This is one evident sense in which the meaning of my words is not determined by my private intentions – in which I cannot just choose to make my words mean anything at all, as Humpty-Dumpty in *Alice* mistakenly thought he could. The meaning of language is a social matter: there is a real sense in which language belongs to my society before it belongs to me.

It is this which Heidegger understood, and which Hans-Georg Gadamer goes on to elaborate in *Truth and Method*. For Gadamer, the meaning of a literary work is never exhausted by the intentions of its author; as the work passes from one cultural or historical context to another, new meanings may be culled from it which were perhaps never anticipated by its author or contemporary audience. Hirsch would admit this in one sense but relegate it to the realm of 'significance'; for Gadamer, this instability is part of the very character of the work itself. All interpretation is situational, shaped and constrained by the historically relative criteria of a particular culture; there is no possibility of knowing the literary text 'as it is'. It is this 'scepticism' which Hirsch finds most unnerving in Heideggerian hermeneutics, and against which he wages his rearguard action.

For Gadamer, all interpretation of a past work consists in a dialogue between past and present. Confronted with such a work, we listen with wise Heideggerian passivity to its unfamiliar voice, allowing it to question our present concerns; but what the work 'says' to us will in turn depend on the kind of questions which we are able to address to it, from our own vantage-point in history. It will also depend on our ability to reconstruct the 'question' to which the work itself is an 'answer', for the work is also a dialogue with its own history. All understanding is *productive*: it is always 'understanding otherwise', realizing new potential in the text, making a difference to it. The present is only ever understandable through the past, with which it forms a living continuity; and the past is always grasped from our own partial viewpoint within the present. The event of understanding comes about when our own 'horizon' of historical meanings and assumptions 'fuses' with the 'horizon' within which the work itself is placed. At such a moment we enter the alien world of the artefact, but at the same time gather it into our own realm, reaching a more complete understanding of ourselves. Rather than 'leaving home', Gadamer remarks, we 'come home'.

It is hard to see why Hirsch should find all this so unnerving. On the contrary, it all seems considerably too smooth. Gadamer can equally surrender himself and literature to the winds of history because these scattered leaves will always in the end come home – and they will do so because beneath all history, silently spanning past, present and future, runs a unifying essence known as 'tradition'. As with T. S. Eliot, all 'valid' texts belong to this tradition, which both speaks through the work of the past that I am contemplating, and speaks through me in the act of 'valid' contemplation. Past and present, subject and object, the alien and the intimate are thus securely coupled together by a Being which encompasses them both. Gadamer is not worried that our tacit cultural preconceptions or 'pre-understandings' may prejudice the reception of the past literary work, since these pre-understandings come to us from the tradition itself, of which the literary work is a part. Prejudice is a positive rather than a negative factor: it was the Enlightenment, with its dream of a wholly disinterested knowledge, which led to the modern 'prejudice against prejudice'. Creative prejudices, as against ephemeral and distorting ones, are those which arise from the tradition and bring us into contact with it. The authority of the tradition itself, linked with our own strenuous self-reflection, will sort out which of our preconceptions are legitimate and which are not – just as the historical distance between ourselves and a work of the past, far from creating an obstacle to true understanding, actually aids such cognition by stripping the work of all that was of merely passing significance about it.

It might be as well to ask Gadamer whose and what 'tradition' he actually has in mind. For his theory holds only on the enormous assumption that there is indeed a single 'mainstream' tradition; that all 'valid' works participate in it; that history forms an unbroken continuum, free of decisive rupture, conflict and contradiction; and that the prejudices which 'we' (who?) have inherited from the 'tradition' are to be cherished. It assumes, in other words, that history is a place where 'we' can always and everywhere be at home; that the work of the past will deepen – rather than, say, decimate – our present self-understanding; and that the alien is always secretly familiar. It is, in short, a grossly complacent theory of history, the projection on to the world at large of a viewpoint for which 'art' means chiefly the classical monuments of the high German tradition. It has little conception of history and tradition as oppressive as well as liberating forces, areas rent by conflict and domination. History for Gadamer is not a place of struggle, discontinuity and exclusion but a 'continuing chain', an ever-flowing river, almost, one might say, a club of the like-minded. Historical differences are tolerantly conceded, but only because they are effectively liquidated by an understanding which 'bridg[es] the temporal distance which separates the interpreter from the text; thus it overcomes . . . the alienation of meaning which has befallen the text'.[5] There is no need to strive to surmount temporal distance by projecting oneself empathetically into the past, as Wilhelm Dilthey among others had believed, since this distance is already bridged by custom, prejudice and tradition. Tradition holds an authority to which we must submit: there is little possibility of critically challenging that authority, and no speculation that its influence may be anything but benevolent. Tradition, Gadamer argues, 'has a justification that is outside the arguments of reason'.[6]

'The conversation that we are', was how Gadamer once described history. Hermeneutics sees history as a living dialogue between past, present and future, and seeks patiently to remove obstacles to this endless mutual communication. But it cannot tolerate the idea of a failure of communication which is not merely ephemeral, which cannot be righted merely by more sensitive textual interpretation, but which is somehow *systematic*: which is, so to speak, built into the communication structures of whole societies. It cannot, in other words, come to terms with the problem of ideology – with the fact that the unending 'dialogue' of human history is as often as not a monologue by the powerful to the powerless, or that if it is indeed a 'dialogue' then the partners – men and women, for example – hardly occupy equal positions. It refuses to recognize that discourse is always caught up with a power which may be by no means benign; and the discourse in which it most signally fails to recognize this fact is its own.

Hermeneutics, as we have seen, tends to concentrate on works of the past: the theoretical questions it asks arise mainly from this perspective. This is hardly surprising, given its scriptural beginnings, but it is also significant: it suggests that criticism's main role is to make sense of the classics. It would be difficult to imagine Gadamer grappling with Norman Mailer. Along with this traditionalist emphasis goes another: the assumption that works of literature form an 'organic' unity. The hermeneutical method seeks to fit each element of a text into a complete whole, in a process commonly known as the 'hermeneutical circle': individual features are intelligible in terms of the entire context, and the entire context becomes intelligible through the individual features. Hermeneutics does not generally consider the possibility that literary works may be diffuse, incomplete and internally contradictory, though there are many reasons to assume that they are.[7] It is worth noting that E. D. Hirsch, for all his antipathy to Romantic organicist concepts, also shares the prejudice that literary texts are integrated wholes, and logically so: the unity of the work resides in the author's all-pervasive intention. There is in fact no reason why the author should not have had several mutually contradictory intentions, or why his intention may not have been somehow self-contradictory, but Hirsch does not consider these possibilities.

The most recent development of hermeneutics in Germany is known as 'reception aesthetics' or 'reception theory', and unlike Gadamer it does not concentrate exclusively on works of the past. Reception theory examines the reader's role in literature, and as such is a fairly novel development. Indeed one might very roughly periodize the history of modern literary theory in three stages: a preoccupation with the author (Romanticism and the nineteenth century); an exclusive concern with the text (New Criticism); and a marked shift of attention to the reader over recent years. The reader has always been the most underprivileged of this trio – strangely, since without him or her there would be no literary texts at all. Literary texts do not exist on bookshelves: they are processes of signification materialized only in the practice of reading. For literature to happen, the reader is quite as vital as the author.

What is involved in the act of reading? Let me take, almost literally at random, the first two sentences of a novel: '"What did you make of the new couple?" The Hanemas, Piet and Angela, were undressing.' (John Updike, *Couples*.) What are we to make of this? We are puzzled for a moment, perhaps, by an apparent lack of connection between the two sentences, until we grasp that what is at work here is the literary convention by which we may attribute a piece of direct speech to a character even if the text does not explicitly do this itself. We gather that some character, probably Piet or Angela Hanema, makes the opening statement; but why do we presume this? The sentence in quotation marks may not be spoken at all: it may be a thought, or a question which someone else has asked, or a kind of epigraph placed at the opening of the novel. Perhaps it is addressed to Piet and Angela Hanema by somebody else, or by a sudden voice from the sky. One reason why the latter solution seems unlikely is that the question is a little colloquial for a voice from the sky, and we might know that Updike is in general a realist writer who does not usually go in for such devices; but a writer's texts do not necessarily form a consistent whole and it may be unwise to lean on this assumption too heavily. It is unlikely on realist grounds that the question is asked by a chorus of people speaking in unison, and slightly unlikely that it is asked by somebody other than Piet or Angela Hanema, since we learn the next moment that they are undressing, perhaps speculate that they are a married couple, and know that married couples, in our suburb of Birmingham at least, do not make a practice of undressing together before third parties, whatever they might do individually.

We have probably already made a whole set of inferences as we read these sentences. We may infer, for example, that the 'couple' referred to is a man and woman, though there is nothing so far to tell us that they are not two women or two tiger cubs. We assume that whoever poses the question cannot mind-read, as then there would be no need to ask. We may suspect that the questioner values the judgement of the addressee, though there is not sufficient context as yet for us to judge that the question is not taunting or aggressive. The phrase 'The Hanemas', we imagine, is probably in grammatical apposition to the phrase 'Piet and Angela', to indicate that this is their surname, which provides a significant piece of evidence for their being married. But we cannot rule out the possibility that there is some group of people called the Hanemas in addition to Piet and Angela, perhaps a whole tribe of them, and that they are all undressing together in some immense hall. The fact that Piet and Angela may share the same surname does not confirm that they are husband and wife: they may be a particularly liberated or incestuous brother and sister, father and daughter or mother and son. We have assumed, however, that they are undressing in sight of each other, whereas nothing has yet told us that the question is not shouted from one bedroom or beach-hut to another. Perhaps Piet and Angela are small children, though the relative sophistication of the question makes this unlikely. Most readers will by now probably have assumed that Piet and Angela Hanema are a married couple undressing together in their bedroom after some event, perhaps a party, at which a new married couple was present, but none of this is actually said.

The fact that these are the first two sentences of the novel means, of course, that many of these questions will be answered for us as we read on. But the process of speculating and inferring to which we are driven by our ignorance here is simply a more intense and dramatic example of what we do all the time when reading. As we read on we shall encounter many more problems, which can be solved only by making further assumptions. We will be given the kinds of *facts* which are withheld from us in these sentences, but we will still have to construct questionable interpretations of them. Reading the opening of Updike's novel involves us in a surprising amount of complex, largely unconscious labour: although we rarely notice it, we are all the time engaged in constructing hypotheses about the meaning of the text. The reader makes implicit connections, fills in gaps, draws inferences and tests out hunches; and to do this means drawing on a tacit knowledge of the world in general and of literary conventions in particular. The text itself is really no more than a series of 'cues' to the reader, invitations to construct a piece of language into meaning. In the terminology of reception theory, the reader 'concretizes' the literary work, which is in itself no more than a chain of organized black marks on a page. Without this continuous active participation on the reader's part, there would be no literary work at all. However solid it may seem, any work for reception theory is actually made up of 'gaps', just as tables are for modern physics – the gap, for instance, between the first and second sentences of *Couples*, where the reader must supply a missing connection. The work is full of 'indeterminacies', elements which depend for their effect upon the reader's interpretation, and which can be interpreted in a number of different, perhaps mutually conflicting ways. The paradox of this is that the more information the work provides, the more indeterminate it becomes. Shakespeare's 'secret black and midnight hags' in one sense narrows down what kind of hags are in question, makes them more determinate, but because all three adjectives are richly suggestive, evoking different responses in different readers, the text has also rendered itself less determinate in the act of trying to become more so.

The process of reading, for reception theory, is always a dynamic one, a complex movement and unfolding through time. The literary work itself exists merely as what the Polish theorist Roman Ingarden calls a set of 'schemata' or general directions, which the reader must actualize. To do this, the reader will bring to the work certain 'pre-understandings', a dim context of beliefs and expectations within which the work's various features will be assessed. As the reading process proceeds, however, these expectations will themselves be modified by what we learn, and the hermeneutical circle – moving from part to whole and back to part – will begin to revolve. Striving to construct a coherent sense from the text, the reader will select and organize its elements into consistent wholes, excluding some and foregrounding others, 'concretizing' certain items in certain ways; he or she will try to hold different perspectives within the work together, or shift from perspective to perspective in order to build up an integrated 'illusion'. What we have learnt on page one will fade and become 'foreshortened' in memory, perhaps to be radically qualified by what we learn later. Reading is not a straightforward linear movement, a merely cumulative affair: our initial speculations generate a frame of reference within which to interpret what comes next, but what comes next may retrospectively transform our original understanding, highlighting some features of it and backgrounding others. As we read on we shed assumptions, revise beliefs, make more and more complex inferences and anticipations; each sentence opens up a horizon which is confirmed, challenged or undermined by the next. We read backwards and forwards simultaneously, predicting and recollecting, perhaps aware of other possible realizations of the text which our reading has negated. Moreover, all of this complicated activity is carried out on many levels at once, for the text has 'backgrounds' and 'foregrounds', different narrative viewpoints, alternative layers of meaning between which we are constantly moving.

Wolfgang Iser, of the so-called Constance school of reception aesthetics, whose theories I have been largely discussing, speaks in *The Act of Reading* (1978) of the 'strategies' which texts put to work, and of the 'repertoires' of familiar themes and allusions which they contain. To read at all, we need to be familiar with the literary techniques and conventions which a particular work deploys; we must have some grasp of its 'codes', by which is meant the rules which systematically govern the ways it produces its meanings. Recall once more the London Underground sign I discussed in the Introduction: 'Dogs must be carried on the escalator.' To understand this notice I need to do a great deal more than simply read its words one after the other. I need to know, for example, that these words belong to what might be called a 'code of reference' – that the sign is not just a decorative piece of language there to entertain travellers, but is to be taken as referring to the behaviour of actual dogs and passengers on actual escalators. I must mobilize my general social knowledge to recognize that the sign has been placed there by the authorities, that these authorities have the power to penalize offenders, that I as a member of the public am being implicitly addressed, none of which is evident in the words themselves. I have to rely, in other words, upon certain social codes and contexts to understand the notice properly. But I also need to bring these into interaction with certain codes or conventions of reading – conventions which tell me that by 'the escalator' is meant *this* escalator and not one in Paraguay, that 'must be carried' means 'must be carried *now*', and so on. I must recognize that the 'genre' of the sign is such as to make it highly improbable that the ambiguity I mentioned in the Introduction is actually 'intended'. It is not easy to distinguish between 'social' and 'literary' codes here: concretizing 'the escalator' as 'this escalator', adopting a reading convention which eradicates ambiguity, itself depends upon a whole network of social knowledge.

I understand the notice, then, by interpreting it in terms of certain codes which seem appropriate; but for Iser this is not all of what happens in reading literature. If there were a perfect 'fit' between the codes which governed literary works and the codes we applied to interpret them, all literature would be as uninspiring as the London Underground sign. The most effective literary work for Iser is one which forces the reader into a new critical awareness of his or her customary codes and expectations. The work interrogates and transforms the implicit beliefs we bring to it, 'disconfirms' our routine habits of perception and so forces us to acknowledge them for the first time for what they are. Rather than merely reinforce our given perceptions, the valuable work of literature violates or transgresses these normative ways of seeing, and so teaches us new codes for understanding. There is a parallel here with Russian Formalism: in the act of reading, our conventional assumptions are 'defamiliarized', objectified to the point where we can criticize and so revise them. If we modify the text by our reading strategies, it simultaneously modifies us: like objects in a scientific experiment, it may return an unpredictable 'answer' to our 'questions'. The whole point of reading, for a critic like Iser, is that it brings us into deeper self-consciousness, catalyzes a more critical view of our own identities. It is as though what we have been 'reading', in working our way through a book, is ourselves.

Iser's reception theory, in fact, is based on a liberal humanist ideology: a belief that in reading we should be flexible and open-minded, prepared to put our beliefs into question and allow them to be transformed. Behind this case lies the influence of Gadamerian hermeneutics, with its trust in that enriched self-knowledge which springs from an encounter with the unfamiliar. But Iser's liberal humanism, like most such doctrines, is less liberal than it looks at first sight. He writes that a reader with strong ideological commitments is likely to be an inadequate one, since he or she is less likely to be open to the transformative power of literary works. What this implies is that in order to undergo transformation at the hands of the text, we must only hold our beliefs fairly provisionally in the first place. The only good reader would *already* have to be a liberal: the act of reading produces a kind of human subject which it also presupposes. This is also paradoxical in another way: for if we only hold our convictions rather lightly in the first place, having them interrogated and subverted by the text is not really very significant. Nothing much, in other words, will have actually happened. The reader is not so much radically upbraided, as simply returned to himself or herself as a more thoroughly liberal subject. Everything about the reading subject is up for question in the act of reading, except what kind of (liberal) subject it is: these ideological limits can be in no way criticized, for then the whole model would collapse. In this sense, the plurality and open-endedness of the process of reading are permissible because they presuppose a certain kind of closed unity which always remains in place: the unity of the reading subject, which is violated and transgressed only to be returned more fully to itself. As with Gadamer, we can foray out into foreign territory because we are always secretly at home. The kind of reader whom literature is going to affect most profoundly is one already equipped with the 'right' kind of capacities and responses, proficient in operating certain critical techniques and recognizing certain literary conventions; but this is precisely the kind of reader who needs to be affected least. Such a reader is 'transformed' from the outset, and is ready to risk further transformation just because of this fact. To read literature 'effectively' you must exercise certain critical capacities, capacities which are always problematically defined; but it is precisely these capacities which 'literature' will be unable to call into question, because its very existence depends on them. What you have defined as a 'literary' work will always be closely bound up with what you consider 'appropriate' critical techniques: a 'literary' work will mean, more or less, one which can be usefully illuminated by such methods of enquiry. But in that case the hermeneutical circle really is a vicious rather than virtuous one: what you get out of the work will depend in large measure on what you put into it in the first place, and there is little room here for any deep-seated 'challenge' to the reader. Iser would seem to avoid this vicious circle by stressing the power of literature to disrupt and transfigure the reader's codes; but this itself, as I have argued, silently assumes exactly the kind of 'given' reader that it hopes to generate through reading. The closedness of the circuit between reader and work reflects the closedness of the academic institution of Literature, to which only certain kinds of texts and readers need apply.

The doctrines of the unified self and the closed text surreptitiously underlie the apparent open-endedness of much reception theory. Roman Ingarden in *The Literary Work of Art* (1931) dogmatically presumes that literary works form organic wholes, and the point of the reader's filling in their 'indeterminacies' is to complete this harmony. The reader must link up the different segments and strata of the work in a 'proper' fashion, rather in the manner of those children's picture books which you colour in according to the manufacturer's instructions. The text for Ingarden comes ready-equipped with its indeterminacies, and the reader must concretize it 'correctly'. This rather limits the reader's activity, reducing him at times to little more than a kind of literary handyman, pottering around and filling in the odd indeterminacy. Iser is a much more liberal kind of employer, granting the reader a greater degree of co-partnership with the text: different readers are free to actualize the work in different ways, and there is no single correct interpretation which will exhaust its semantic potential. But this generosity is qualified by one rigorous instruction: the reader must construct the text so as to render it internally *consistent*. Iser's model of reading is fundamentally functionalist: the parts must be made to adapt coherently to the whole. Behind this arbitrary prejudice, in fact, lies the influence of *Gestalt* psychology, with its concern to integrate discrete perceptions into an intelligible whole. It is true that this prejudice runs so deep in modern critics that it is difficult to see it as just that – a doctrinal predilection, which is no less arguable and contentious than any other. There is absolutely no need to suppose that works of literature either do or should constitute harmonious wholes, and many suggestive frictions and collisions of meaning must be blandly 'processed' by literary criticism to induce them to do so. Iser sees that Ingarden is a good deal too 'organicist' in his views of the text, and appreciates modernist, multiple works partly because they make us more self-conscious about the labour of interpreting them. But at the same time the 'openness' of the work is something which is to be gradually eliminated, as the reader comes to construct a working hypothesis which can account for and render mutually coherent the greatest number of the work's elements.

Textual indeterminacies just spur us on to the act of abolishing them, replacing them with a stable meaning. They must, in Iser's revealingly authoritarian term, be 'normalized' – tamed and subdued to some firm structure of sense. The reader, it would seem, is engaged in fighting the text as much as interpreting it, struggling to pin down its anarchic 'polysemantic' potential within some manageable framework. Iser speaks quite openly of 'reducing' this polysemantic potential to some kind of order – a curious way, one might have thought, for a 'pluralist' critic to speak. Unless this is done, the unified reading subject will be jeopardized, rendered incapable of returning to itself as a well-balanced entity in the 'self-correcting' therapy of reading.

It is always worth testing out any literary theory by asking: How would it work with Joyce's *Finnegans Wake*? The answer in Iser's case is bound to be: Not too well. He deals, admittedly, with Joyce's *Ulysses*; but his major critical interests are in realist fiction since the eighteenth century, and there are ways in which *Ulysses* can be made to conform to this model. Would Iser's opinion that the most valid literature disturbs and transgresses received codes do for the contemporary readers of Homer, Dante or Spenser? Is it not a viewpoint more typical of a modern-day European liberal, for whom 'systems of thought' is bound to have something of a negative rather than positive ring, and who will therefore look to the kind of art which appears to undermine them? Has not a great deal of 'valid' literature precisely confirmed rather than troubled the received codes of its time? To locate the power of art primarily in the negative – in the transgressive and defamiliarizing – is with both Iser and the Formalists to imply a definite attitude to the social and cultural systems of one's epoch: an attitude which, in modern liberalism, amounts to suspecting thought-systems as such. That it can do so is eloquent testimony to liberalism's obliviousness of one particular thought-system: that which sustains its own position.

To grasp the limits of Iser's liberal humanism, we may contrast him briefly with another theorist of reception, the French critic Roland Barthes. The approach of Barthes's *The Pleasure of the Text* (1973) is about as different from Iser's as one could imagine – the difference, stereotypically speaking, between a French hedonist and a German rationalist. Whereas Iser focuses mainly on the realist work, Barthes offers a sharply contrasting account of reading by taking the modernist text, one which dissolves all distinct meaning into a free play of words, which seeks to undo repressive thought-systems by a ceaseless slipping and sliding of language. Such a text demands less a 'hermeneutics' than an 'erotics': since there is no way to arrest it into determinate sense, the reader simply luxuriates in the tantalizing glide of signs, in the provocative glimpses of meanings which surface only to submerge again. Caught up in this exuberant dance of language, delighting in the textures of words themselves, the reader knows less the purposive pleasures of building a coherent system, binding textual elements masterfully together to shore up a unitary self, than the masochistic thrills of feeling that self shattered and dispersed through the tangled webs of the work itself. Reading is less like a laboratory than a boudoir. Far from returning the reader to himself, in some final recuperation of the selfhood which the act of reading has thrown into question, the modernist text explodes his or her secure cultural identity, in a *jouissance* which for Barthes is both readerly bliss and sexual orgasm.

Barthes's theory is not, as the reader might have suspected, without its problems. There is something a little disturbing about this self-indulgent avant-garde hedonism in a world where others lack not only books but food. If Iser offers us a grimly 'normative' model which reins in the unbounded potential of language, Barthes presents us with a private, asocial, essentially anarchic experience which is perhaps no more than the flip-side of the first. Both critics betray a liberal distaste for systematic thought; both in their different ways ignore the position of the reader in history. For readers do not of course encounter texts in a void: all readers are socially and historically positioned, and how they interpret literary works will be deeply shaped by this fact. Iser is aware of the social dimension of reading, but chooses to concentrate largely on its 'aesthetic' aspects; a more historically-minded member of the school of Constance is Hans Robert Jauss, who seeks in Gadamerian fashion to situate a literary work within its historical 'horizon', the context of cultural meanings within which it was produced, and then explores the shifting relations between this and the changing 'horizons' of its historical readers. The aim of this work is to produce a new kind of literary history – one centred not on authors, influences and literary trends, but on literature as defined and interpreted by its various moments of historical 'reception'. It is not that literary works themselves remain constant, while interpretations of them change: texts and literary traditions are themselves actively altered according to the various historical 'horizons' within which they are received.

A more detailed historical study of literary reception is Jean-Paul Sartre's *What is Literature?* (1948). What Sartre's book makes clear is the fact that a work's reception is never just an 'external' fact about it, a contingent matter of book reviews and bookshop sales. It is a constitutive dimension of the work itself. Every literary text is built out of a sense of its potential audience, includes an image of whom it is written *for*: every work encodes within itself what Iser calls an 'implied reader', intimates in its every gesture the kind of 'addressee' it anticipates. 'Consumption', in literary as in any other kind of production, is part of the process of production itself. If a novel opens with the sentence 'Jack staggered red-nosed out of the pub', it already implies a reader who understands fairly advanced English, knows what a pub is and has cultural knowledge of the connection between alcohol and facial inflammation. It is not just that a writer 'needs an audience': the language he uses already implies one range of possible audiences rather than another, and this is not a matter in which he necessarily has much choice. A writer may not have in mind a particular kind of reader at all, he may be superbly indifferent to who reads his work, but a certain kind of reader is already included within the very act of writing itself, as an internal structure of the text. Even when I talk to myself, my utterances would not be utterances at all unless they, rather than I, anticipated a potential listener. Sartre's study, then, sets out to pose the question 'For whom does one write?', but in an historical rather than 'existential' perspective. It traces the destiny of the French writer from the seventeenth century, where the 'classical' style signalled a settled contract or shared framework of assumptions between author and audience, to the ingrown self-consciousness of a nineteenth-century literature ineluctably addressed to a bourgeoisie it despised. It ends with the dilemma of the contemporary 'committed' writer, who can address his work neither to the bourgeoisie, the working class, nor some myth of 'man in general'.

Reception theory of the Jauss and Iser kind seems to raise a pressing epistemological problem. If one considers the 'text in itself' as a kind of skeleton, a set of 'schemata' waiting to be concretized in various ways by various readers, how can one discuss these schemata at all without having already concretized them? In speaking of the 'text itself', measuring it as a norm against particular interpretations of it, is one ever dealing with anything more than one's own concretization? Is the critic claiming some God-like knowledge of the 'text in itself', a knowledge denied to the mere reader who has to make do with his or her inevitably partial construction of the text? It is a version, in other words, of the old problem of how one can know the light in the refrigerator is off when the door is closed. Roman Ingarden considers this difficulty but can provide no adequate solution to it; Iser permits the reader a fair degree of freedom, but we are not free simply to interpret as we wish. For an interpretation to be an interpretation of *this* text and not of some other, it must be in some sense logically constrained by the text itself. The work, in other words, exercises a degree of determinacy over readers' responses to it, otherwise criticism would seem to fall into total anarchy. *Bleak House* would be nothing more than the millions of different, often discrepant readings of the novel which readers have come up with, and the 'text itself' would drop out, as a kind of mysterious X. What if the literary work were not a determinate structure containing certain indeterminacies, but if everything in the text was indeterminate, dependent on which way the reader chose to construct it? In what sense could we then speak of interpreting the 'same' work?

Not all reception theorists find this an embarrassment. The American critic Stanley Fish is quite happy to accept that, when you get down to it, there is no 'objective' work of literature there on the seminar table at all. *Bleak House* is just all the assorted accounts of the novel that have been or will be given. The true writer is the reader: dissatisfied with mere Iserian co-partnership in the literary enterprise, the readers have now overthrown the bosses and installed themselves in power. For Fish, reading is not a matter of discovering what the text means, but a process of experiencing what it *does* to you. His notion of language is pragmatist: a linguistic inversion, for example, will perhaps generate in us a feeling of surprise or disorientation, and criticism is no more than an account of the reader's developing responses to the succession of words on the page. What the text 'does' to us, however, is actually a matter of what we do to it, a question of interpretation; the object of critical attention is the structure of the reader's experience, not any 'objective' structure to be found in the work itself. Everything in the text – its grammar, meanings, formal units – is a product of interpretation, in no sense 'factually' given; and this raises the intriguing question of what it is that Fish believes he is interpreting when he reads. His refreshingly candid answer to this question is that he does not know; but neither, he thinks, does anybody else.

Fish is in fact careful to guard against the hermeneutical anarchy to which his theory appears to lead. To avoid dissolving the text into a thousand competing readings, he appeals to certain 'interpretative strategies' which readers have in common, and which will govern their personal responses. Not any old reading response will do: the readers in question are 'informed or at-home' readers bred in the academic institutions, whose responses are thus unlikely to prove too wildly divergent from each other to forestall all reasoned debate. He is, however, insistent that there is nothing whatsoever 'in' the work itself – that the whole idea of meaning being somehow 'immanent' in the text's language, awaiting its release by the readers' interpretation, is an objectivist illusion. It is to this illusion, he considers, that Wolfgang Iser has fallen prey.

The argument between Fish and Iser is to some extent a verbal one. Fish is quite right to claim that nothing, in literature or the world at large, is 'given' or 'determinate', if by that is meant 'non-interpreted'. There are no 'brute' facts, independent of human meanings; there are no facts that we do not know about. But this is not what 'given' necessarily or even usually means: few philosophers of science would nowadays deny that the data in the laboratory are the product of interpretation, just that they are not interpretations in the sense that the Darwinian theory of evolution is. There is a difference between scientific hypotheses and scientific data, though both are indubitably 'interpretations', and the uncrossable gulf which much traditional philosophy of science has imagined between them is certainly an illusion.[8] You can say that perceiving eleven black marks as the word 'nightingale' is an interpretation, or that perceiving something as black or eleven or a word is an interpretation, and you would be right; but if in most circumstances you read those marks to mean 'nightgown' you would be wrong. An interpretation on which everyone is likely to agree is one way of defining a fact. It is less easy to show that interpretations of Keats's 'Ode to a Nightingale' are wrong. Interpretation in this second, broader sense usually runs up against what philosophy of science calls the 'underdetermination of theory', meaning that any set of data can be explained by more theories than one. This does not seem to be the case in deciding whether the eleven marks I have mentioned form the word 'nightingale' or 'nightgown'.

The fact that these marks denote a certain kind of bird is quite arbitrary, a matter of linguistic and historical convention. If the English language had developed differently, they might not; or there may be some language unknown to me in which they denote 'dichotomous'. There may be some culture which would not perceive these marks as imprints at all, as 'marks' in our sense, but see them as bits of black immanent in the white paper which have somehow emerged. This culture may also have a different counting-system from ours and reckon them not as eleven but as three plus an indefinite number. In *its* form of script, there may well be no distinction between their words for 'nightingale' and 'nightgown'. And so on: there is nothing divinely given or immutably fixed about language, as the fact that the English word 'nightingale' has had more meanings than one in its time would suggest. But interpreting these marks is a constrained affair, because the marks are often used by people in their social practices of communication in certain ways, and these practical social uses *are* the various meanings of the word. When I identify the word in a literary text, these social practices do not simply drop away. I may well come to feel after reading the work that the word now means something quite different, that it denotes 'dichotomous' rather than a kind of bird, because of the transformed context of meanings into which it has been inserted. But identifying the word in the first place involves some sense of what its practical social uses are.

The claim that we can make a literary text mean whatever we like is in one sense quite justified. What after all is there to stop us? There is literally no end to the number of contexts we might invent for its words in order to make them signify differently. In another sense, the idea is a simple fantasy bred in the minds of those who have spent too long in the classroom. For such texts belong to language as a whole, have intricate relations to other linguistic practices, however much they might also subvert and violate them; and language is not in fact something we are free to do what we like with. If I cannot read the word 'nightingale' without imagining how blissful it would be to retreat from urban society to the solace of Nature, then the word has a certain power for me, or over me, which does not magically evaporate when I encounter it in a poem. This is part of what is meant by saying that the literary work constrains our interpretations of it, or that its meaning is to some extent 'immanent' in it. Language is a field of social forces which shape us to our roots, and it is an academicist delusion to see the literary work as an arena of infinite possibility which escapes it.

Nevertheless, interpreting a poem *is* in an important sense freer than interpreting a London Underground notice. It is freer because in the latter case the language is part of a practical situation which tends to rule out certain readings of the text and legitimate others. This, as we have seen, is by no means an absolute constraint, but it is a significant one. In the case of literary works, there is also sometimes a practical situation which excludes certain readings and licenses others, known as the teacher. It is the academic institution, the stock of socially legitimated ways of reading works, which operates as a constraint. Such licensed ways of reading are never of course 'natural', and never simply academic either: they relate to dominant forms of valuation and interpretation in a society as a whole. They are still active when I read a popular novel on a train, not just a poem in a university class. But reading a novel remains different from reading a road sign because the reader is not supplied with a ready-made context to render the language intelligible. A novel which opens with the sentence: 'Lok was running as fast as he could' is implicitly saying to the reader: 'I invite you to imagine a context in which it makes sense to say "Lok was running as fast as he could".'[9] The novel will gradually construct that context, or if you like the reader will gradually construct it for the novel. Even here it is not a matter of total interpretative freedom: since I speak the English language, the social uses of words like 'running' govern my search for appropriate contexts of meaning. But I am not as constrained as I am by 'No Exit'; and this is one reason why people often have major disagreements over the meaning of language they treat in a 'literary' way.

I began this book by challenging the idea that 'literature' was an unchanging object. I also argued that literary values are a good deal less guaranteed than people sometimes think. Now we have seen that the literary work itself is much less easy to nail down than we often assume. One nail which can be driven through it to give it a fixed meaning is that of authorial intention: we have seen some of the problems of this tactic in discussing E. D. Hirsch. Another nail is Fish's appeal to a shared 'interpretative strategy', a kind of common competence which readers, at least academic ones, are likely to have. That there *is* an academic institution which powerfully determines what readings are generally permissible is certainly true; and the 'literary institution' includes publishers, literary editors and reviewers as well as academia. But within this institution there can be a *struggle* of interpreta- tions, which Fish's model would not seem to account for – a struggle not just between this reading of Hölderlin and that, but one waged around the categories, conventions and strategies of interpretation itself. Few teachers or reviewers are likely to penalize an account of Hölderlin or Beckett becasue it differs from their own. Rather more of them, however, might penalize such an account because it seemed to them 'non-literary' – because it transgressed the accepted boundaries and procedures of 'literary criticism'. Literary criticism does not usually dictate any particular reading as long as it is 'literary critical'; and what counts as literary criticism is determined by the literary institution. It is thus that the liberalism of the literary institution, like Wolfgang Iser's, is in general blind to its own constitutive limits.

Some literary students and critics are likely to be worried by the idea that a literary text does not have a single 'correct' meaning, but probably not many. They are more likely to be engaged by the idea that the meanings of a text do not lie within them like wisdom teeth within a gum, waiting patiently to be extracted, but that the reader has some active role in this process. Nor would many people today be disturbed by the notion that the reader does not come to the text as a kind of cultural virgin, immaculately free of previous social and literary entanglements, a supremely disinterested spirit or blank sheet on to which the text will transfer its own inscriptions. Most of us recognize that no reading is innocent or without presuppositions. But fewer people pursue the full implications of this readerly guilt. One of the themes of this book has been that there is no such thing as a purely 'literary' response: all such responses, not least those to literary *form*, to the aspects of a work which are sometimes jealously reserved to the 'aesthetic', are deeply imbricated with the kind of social and historical individuals we are. In the various accounts of literary theories I have given so far, I have tried to show that there is always a great deal more at stake here than views of literature – that informing and sustaining all such theories are more or less definite readings of social reality. It is *these* readings which are in a real sense guilty, all the way from Matthew Arnold's patronizing attempts to pacify the working class to Heidegger's Nazism. Breaking with the literary institution does not just mean offering different accounts of Beckett; it means breaking with the very ways literature, literary criticism and its supporting social values are defined.

The twentieth century had another enormous nail in its literary theoretical armoury with which to fix the literary work once and for all. That nail was called structuralism, which we can now investigate.

3

Structuralism and Semiotics

We left American literary theory at the end of the Introduction in the grip of New Criticism, honing its increasingly sophisticated techniques and fighting a rearguard action against modern science and industrialism. But as North American society developed over the 1950s, growing more rigidly scientistic and managerial in its modes of thought, a more ambitious form of critical technocracy seemed demanded. New Criticism had done its job well, but it was in a sense too modest and particularist to qualify as a hard-nosed academic discipline. In its obsessive concentration on the isolated literary text, its delicate nurturings of sensibility, it had tended to leave aside the broader, more structural aspects of literature. What had happened to literary *history*? What was needed was a literary theory which, while preserving the *formalist* bent of New Criticism, its dogged attention to literature as aesthetic object rather than social practice, would make something a good deal more systematic and 'scientific' out of all this. The answer arrived in 1957, in the shape of the Canadian Northrop Frye's mighty 'totalization' of all literary genres, *Anatomy of Criticism*.

Frye's belief was that criticism was in a sorry unscientific mess and needed to be smartly tidied up. It was a matter of subjective value-judgements and idle gossip, and badly required the discipline of an objective system. This was possible, Frye held, because literature itself formed such a system. It was not in fact just a random collection of writings strewn throughout history: if you examined it closely you could see that it worked by certain objective laws, and criticism could itself become systematic by formulating them. These laws were the various modes, archetypes, myths and genres by which all literary works were structured. At the root of all literature lay four 'narrative categories', the comic, romantic, tragic and ironic, which could be seen to correspond respectively to the four *mythoi* of spring, summer, autumn and winter. A theory of literary 'modes' could be outlined, whereby in myth the hero is superior in kind to others, in romance superior in degree, in the 'high mimetic' modes of tragedy and epic superior in degree to others but not to his environment, in the 'low mimetic' modes of comedy and realism equal to the rest of us, and in satire and irony inferior. Tragedy and comedy can be subdivided into high mimetic, low mimetic and ironic; tragedy is about human isolation, comedy about human integration. Three recurrent patterns of symbolism – the apocalyptic, demonic and analogical – are identified. The whole system can then be put into motion as a cyclical theory of literary history: literature passes from myth to irony and then reverts to myth, and in 1957 we were evidently somewhere in the ironic phase with signs of an impending return to the mythic.

To establish his literary system, of which the above is only a partial account, Frye must first of all clear value-judgements out of the way, since these are merely subjective noises. When we analyse literature we are speaking of literature; when we evaluate it we are speaking of ourselves. The system must also expel any history other than literary history: literary works are made out of other literary works, not out of any material external to the literary system itself. The advantage of Frye's theory, then, is that it keeps literature untainted by history in New Critical fashion, viewing it as an enclosed ecological recycling of texts, but unlike New Criticism finds in literature a *substitute* history, with all the global span and collective structures of history itself. The modes and myths of literature are transhistorical, collapsing history to sameness or a set of repetitive variations on the same themes. For the system to survive it must be kept rigorously closed: nothing external can be allowed to infiltrate it lest its categories are deranged. This is why Frye's 'scientific' impulse demands a formalism even more full-blooded than that of New Criticism. The New Critics allowed that literature was in some significant sense cognitive, yielding a sort of knowledge of the world; Frye insists that literature is an 'autonomous verbal structure' quite cut off from any reference beyond itself, a sealed and inward-looking realm which 'contain[s] life and reality in a system of verbal relationships'.[1] All the system ever does is reshuffle its symbolic units in relation to each other, rather than in relation to any kind of reality outside it. Literature is not a way of knowing reality but a kind of collective utopian dreaming which has gone on throughout history, an expression of those fundamental human desires which have given rise to civilization itself, but which are never fully satisfied there. It is not to be seen as the self-expression of individual authors, who are no more than functions of this universal system: it springs from the collective subject of the human race itself, which is how it comes to embody 'archetypes' or figures of universal significance.

Frye's work emphasizes as it does the utopian root of literature because it is marked by a deep fear of the actual social world, a distaste for history itself. In literature, and in literature alone, one can shake off the sordid 'externalities' of referential language and discover a spiritual home. The *mythoi* of the theory are, significantly, pre-urban images of the natural cycles, nostalgic memories of a history before industrialism. Actual history is for Frye bondage and determinism, and literature remains the one place where we can be free. It is worth asking what kind of history we have been living through for this theory to be even remotely convincing. The beauty of the approach is that it deftly combines an extreme aestheticism with an efficiently classifying 'scientificity', and so maintains literature as an imaginary alternative to modern society while rendering criticism respectable in that society's terms. It displays an iconoclastic briskness towards literary waffle, dropping each work into its appointed mythological slot with computerized efficiency, but blends this with the most Romantic of yearnings. In one sense it is scornfully 'anti-humanist', decentring the individual human subject and centring all on the collective literary system itself; in another sense it is the work of a committed Christian humanist (Frye is a clergyman), for whom the dynamic which drives literature and civilization – desire – will finally be fulfilled only in the kingdom of God.

Like several of the literary theorists we have looked at, then, Frye offers literature as a displaced version of religion. Literature becomes an essential palliative for the failure of religious ideology, and supplies us with various myths which are of relevance to social life. In *The Critical Path* (1971), Frye contrasts conservative 'myths of concern' with liberal 'myths of freedom', and desires an equable balance between the two: the authoritarian tendencies of conservatism must be corrected by myths of freedom, while a conservative sense of order must temper liberalism's tendencies to social irresponsibility. What the mighty mythological system from Homer to the kingdom of God comes down to, in short, is a position somewhere between liberal Republican and conservative Democrat. The only mistake, Frye informs us, is that of the revolutionary, who naively misinterprets myths of freedom as historically realizable goals. The revolutionary is just a bad critic, mistaking myth for reality as a child might mistake the actress for a real fairy princess. It is remarkable that literature, severed from any sordid practical concern as it is, is in the end more or less capable of telling us which way to vote. Frye stands in the liberal humanist tradition of Arnold, desiring, as he says, 'society as free, classless and urbane'. What he means by 'classless', like Arnold before him, is in effect a society which universally subscribes to his own middle-class liberal values.

There is a loose sense in which Northrop Frye's work can be described as 'structuralist', and it is significantly contemporary with the growth of 'classical' structuralism in Europe. Structuralism, as the term suggests, is concerned with structures, and more particularly with examining the general laws by which they work. It also like Frye tends to *reduce* individual phenomena to mere instances of such laws. But structuralism proper contains a distinctive doctrine which is not to be found in Frye: the belief that the individual units of any system have meaning only by virtue of their relations to one another. This does not follow from a simple belief that you should look at things 'structurally'. You can examine a poem as a 'structure' while still treating each of its items as more or less meaningful in itself. Perhaps the poem contains one image about the sun and another about the moon, and you are interested in how these two images fit together to form a structure. But you become a card-carrying structuralist only when you claim that the meaning of each image is wholly a matter of its relation to the other. The images do not have a 'substantial' meaning, only a 'relational' one. You do not need to go outside the poem, to what you know of suns and moons, to explain them; they explain and define each other.

Let me try to illustrate this by a simple example. Suppose we are analysing a story in which a boy leaves home after quarrelling with his father, sets out on a walk through the forest in the heat of the day and falls down a deep pit. The father comes out in search of his son, peers down the pit, but is unable to see him because of the darkness. At that moment the sun has risen to a point directly overhead, illuminates the pit's depths with its rays and allows the father to rescue his child. After a joyous reconciliation, they return home together.

This may not be a particularly gripping narrative, but it has the advantage of simplicity. Clearly it could be interpreted in all sorts of ways. A psychoanalytical critic might detect definite hints of the Oedipus complex in it, and show how the child's fall into the pit is a punishment he unconsciously wishes upon himself for the rift with his father, perhaps a form of symbolic castration or a symbolic recourse to his mother's womb. A humanist critic might read it as a poignant dramatization of the difficulties implicit in human relationships. Another kind of critic might see it as an extended, rather pointless word-play on 'son/sun'. What a structuralist critic would do would be to schematize the story in diagrammatic form. The first unit of signification, 'boy quarrels with father', might be rewritten as 'low rebels against high'. The boy's walk through the forest is a movement along a horizontal axis, in contrast to the vertical axis 'low/high', and could be indexed as 'middle'. The fall into the pit, a place below ground, signifies 'low' again, and the zenith of the sun 'high'. By shining into the pit, the sun has in a sense stooped 'low', thus inverting the narrative's first signifying unit, where 'low' struck against 'high'. The reconciliation between father and son restores an equilibrium between 'low' and 'high', and the walk back home together, signifying 'middle', marks this achievement of a suitably intermediate state. Flushed with triumph, the structuralist rearranges his rulers and reaches for the next story.

What is notable about this kind of analysis is that, like Formalism, it brackets off the actual *content* of the story and concentrates entirely on the form. You could replace father and son, pit and sun, with entirely different elements – mother and daughter, bird and mole – and still have the *same* story. As long as the structure of *relations* between the units is preserved, it does not matter which items you select. This is not the case with the psychoanalytical or humanist readings of the tale, which depend on these items having a certain *intrinsic* significance, to understand which we have to resort to our knowledge of the world outside the text. Of course there is a sense in which the sun is high and pits are low anyway, and to that extent what is chosen as 'content' does matter; but if we took a narrative structure in which what was required was the symbolic role of 'mediator' between two items, the mediator could be anything from a grasshopper to a waterfall.

The relations between the various items of the story may be ones of parallelism, opposition, inversion, equivalence and so on; and as long as this structure of internal relations remains intact, the individual units are re-placeable. Three other points may be noted about the method. First, it does not matter to structuralism that this story is hardly an example of great literature. The method is quite indifferent to the cultural value of its object: anything from *War and Peace* to the *War Cry* will do. The method is analytical, not evaluative. Second, structuralism is a calculated affront to common sense. It refuses the 'obvious' meaning of the story and seeks instead to isolate certain 'deep' structures within it, which are not apparent on the surface. It does not take the text at face value, but 'displaces' it into a quite different kind of object. Third, if the particular contents of the text are replaceable, there is a sense in which one can say that the 'content' of the narrative is its structure. This is equivalent to claiming that the narrative is in a way about itself: its 'subject' is its own internal relations, its own modes of sense-making.

Literary structuralism flourished in the 1960s as an attempt to apply to literature the methods and insights of the founder of modern structural linguistics, Ferdinand de Saussure. Since many popularizing accounts of Saussure's epoch-making *Course in General Linguistics* (1916) are now available, I shall merely sketch in a few of his central positions. Saussure viewed language as a system of signs, which was to be studied 'synchronically' – that is to say, studied as a complete system at a given point in time – rather than 'diachronically', in its historical development. Each sign was to be seen as being made up of a 'signifier' (a sound-image, or its graphic equivalent), and a 'signified' (the concept or meaning). The three black marks $c - a - t$ are a signifier which evoke the signified 'cat' in an English mind. The relation between signifier and signified is an arbitrary one: there is no inherent reason why these three marks should mean 'cat', other than cultural and historical convention. Contrast *chat* in French. The relation between the whole sign and what it refers to (what Saussure calls the 'referent', the real furry four-legged creature) is therefore also arbitrary. Each sign in the system has meaning only by virtue of its difference from the others. 'Cat' has meaning not 'in itself', but because it is not 'cap' or 'cad' or 'bat'. It does not matter how the signifier alters, as long as it preserves its difference from all the other signifiers; you can pronounce it in many different accents as long as this difference is maintained. 'In the linguistic system,' says Saussure, 'there are only differences': meaning is not mysteriously immanent in a sign but is functional, the result of its difference from other signs. Finally, Saussure believed that linguistics would get into a hopeless mess if it concerned itself with actual speech, or *parole* as he called it. He was not interested in investigating what people actually said; he was concerned with the objective structure of signs which made their speech possible in the first place, and this he called *langue*. Neither was Saussure concerned with the real objects which people spoke about: in order to study language effectively, the referents of the signs, the things they actually denoted, had to be placed in brackets.

Structuralism in general is an attempt to apply this linguistic theory to objects and activities other than language itself. You can view a myth, wrestling match, system of tribal kinship, restaurant menu or oil painting as a system of signs, and a structuralist analysis will try to isolate the underlying set of laws by which these signs are combined into meanings. It will largely ignore what the signs actually 'say', and concentrate instead on their internal relations to one another. Structuralism, as Fredric Jameson has put it, is an attempt 'to rethink everything through once again in terms of linguistics'.[2] It is a symptom of the fact that language, with its problems, mysteries and implications, has become both paradigm and obsession for twentieth-century intellectual life.

Saussure's linguistic views influenced the Russian Formalists, although Formalism is not itself exactly a structuralism. It views literary texts 'structurally', and suspends attention to the referent to examine the sign itself, but it is not particularly concerned with meaning as differential or, in much of its work, with the 'deep' laws and structures underlying literary texts. It was one of the Russian Formalists, however – the linguist Roman Jakobson – who was to provide the major link between Formalism and modern-day structuralism. Jakobson was leader of the Moscow Linguistic Circle, a Formalist group founded in 1915, and in 1920 migrated to Prague to become one of the major theoreticians of Czech structuralism. The Prague Linguistic Circle was founded in 1926, and survived until the outbreak of the Second World War. Jakobson later migrated once more, this time to the United States, where he encountered the French anthropologist Claude Lévi-Strauss during the Second World War, an intellectual relationship out of which much of modern structuralism was to develop.

Jakobson's influence can be detected everywhere within Formalism, Czech structuralism and modern linguistics. What he contributed in particular to poetics, which he regarded as part of the field of linguistics, was the idea that the 'poetic' consisted above all in language's being placed in a certain kind of self-conscious relationship to itself. The poetic functioning of language 'promotes the palpability of signs', draws attention to their material qualities rather than simply using them as counters in communication. In the 'poetic', the sign is dislocated from its object: the usual relation between sign and referent is disturbed, which allows the sign a certain independence as an object of value in itself. All communication for Jakobson involves six elements: an addresser, an addressee, a message passed between them, a shared code which makes that message intelligible, a 'contact' or physical medium of communication, and a 'context' to which the message refers. Any one of these elements may dominate in a particular communicative act: language seen from the addresser's viewpoint is 'emotive' or expressive of a state of mind; from the addressee's standpoint it is 'conative', or trying for an effect; if communication concerns the context it is 'referential', if it is oriented to the code itself it is 'metalinguistic' (as when two individuals discuss whether they are understanding each other), and communication angled towards the contact itself is 'phatic' (e.g. 'Well, here we are chatting away at last'). The 'poetic' function is dominant when the communication focuses on the message itself – when the words themselves, rather than what is said by whom for what purpose in what situation, are 'foregrounded' in our attention.[3]

Jakobson also makes much of a distinction implicit in Saussure between the metaphorical and the metonymic. In metaphor, one sign is *substituted* for another because it is somehow similar to it: 'passion' becomes 'flame'. In metonymy, one sign is *associated* with another: 'wing' is associated with 'aircraft' because it is part of it, 'sky' with 'aircraft' because of physical contiguity. We can make metaphors because we have a series of signs which are 'equivalent': 'passion', 'flame', 'love' and so on. When we speak or write, we select signs from a possible range of equivalences, and then combine them together to form a sentence. What happens in poetry, however, is that we pay attention to 'equivalences' in the process of *combining* words together as well as in selecting them: we string together words which are semantically or rhythmically or phonetically or in some other way equivalent. This is why Jakobson is able to say, in a famous definition, that 'The poetic function projects the principle of equivalence from the axis of selection to the axis of combination.'[4] Another way of saying this is that, in poetry, 'similarity is superinduced upon contiguity': words are not just strung together for the sake of the thoughts they convey, as in ordinary speech, but with an eye to the patterns of similarity, opposition, parallelism and so on created by their sound, meaning, rhythm and connotations. Some literary forms – realist prose, for example – tend to be metonymic, linking signs by their associations with each other; other forms, such as Romantic and Symbolist poetry, are highly metaphorical.[5]

The Prague school of linguistics – Jakobson, Jan Mukařovský, Felix Vodička and others – represent a kind of transition from Formalism to modern structuralism. They elaborated the ideas of the Formalists, but systematized them more firmly within the framework of Saussurean linguistics. Poems were to be viewed as 'functional structures', in which signifiers and signifieds are governed by a single complex set of relations. These signs must be studied in their own right, not as reflections of an external reality: Saussure's stress on the arbitrary relation between sign and referent, word and thing, helped to detach the text from its surroundings and make of it an autonomous object. Yet the literary work was still related to the world by the Formalist concept of 'defamiliarization': art estranges and undermines conventional sign-systems, compels our attention to the material process of language itself, and so renews our perceptions. In not taking language for granted, we are also transforming our consciousness. More than the Formalists, however, the Czech structuralists insisted on the structural unity of the work: its elements were to be grasped as functions of a dynamic whole, with one particular level of the text (what the Prague school called the 'dominant') acting as the determining influence which 'deformed', or pulled into its own field of force, all the others.

So far the Prague structuralists might sound like little more than a more scientific version of New Criticism, and there is a seed of truth in this suggestion. But though the artefact was to be seen as a closed system, what *counted* as an artefact was a matter of social and historical circumstances. According to Jan Mukařovský, the work of art is perceived as such only against a more general background of significations, only as a systematic 'deviation' from a linguistic norm; as this background changes, interpretation and evaluation of the work change accordingly, to the point where it may cease to be perceived as a work of art at all. There is nothing, Mukařovský argues in *Aesthetic Function, Norm and Value as Social Facts* (1936) which possesses an aesthetic function regardless of place, time or the person evaluating it, and nothing which could not possess such a function in appropriate conditions. Mukařovský distinguishes between the 'material artefact', which is the physical book, painting or sculpture itself, and the 'aesthetic object', which exists only in human interpretation of this physical fact.

With the work of the Prague school, the term 'structuralism' comes more or less to merge with the word 'semiotics'. 'Semiotics', or 'semiology', means the systematic study of signs, and this is what literary structuralists are really doing. The word 'structuralism' itself indicates a *method* of enquiry, which can be applied to a whole range of objects from football matches to economic modes of production; 'semiotics' denotes rather a particular *field* of study, that of systems which would in an ordinary sense be regarded as signs: poems, bird calls, traffic lights, medical symptoms and so on. But the two words overlap, since structuralism treats something which may not usually be thought of as a system of signs as though it were – the kinship relations of tribal societies, for example – while semiotics commonly uses structuralist methods.

The American founder of semiotics, the philosopher C. S. Peirce, distinguished between three basic kinds of sign. There was the 'iconic', where the sign somehow resembled what it stood for (a photograph of a person, for example); the 'indexical', in which the sign is somehow associated with what it is a sign of (smoke with fire, spots with measles), and the 'symbolic', where as with Saussure the sign is only arbitrarily or conventionally linked with its referent. Semiotics takes up this and many other classifications: it distinguishes between 'denotation' (what the sign stands for) and 'connotation' (other signs associated with it); between codes (the rule-governed structures which produce meanings) and the messages transmitted by them; between the 'paradigmatic' (a whole class of signs which may stand in for one another) and the 'syntagmatic' (where signs are coupled together with each other in a 'chain'). It speaks of 'metalanguages', where one sign-system denotes another sign-system (the relation between literary criticism and literature, for instance), 'polysemic' signs which have more than one meaning, and a great many other technical concepts. To see what this kind of analysis looks like in practice, we may briefly consider the work of the leading Soviet semiotician of the so-called school of Tartu, Yury Lotman.

In his works *The Structure of the Artistic Text* (1970) and *The Analysis of the Poetic Text* (1972), Lotman sees the poetic text as a stratified system in which meaning only exists contextually, governed by sets of similarities and oppositions. Differences and parallelisms in the text are themselves relative terms, and can only be perceived in relation to one another. In poetry, it is the nature of the signifier, the patterns of sound and rhythm set up by the marks on the page themselves, which determines what is signified. A poetic text is 'semantically saturated', condensing more 'information' than any other discourse; but whereas for modern communication theory in general an increase in 'information' leads to a decrease in 'communication' (since I cannot 'take in' all that you so intensively tell me), this is not so in poetry because of its unique kind of internal organization. Poetry has a minimum of 'redundancy' – of those signs which are present in a discourse to facilitate communication rather than convey information – but still manages to produce a richer set of messages than any other form of language. Poems are bad when they do not carry sufficient information, for, as Lotman remarks, 'information is beauty'. Every literary text is made up of a number of 'systems' (lexical, graphic, metrical, phonological and so on), and gains its effects through constant clashes and tensions between these systems. Each of the systems comes to represent a 'norm' from which the others deviate, setting up a code of expectations which they transgress. Metre, for example, creates a certain pattern which the poem's syntax may cut across and violate. In this way, each system in the text 'defamiliarizes' the others, breaking up their regularity and throwing them into more vivid relief. Our perception of the poem's grammatical structure, for example, may heighten our awareness of its meanings. Just as one of the poem's systems threatens to become too predictable, another cuts across it to disrupt it into new life. If two words are associated together because of their similar sound or position in the metrical scheme, this will produce a sharper awareness of their similarity or difference of meaning. The literary work continually enriches and transforms mere dictionary meaning, generating new significances by the clash and condensation of its various 'levels'. And since any two words whatsoever may be juxtaposed on the basis of some equivalent feature, this possibility is more or less unlimited. Each word in the text is linked by a whole set of formal structures to several other words, and its meaning is thus always 'overdetermined', always the result of several different determinants acting together. An individual word may relate to another word through assonance, to another through syntactical equivalence, to yet another through morphological parallelism, and so on. Each sign thus participates in several different 'paradigmatic patterns' or systems simultaneously, and this complexity is greatly compounded by the 'syntagmatic' chains of association, the 'lateral' rather than 'vertical' structures, in which signs are placed.

The poetic text for Lotman is thus a 'system of systems', a relation of relations. It is the most complex form of discourse imaginable, condensing together several systems each of which contains its own tensions, parallelisms, repetitions and oppositions, and each of which is continually modifying all of the others. A poem, in fact, can only be re-read, not read, since some of its structures can only be perceived retrospectively. Poetry activates the full body of the signifier, presses the word to work to its utmost under the intense pressure of surrounding words, and so to release its richest potential. Whatever we perceive in the text is perceived only by contrast and difference: an element which had no differential relation to any other would remain invisible. Even the *absence* of certain devices may produce meaning: if the codes which the work has generated lead us to expect a rhyme or a happy ending which does not materialize, this 'minus device', as Lotman terms it, may be as effective a unit of meaning as any other. The literary work, indeed, is a continual generating and violating of expectations, a complex interplay of the regular and the random, norms and deviations, routinized patterns and dramatic defamiliarizations.

Despite this unique verbal richness, Lotman does not consider that poetry or literature can be defined by their inherent linguistic properties. The meaning of the text is not just an internal matter: it also inheres in the text's relation to wider systems of meaning, to other texts, codes and norms in literature and society as a whole. Its meaning is also relative to the reader's 'horizon of expectations': Lotman has learned the lessons of reception theory well. It is the reader who by virtue of certain 'receptive codes' at his or her disposal identifies an element in the work as a 'device'; the device is not simply an internal feature but one perceived through a particular code and against a definite textual background. One person's poetic device may be another's daily speech.

It is obvious from all this that literary criticism has come a long way from the days when we had to do little more than thrill to the beauty of the imagery. What semiotics represents, in fact, is literary criticism transfigured by structural linguistics, rendered a more disciplined and less impressionistic enterprise which, as Lotman's work testifies, is *more* rather than less alive to the wealth of form and language than most traditional criticism. But if structuralism transformed the study of poetry, it also revolutionized the study of narrative. Indeed it created a whole new literary science – narratology – of which the most influential practitioners have been the Lithuanian A. J. Greimas, the Bulgarian Tzvetan Todorov, and the French critics Gérard Genette, Claude Bremond and Roland Barthes. The modern structuralist analysis of narrative began with the pioneering work on myth of the French structural anthropologist Claude Lévi-Strauss, who viewed apparently different myths as variations on a number of basic themes. Beneath the immense heterogeneity of myths were certain constant universal structures, to which any particular myth could be reduced. Myths were a kind of language: they could be broken down into individual units ('mythemes') which like the basic sound units of language (phonemes) acquired meaning only when combined together in particular ways. The rules which governed such combinations could then be seen as a kind of grammar, a set of relations beneath the surface of the narrative which constituted the myth's true 'meaning'. These relations, Lévi-Strauss considered, were inherent in the human mind itself, so that in studying a body of myth we are looking less at its narrative contents than at the universal mental operations which structure it. These mental operations, such as the making of binary oppositions, are in a way what myths are about: they are devices to think with, ways of classifying and organizing reality, and this, rather than the recounting of any particular tale, is their point. The same, Lévi-Strauss believes, can be said of totemic and kinship systems, which are less social and religious institutions than networks of communication, codes which permit the transmission of 'messages'. The mind which does all this thinking is not that of the individual subject: myths think themselves through people, rather than vice versa. They have no origin in a particular consciousness, and no particular end in view. One result of structuralism, then, is the 'decentring' of the individual subject, who is no longer to be regarded as the source or end of meaning. Myths have a quasi-objective collective existence, unfold their own 'concrete logic' with supreme disregard for the vagaries of individual thought, and reduce any particular consciousness to a mere function of themselves.

Narratology consists in generalizing this model beyond the unwritten 'texts' of tribal mythology to other kinds of story. The Russian Formalist Vladimir Propp had already made a promising start with his *Morphology of the Folk Tale* (1928), which boldly reduced all folk tales to seven 'spheres of action' and thirty-one fixed elements or 'functions'. Any individual folk tale merely combined these 'spheres of action' (the hero, the helper, the villain, the person sought-for and so on) in specific ways. Drastically economical as this model was, it was possible to reduce it even further. A. J. Greimas's *Sémantique structurale* (1966), finding Propp's scheme still too empirical, is able to abstract his account even further by the concept of an *actant*, which is neither a specific narrative even nor a character but a structural unit. The six *actants* of Subject and Object, Sender and Receiver, Helper and Opponent can subsume Propp's various spheres of action and make for an even more elegant simplicity. Tzvetan Todorov attempts a similar 'grammatical' analysis of Boccaccio's *Decameron*, in which characters are seen as nouns, their attributes as adjectives and their actions as verbs. Each story of *The Decameron* can thus be read as a kind of extended sentence, combining these units in different ways. And just as the work thus comes to be about its own quasi-linguistic structure, so for structuralism every literary work, in the act of apparently describing some external reality, is secretly casting a sideways glance at its own processes of construction. In the end, structuralism does not only think everything through again, this time as language; it thinks everything through again as though language were its very subject matter.

To clarify our view of narratology, we may look finally at the work of Gérard Genette. In his *Narrative Discourse* (1972), Genette draws on a distinction in narrative between *récit*, by which he means the actual order of events in the text; *histoire*, which is the sequence in which those events 'actually' occurred, as we can infer this from the text; and *narration*, which concerns the act of narrating itself. The first two categories are equivalent to a classic Russian Formalist distinction between 'plot' and 'story': a detective story usually opens with the discovery of a body and finally backtracks to expose how the murder happened, but this plot of events reverses the 'story' or actual chronology of the action. Genette discerns five central categories of narrative analysis. 'Order' refers to the time-order of the narrative, how it may operate by prolepsis (anticipation), analepsis (flashback) or anachrony, which refers to discordances between 'story' and 'plot'. 'Duration' signifies how the narrative may elide episodes, expand them, summarize, pause a little and so on. 'Frequency' involves questions of whether an event happened once in the 'story' and is narrated once, happened once but is narrated several times, happened several times and is narrated several times, or happened several times and is narrated only once. The category of 'mood' can be subdivided into 'distance' and 'perspective'. Distance concerns the relation of the narration to its own materials: is it a matter of recounting the story ('diagesis') or representing it ('mimesis'), is the narrative told in direct, indirect or 'free indirect' speech? 'Perspective' is what might traditionally be called 'point of view', and can also be variously subdivided: the narrator may know more than the characters, less than them, or move on the same level; the narrative may be 'non-focalized', delivered by an omniscient narrator outside the action, or 'internally focalized', recounted by one character from a fixed position, from variable positions, or from several character-view-points. A form of 'external focalization' is possible, in which the narrator knows less than the characters do. Finally there is the category of 'voice', which concerns the act of narrating itself, what kind of narrator and narratee are implied. Various combinations are possible here between the 'time of the narrative' and the 'narrated time', between the action of recounting the story and the events which you recount: you may tell of the events before, after or (as in the epistolary novel) while they happen. A narrator may be 'heterodiegetic' (i.e. absent from his own narrative), 'homodiegetic' (inside his narrative as in first-person stories), or 'autodiegetic' (where he is not only inside the narrative but figures as its principal character). These are only some of Genette's classifications; but one important aspect of discourse to which they alert us is the difference between *narration* – the act and process of telling a story – and *narrative* – what it is you actually recount. When I tell a story about myself, as in autobiography, the 'I' who does the telling seems in one sense identical with the 'I' whom I describe, and in another sense different from it. We shall see later how this paradox has interesting impli-cations beyond literature itself.

What are the gains of structuralism? To begin with, it represents a remorse-less *demystification* of literature. It is less easy after Greimas and Genette to hear the cut and thrust of the rapiers in line three, or feel that you know just what it feels like to be a scarecrow after reading *The Hollow Men*. Loosely subjective talk was chastized by a criticism which recognized that the literary work, like any other product of language, is a *construct*, whose mechanisms could be classified and analysed like the objects of any other science. The Romantic prejudice that the poem, like a person, harboured a vital essence, a soul which it was discourteous to tamper with, was rudely unmasked as a bit of disguised theology, a superstitious fear of reasoned enquiry which made a fetish of literature and reinforced the authority of a 'naturally' sensitive critical elite. Moreover, the structuralist method implicitly questioned literature's claim to be a unique form of discourse: since deep structures could be dug out of Mickey Spillane as well as Sir Philip Sidney, and no doubt the same ones at that, it was no longer easy to assign literature an ontologically privileged status. With the advent of structuralism, the world of the great aestheticians and humanist literary scholars of twentieth-century Europe – the world of Croce, Curtius, Auerbach, Spitzer and Wellek – seemed one whose hour had passed.[6] These men, with their formidable erudition, imaginative insight and cosmopolitan range of allusion, appeared suddenly in historical perspective, as luminaries of a high European humanism which pre-dated the turmoil and conflagration of the mid-twentieth century. It seemed clear that such a rich culture could not be reinvented – that the choice was between learning from it and passing on, or clinging with nostalgia to its remnants in our time, denouncing a 'modern world' in which the paperback has spelt the death of high culture, and where there are no longer domestic servants to protect one's door while one reads in privacy.

The structuralist emphasis on the 'constructedness' of human meaning represented a major advance. Meaning was neither a private experience nor a divinely ordained occurrence: it was the product of certain shared systems of signification. The confident bourgeois belief that the isolated individual subject was the fount and origin of all meaning took a sharp knock: language pre-dated the individual, and was much less his or her product than he or she was the product of it. Meaning was not 'natural', a question of just looking and seeing, or something eternally settled; the way you interpreted your world was a function of the languages you had at your disposal, and there was evidently nothing immutable about these. Meaning was not something which all men and women everywhere intuitively shared, and then articulated in their various tongues and scripts: what meaning you were able to articulate depended on what script or speech you shared in the first place. There were the seeds here of a social and historical theory of meaning, whose implications were to run deep within contemporary thought. It was impossible any longer to see reality simply as something 'out there', a fixed order of things which language merely reflected. On that assumption, there was a natural bond between word and thing, a given set of correspondences between the two realms. Our language laid bare for us how the world was, and this could not be questioned. This rationalist or empiricist view of language suffered severely at the hands of structuralism: for if, as Saussure had argued, the relation between sign and referent was an arbitrary one, how could any 'correspondence' theory of knowledge stand? Reality was not reflected by language but *produced* by it: it was a particular way of carving up the world which was deeply dependent on the sign-systems we had at our command, or more precisely which had us at theirs. The suspicion began to arise, then, that structuralism was only not an empiricism because it was yet one more form of philosophical idealism – that its view of reality as essentially a product of language was simply the latest version of the classical idealist doctrine that the world was constituted by human consciousness.

Structuralism scandalized the literary Establishment with its neglect of the individual, its clinical approach to the mysteries of literature, and its clear incompatibility with common sense. The fact that structuralism offends common sense has always been a point in its favour. Common sense holds that things generally have only one meaning and that this meaning is usually obvious, inscribed on the faces of the objects we encounter. The world is pretty much as we perceive it, and our way of perceiving it is the natural, self-evident one. We know the sun goes round the earth because we can see that it does. At different times common sense has dictated burning witches, hanging sheep-stealers and avoiding Jews for fear of fatal infection, but this statement is not itself commonsensical since common sense believes itself to be historically invariable. Thinkers who have argued that the apparent meaning is not necessarily the real one have usually been met with scorn: Copernicus was followed by Marx, who claimed that the true significance of social processes went on 'behind the backs' of individual agents, and after Marx Freud argued that the real meanings of our words and actions were quite imperceptible to the conscious mind. Structuralism is a modern inheritor of this belief that reality, and our experience of it, are discontinuous with each other; as such, it threatens the ideological security of those who wish the world to be within their control, to carry its singular meaning on its face and to yield it up to them in the unblemished mirror of their language. It undermines the empiricism of the literary humanists – the belief that what is most 'real' is what is experienced, and that the home of this rich, subtle, complex experience is literature itself. Like Freud, it exposes the shocking truth that even our most intimate experience is the effect of a structure.

I have said that structuralism contained the seeds of a social and historical theory of meaning, but they were not, on the whole, able to sprout. For if the sign-systems by which individuals lived could be seen as culturally variable, the deep laws which governed the workings of these systems were not. For the 'hardest' forms of structuralism they were universal, embedded in a collective mind which transcended any particular culture, and which Lévi-Strauss suspected to be rooted in the structures of the human brain itself. Structuralism, in a word, was hair-raisingly unhistorical: the laws of the mind it claimed to isolate – parallelisms, oppositions, inversions and the rest – moved at a level of generality quite remote from the concrete differences of human history. From this Olympian height, all minds looked pretty much alike. Having characterized the underlying rule-systems of a literary text, all the structuralist could do was sit back and wonder what to do next. There was no question of relating the work to the realities of which it treated, or to the conditions which produced it, or to the actual readers who studied it, since the founding gesture of structuralism had been to bracket off such realities. In order to reveal the nature of language, Saussure, as we have seen, had first of all to repress or forget what it talked about: the referent, or real object which the sign denoted, was put in suspension so that the structure of the sign itself could be better examined. It is notable how similar this gesture is to Husserl's bracketing of the real object in order to get to closer grips with the way the mind experiences it. Structuralism and phenomenology, dissimilar though they are in central ways, both spring from the ironic act of shutting out the material world in order the better to illuminate our consciousness of it. For anyone who believes that consciousness is in an important sense *practical*, inseparably bound up with the ways we act in and on reality, any such move is bound to be self-defeating. It is rather like killing a person in order to examine more conveniently the circulation of the blood.

But it was not just a matter of shutting out something as general as 'the world': it was a question of discovering some toehold of certainty in a particular world where certainty seemed hard to come by. The lectures which make up Saussure's *Course in General Linguistics* were delivered in the heart of Europe between 1907 and 1911, on the brink of an historical collapse which Saussure himself did not live to see. These were precisely the years in which Edmund Husserl was formulating the major doctrines of phenomenology, in a European centre not far removed from Saussure's Geneva. At about the same time, or a little later, the major writers of twentieth-century English literature – Yeats, Eliot, Pound, Lawrence, Joyce – were developing their own closed symbolic systems, in which Tradition, theosophy, the male and female principles, medievalism and mythology were to provide the keystones of complete 'synchronic' structures, exhaustive models for the control and explanation of historical reality. Saussure himself was to posit the existence of a 'collective consciousness' underlying the system of *langue*. It is not difficult to see the flight from contemporary history in the recourse to myth of the major writers of English literature; it is less obviously detectable in a textbook of structural linguistics or an esoteric piece of philosophy.

Where it *is* more obviously detectable, perhaps, is in structuralism's embarrassment with the problem of historical change. Saussure looked at the development of language in terms of one synchronic system following another, rather like the Vatican official who remarked that whether the Pope's imminent pronouncement on the question of birth control turned out to uphold the previous teaching or not, the Church would nevertheless have moved from one state of certainty to another state of certainty. For Saussure, historical change was something which afflicted the individual elements of a language, and could only in this indirect way affect the whole: the language as a whole would reorganize itself to accommodate such disturbances, like learning to live with a wooden leg or like Eliot's Tradition welcoming a new masterpiece to the club. Behind this linguistic model lies a definite view of human society: change is disturbance and disequilibrium in an essentially conflict-free system, which will stagger for a moment, regain its balance and take the change in its stride. Linguistic change for Saussure seems a matter of accident: it happens 'blindly', and it was left to the later Formalists to explain how change itself might be grasped systematically. Jakobson and his colleague Yury Tynyanov saw the history of literature as itself forming a system, in which at any given point some forms and genres were 'dominant' while others were subordinate. Literary development took place by way of shifts within this hierarchical system, such that a previously dominant form became subordinate or vice versa. The dynamic of this process was 'defamiliarization': if a dominant literary form had grown stale and 'imperceptible' – if, for example, some of its devices had been taken over by a sub-genre such as popular journalism, thus blurring its difference from such writings – a previously subordinate form would emerge to 'defamiliarize' this situation. Historical change was a matter of the gradual realignment of fixed elements within the system: nothing ever disappeared, it merely changed shape by altering its relations to other elements. The history of a system, Jakobson and Tynyanov comment, is itself a system: diachrony can be studied synchronically. Society itself was made up of a whole set of systems (or 'series', as the Formalists called them), each of which was powered by its own internal laws, and evolved in relative autonomy of all the others. There were, however, 'correlations' between the various series: at any given time the literary series would encounter several possible paths along which it could develop, but which path was actually selected was the result of correlations between the literary system itself and other historical series. This was not a suggestion which all later structuralists took up: in their resolutely 'synchronic' approach to the object of study, historical change sometimes became as mysteriously inexplicable as the Romantic symbol.

Structuralism broke with conventional literary criticism in many ways, while remaining mortgaged to it in many others. Its preoccupation with language was, as we have seen, radical in its implications, but it was at the same time a familiar obsession of academics. Was language really all there was? What about labour, sexuality, political power? These realities might themselves be inextricably caught up in discourse, but they were certainly not reducible to it. What political conditions themselves determined this extreme 'foregrounding' of language itself? Was the structuralist view of the literary text as a closed system really much different from the New Critical treatment of it as an isolated object? What had happened to the concept of literature as a social *practice*, a form of *production* which was not necessarily exhausted by the product itself? Structuralism could dissect that product, but it refused to enquire into the material conditions of its making, since this might mean surrendering to the myth of an 'origin'. Nor were many structuralists worried about how the product was actually consumed – about what happened when people actually read works of literature, what role such works played in social relations as a whole. Moreover, was not structuralism's stress on the *integrated* nature of a sign-system just another version of the work as 'organic unity'? Lévi-Strauss spoke of myths as imaginary resolutions of real social contradictions; Yury Lotman used the imagery of cybernetics to show how the poem formed a complex organic totality; the Prague school developed a 'functionalist' view of the work in which all the parts laboured inexorably together for the good of the whole. Traditional criticism had sometimes reduced the literary work to little more than a window on to the author's psyche; structuralism seemed to make it a window on to the universal mind. The 'materiality' of the text itself, its detailed linguistic processes, was in danger of being abolished: the 'surface' of a piece of writing was little more than the obedient reflection of its concealed depths. What Lenin once called the 'reality of appearances' was at risk of being overlooked: all 'surface' features of the work could be reduced to an 'essence', a single central meaning which informed all the work's aspects, and this essence was no longer the writer's soul or the Holy Spirit but the 'deep structure' itself. The text was really just a 'copy' of this deep structure, and structuralist criticism was a copy of this copy. Finally, if traditional critics composed a spiritual elite, structuralists appeared to constitute a scientific one, equipped with an esoteric knowledge far removed from the 'ordinary' reader.

At the same moment as structuralism bracketed off the real object, it bracketed off the human subject. Indeed it is this double movement which defines the structuralist project. The work neither refers to an object, nor is the expression of an individual subject; both of these are blocked out, and what is left hanging in the air between them is a system of rules. This system has its own independent life, and will not stoop to the beck and call of individual intentions. To say that structuralism has a problem with the individual subject is to put it mildly: that subject was effectively liquidated, reduced to the function of an impersonal structure. To put it another way: the new subject was really the *system itself*, which seemed equipped with all the attributes (autonomy, self-correction, unity and so on) of the traditional individual. Structuralism is 'anti-humanist', which means not that its devotees rob children of their sweets but that they reject the myth that meaning begins and ends in the individual's 'experience'. For the humanist tradition, meaning is something that I create, or that we create together; but how could we create meaning unless the rules which govern it were already there? However far back we push, however much we hunt for the origin of meaning, we will always find a structure already in place. This structure could not have been simply the *result* of speech, for how were we able to speak coherently in the first place without it? We could never discover the 'first sign' from which it all began, because, as Saussure makes clear, one sign presupposes another from which it differs, and that another. If language was ever 'born', Lévi-Strauss speculates, it must have been born 'at a stroke'. Roman Jakobson's communicative model, the reader will remember, starts from an addresser who is the source of the transmitted message; but where did this addresser come from? To be able to transmit a message at all, he or she must already be caught up in and constituted by language. In the beginning was the Word.

To see language in this way is a valuable advance on seeing it simply as the 'expression' of an individual mind. But it also makes for severe difficulties. For though language may not be best understood as individual expression, it certainly in some way involves human subjects and their intentions, and it is this which the structuralist picture leaves out of account. Let us go back for a moment to the situation I outlined earlier, where I tell you to close the door when a gale is howling through the room. I said then that the meaning of my words was independent of any private intention I might have – that the meaning was, so to speak, a function of the language itself, rather than some mental process of mine. In a certain practical situation, the words just do seem to mean what they mean whatever I might whimsically want them to mean. But what if I asked you to close the door having just spent twenty minutes roping you to your chair? What if the door was closed already, or there was no door there at all? Then, surely, you would be quite justified to ask me: 'What do you mean?' It isn't that you don't understand the meaning of my *words*; it is that you don't understand the *meaning* of my words. It will not help if I hand you a dictionary. Asking 'What do you mean?' in this situation is indeed asking about the intentions of a human subject, and unless I understand these then the request to close the door is in an important sense meaningless.

Asking about my intentions, however, is not necessarily asking to peer into my mind and observe the mental processes going on there. It is not necessary to see intentions in the way that E. D. Hirsch does, as essentially private 'mental acts'. To ask in such a situation 'What do you mean?' is really to ask what effects my language is trying to bring about: it is a way of understanding the situation itself, not an attempt to tune into ghostly impulses within my skull. Understanding my intention is grasping my speech and behaviour in relation to a significant context. When we understand the 'intentions' of a piece of language, we interpret it as being in some sense *oriented*, structured to achieve certain effects; and none of this can be grasped apart from the practical conditions in which the language operates. It is to see language as a practice rather than as an object; and there are of course no practices without human subjects.

This way of viewing language is on the whole quite foreign to structuralism, at least in its classical varieties. Saussure, as I have mentioned, was interested not in what people actually said but in the structure which allowed them to say it: he studied *langue* rather than *parole*, seeing the former as an objective social fact and the latter as the random, untheorizable utterance of the individual. But this view of language already encodes a certain questionable way of conceptualizing the relations between individuals and societies. It sees the system as determined and the individual as free; it grasps social pressures and determinants not so much as forces active in our actual speaking, but as a monolithic structure which somehow stands over against us. It presumes that *parole*, individual utterance, really *is* individual, rather than an inevitably social and 'dialogic' affair which catches us up with other speakers and listeners in a whole field of social values and purposes. Saussure strips language of its sociality at the point where it matters most: at the point of linguistic production, the actual speaking, writing, listening and reading of concrete social individuals. The constraints of the language system are consequently fixed and given, aspects of *langue*, rather than forces which we produce, modify and transform in our actual communication. We may also notice that Saussure's model of individual and society, like many classical bourgeois models, has no intermediate terms, no mediations between solitary individual speakers and the linguistic system as a whole. The fact that someone may not only be a 'member of society' but also a woman, shop-steward, Catholic, mother, immigrant and disarmament campaigner is simply slid over. The linguistic corollary of this – that we inhabit many different 'languages' simultaneously, some of them perhaps mutually conflicting – is also ignored.

The shift away from structuralism has been in part, to use the terms of the French linguist Emile Benveniste, a move from 'language' to 'discourse'.[7] 'Language' is speech or writing viewed 'objectively', as a chain of signs without a subject. 'Discourse' means language grasped as *utterance*, as involving speaking and writing subjects and therefore also, at least potentially, readers or listeners. This is not simply a return to the pre-structuralist days when we thought that language belonged to us individually as our eyebrows did; it does not revert to the classical 'contractual' model of language, according to which language is just a sort of instrument essentially isolated individuals use to exchange their pre-linguistic experiences. This was really a 'market' view of language, closely associated with the historical growth of bourgeois individualism: meaning belonged to me like my commodity, and language was just a set of tokens which like money allowed me to exchange my meaning-commodity with another individual who was also a private proprietor of meaning. It was difficult on this empiricist theory of language to know how what got exchanged was the genuine article: if I had a concept, fixed a verbal sign to it and threw the whole package across to someone else, who looked at the sign and rifled through his own verbal filing system for the corresponding concept, how could I ever know that he was matching up signs and concepts in the way that I was? Maybe we were all systematically misunderstanding each other all of the time. Laurence Sterne wrote a novel, *Tristram Shandy*, exploiting the comic potential of just this empiricist model, not long after it had become the standard philosophical view of language in England. There was no question for the critics of structuralism of returning to this sorry state in which we viewed signs in terms of concepts, rather than talking about having concepts as particular ways of handling signs. It was just that a theory of meaning which seemed to squeeze out the human subject was very curious. What had been narrow-minded about previous theories of meaning was their dogmatic insistence that the intention of the speaker or writer was always paramount for interpretation. In countering this dogmatism, there was no need to pretend that intentions did not exist at all; it was simply necessary to point out the arbitrariness of claiming that they were always the *ruling* structure of discourse.

In 1962, Roman Jakobson and Claude Lévi-Strauss published an analysis of Charles Baudelaire's poem *Les chats* which has become something of a classic of high structuralist practice.[8] With toothcombing tenacity, the essay dug out a set of equivalences and oppositions from the poem's semantic, syntactic and phonological levels, equivalences and oppositions which extended right down to individual phonemes. But as Michael Riffaterre pointed out in a famous rejoinder to this critique, some of the structures Jakobson and Lévi-Strauss identified would simply have been imperceptible to even the most vigilant reader.[9] Moreover, the analysis took no account of the reading *process*: it seized the text synchronically, as an object in space rather than a movement in time. A particular meaning in a poem will cause us retrospectively to revise what we have learnt already; a word or image which is repeated does not mean the same as it did the first time, by virtue of the very fact that it is a repetition. No event occurs twice, precisely because it has occurred once already. The Baudelaire essary, Riffaterre argues, also overlooks certain crucial connotations of words which one could recognize only by moving outside the text itself to the cultural and social codes on which it draws; and this move, of course, is forbidden by the authors' structuralist assumptions. In true structuralist fashion, they treat the poem as 'language'; Riffaterre, by appealing to the reading process and the cultural situation in which the work is apprehended, has gone some way towards regarding it as 'discourse'.

One of the most important critics of Saussurean linguistics was the Russian philosopher and literary theorist Mikhail Bakhtin, who under the name of his colleague V. N. Voloshinov published in 1929 a pioneering study entitled *Marxism and the Philosophy of Language*. Bakhtin had also been largely responsible for what remains the most cogent critique of Russian Formalism, *The Formal Method in Literary Scholarship*, published under the names of Bakhtin and P. N. Medvedev in 1928. Reacting sharply against Saussure's 'objectivist' linguistics, but critical also of 'subjectivist' alternatives, Bakhtin shifted attention from the abstract system of *langue* to the concrete utterances of individuals in particular social contexts. Language was to be seen as inherently 'dialogic': it could be grasped only in terms of its inevitable orientation towards another. The sign was to be seen less as a fixed unit (like a signal) than as an active component of speech, modified and transformed in meaning by the variable social tones, valuations and connotations it condensed within itself in specific social conditions. Since such valuations and connotations were constantly shifting, since the 'linguistic community' was in fact a *heterogeneous* society composed of many conflicting interests, the sign for Bakhtin was less a neutral element in a given structure than a focus of struggle and contradiction. It was not simply a matter of asking 'what the sign meant', but of investigating its varied history, as conflicting social groups, classes, individuals and discourses sought to appropriate it and imbue it with their own meanings. Language, in short, was a field of ideological contention, not a monolithic system; indeed signs were the very material medium of ideology, since without them no values or ideas could exist. Bakhtin respected what might be called the 'relative autonomy' of language, the fact that it could not be reduced to a mere reflex of social interests; but he insisted that there was no language which was not caught up in definite social relationships, and that these social relationships were in turn part of broader political, ideological and economic systems. Words were 'multi-accentual' rather than frozen in meaning: they were always the words of one particular human subject for another, and this practical context would shape and shift their meaning. Moreover, since all signs were material – quite as material as bodies or automobiles – and since there could be no human consciousness without them, Bakhtin's theory of language laid the foundation for a materialist theory of consciousness itself. Human consciousness *was* the subject's active, material, semiotic intercourse with others, not some sealed interior realm divorced from these relations; consciousness, like language, was both 'inside' and 'outside' the subject simultaneously. Language was not to be seen either as 'expression', 'reflection' or abstract system, but rather as a material means of production, whereby the material body of the sign was transformed through a process of social conflict and dialogue into meaning.

Some significant work has followed in our own time from this radical anti-structuralist perspective.[10] It also has remote relations with a current of Anglo-Saxon linguistic philosophy which is far from concerned with such alien concepts as 'ideology'. Speech act theory, as this current is known, began in the work of the English philosopher J. L. Austin, and especially in his jocosely entitled *How to Do Things With Words* (1962). Austin had noticed that not all of our language actually describes reality: some of it is 'performative', aimed at getting something done. There are 'illocutionary' acts, which do something *in* the saying: 'I promise to be good,' or 'I hereby pronounce you man and wife.' There are also 'perlocutionary' acts, which bring an effect about *by* the saying: I may succeed in convincing, persuading, intimidating you by my words. In the end, interestingly, Austin came to admit that all language is really performative: even statements of fact, or 'constative' language, are acts of informing or affirming, and to communicate information is as much a 'performance' as naming a ship. For 'illocutionary' acts to be valid, certain conventions must be in place: I must be the kind of person licensed to make such statements, I must be serious about it, the circumstances must be appropriate, the procedures must be correctly executed, and so on. I cannot baptize a badger, and will probably have made things worse if I am not a clergyman anyway. (I choose this baptismal image because Austin's discussion of appropriate conditions, correct procedures and the rest has an odd and not insignificant similarity to theological debates about sacramental validity.) The relevance of all this to literature becomes clear when we realize that literary works themselves can be seen as speech acts, or as an imitation of them. Literature may appear to be describing the world, and sometimes actually does so, but its real function is performative: it uses language within certain conventions in order to bring about certain effects in a reader. It achieves something *in* the saying: it is language as a kind of material practice in itself, discourse as social action. In looking at 'constative' propositions, statements of truth or falsity, we tend to suppress their reality and effectivity as actions in their own right; literature restores to us this sense of linguistic performance in the most dramatic way, for whether what it asserts as existing actually exists or not is unimportant.

There are problems with speech act theory, both in itself and as a model of literature. It is not clear that such theory can finally avoid smuggling in the old 'intending subject' of phenomenology in order to anchor itself, and its preoccupations with language seem unhealthily juridical, a matter of who is allowed to say what to whom in what conditions.[11] The object of Austin's analysis is, as he says, 'the total speech act in the total speech situation'; but Bakhtin shows that there is rather more involved in such acts and situations than speech act theory suspects. It is also dangerous to take 'living speech' situations as models for literature. For literary texts are not of course literally speech acts: Flaubert is not actually talking to me. If anything, they are 'pseudo' or 'virtual' speech acts – 'imitations' of speech acts – and as such were more or less dismissed by Austin himself as 'non-serious' and defective. Richard Ohmann has taken this characteristic of literary texts – that they imitate or represent speech acts which themselves have never happened – as a way of defining 'literature' itself, though this does not in fact cover all that 'literature' is commonly taken to denote.[12] To think of literary discourse in terms of human subjects is not in the first place to think of it in terms of *actual* human subjects: the real historical author, a particular historical reader and so on. Knowing about this may be important; but a literary work is not actually a 'living' dialogue or monologue. It is a piece of language which has been detached from any specific 'living' relationship and thus subject to the 'reinscriptions' and reinterpretations of many different readers. The work itself cannot 'foresee' its own future history of interpretations, cannot control and delimit these readings as we can do, or try to do, in face-to-face conversation. Its 'anonymity' is part of its very structure, not just an unfortunate accident which befalls it; and in this sense to be an 'author' – the 'origin' of one's own meanings, with 'authority' over them – is a myth.

Even so, a literary work can be seen as constructing what have been called 'subject positions'. Homer did not anticipate that I personally would read his poems, but his language, by virtue of the ways it is constructed, unavoidably offers certain 'positions' for a reader, certain vantage-points from which it can be interpreted. To understand a poem means grasping its language as being 'oriented' towards the reader from a certain range of positions: in reading, we build up a sense of what kind of effects this language is trying to achieve ('intention'), what sorts of rhetoric it considers appropriate to use, what assumptions govern the kinds of poetic tactics it employs, what attitudes towards reality these imply. None of this need be identical with the intentions, attitudes and assumptions of the actual historical author at the time of writing, as is obvious if one tries to read William Blake's *Songs of Innocence and Experience* as the 'expression' of William Blake himself. We may know nothing about the author, or the work may have had several authors (who was the 'author' of the Book of Isaiah, or of *Casablanca*?), or to be an acceptable author at all in a certain society may mean writing from a certain 'position'. Dryden could not have written 'free verse' and still have been a poet. Understanding these textual effects, assumptions, tactics and orientations is just to understand the 'intention' of the work. And such tactics and assumptions may not be mutually coherent: a text may offer several mutually conflicting or contradictory 'subject positions' from which to be read. In reading Blake's *Tyger* poem, the process of building up an idea of where the language is coming from and what it is aimed at is inseparable from the process of constructing a 'subject position' for ourselves as readers. What kind of reader do the poem's tone, rhetorical tactics, stock of imagery, armoury of assumptions imply? How does it expect us to take it? Does it seem to expect us to take its propositions at face value, thus confirming us as readers in a position of recognition and assent, or is it inviting us to assume a critical, dissociating position from what it offers? Is it, in other words, ironic or satirical? More disturbingly, is the text trying to stand us ambiguously between the two options, eliciting from us a kind of consent while seeking simultaneously to undermine it?

To see the relation between language and human subjectivity in this way is to concur with the structuralists in avoiding what may be called the 'humanist' fallacy – the naive notion that a literary text is just a kind of transcript of the living voice of a real man or woman addressing us. Such a view of literature always tends to find its distinguishing characteristic – the fact that it is *written* – somehow disturbing: the print, in all its cold impersonality, interposes its ungainly bulk between ourselves and the author. If only we could talk to Cervantes directly! Such an attitude 'dematerializes' literature, strives to reduce its material density as language to the intimate spiritual encounter of living 'persons'. It goes along with the liberal humanist suspicion of all that cannot be immediately reduced to the interpersonal, from feminism to factory production. It is not, in the end, concerned with regarding the literary text as a *text* at all. But if structuralism avoided the humanist fallacy, it did so only to fall into the opposite trap of more or less abolishing human subjects altogether. For the structuralists, the 'ideal reader' of a work was someone who would have at his or her disposal all of the codes which would render it exhaustively intelligible. The reader was thus just a kind of mirror-reflection of the work itself – someone who would understand it 'as it was'. An ideal reader would need to be fully equipped with all the technical knowledge essential for deciphering the work, to be faultless in applying this knowledge, and free of any hampering restrictions. If this model was pressed to an extreme, he or she would have to be stateless, classless, ungendered, free of ethnic characteristics and without limiting cultural assumptions. It is true that one does not tend to meet many readers who fill this bill entirely satisfactorily, but the structuralists conceded that the ideal reader need not do anything so humdrum as actually exist. The concept was merely a convenient heuristic (or exploratory) fiction for determining what it would take to read a particular text 'properly'. The reader, in other words, was just a function of the text itself: to give an exhaustive description of the text was really the same thing as to give a complete account of the kind of reader it would require to understand it.

The ideal reader or 'super-reader' posited by structuralism was in effect a transcendental subject absolved from all limiting social determinants. It owed much as a concept to the American linguist Noam Chomsky's notion of linguistic 'competence', by which was meant the innate capacities which allowed us to master the underlying rules of language. But not even Lévi-Strauss was able to read texts as would the Almighty himself. Indeed it has been plausibly suggested that Lévi-Strauss's initial engagements with structuralism had much to do with his political views about the reconstruction of post-war France, views about which there was nothing divinely assured.[13]

Structuralism is among other things one more of literary theory's series of doomed attempts to replace religion with something as effective: in this case, with the modern religion of science. But the search for a purely objective reading of literary works clearly poses grievous problems. It seems impossible to eradicate some element of interpretation, and so of subjectivity, from even the most rigorously objective analysis. How, for example, did the structuralist identify the various 'signifying units' of the text in the first place? How did he or she decide that a specific sign or set of signs constituted such a basic unit, without recourse to frames of cultural assumption which structuralism in its strictest forms wished to ignore? For Bakhtin, all language, just because it is a matter of social practice, is inescapably shot through with valuations. Words not only denote objects but imply attitudes to them: the tone in which you say 'Pass the cheese' can signify how you regard me, yourself, the cheese and the situation we are in. Structuralism conceded that language moved in this 'connotative' dimension, but it shrank back from the full implications of this. It certainly tended to disown valuations in the broader sense of saying whether you thought a particular literary work was good, bad or indifferent. It did so because this seemed unscientific, and because it was tired of bellelettristic preciosity. There was thus no reason in principle why you should not spend your life as a structuralist working on bus tickets. The science itself gave you no clue as to what might or might not be important. The prudishness of structuralism's evasion of value-judgements, like the prudishness of behaviourist psychology, with its coy, euphemistic, circumlocutory avoidance of any language which smacks of the human, was more than just a fact about its method. It suggested the extent to which structuralism was the dupe of an alienated theory of scientific practice, one powerfully dominant in late capitalist society.

That structuralism has in some ways become complicit with the aims and procedures of such society is obvious enough in the reception it has received in England. Conventional English literary criticism has tended to divide into two camps over structuralism. On the one hand there are those who see in it the end of civilization as we have known it. On the other hand, there are those erstwhile or essentially conventional critics who have scrambled with varying degrees of dignity on a bandwagon which in Paris at least has been disappearing down the road for some time. The fact that structuralism was effectively over as an intellectual movement in Europe some years ago has not seemed to deter them: a decade or so is perhaps the customary time-lapse for ideas in transit across the Channel. These critics operate, one might say, rather like intellectual immigration officers: their job is to stand at Dover as the new-fangled ideas are unloaded from Paris, examine them for the bits and pieces which seem more or less reconcilable with traditional critical techniques, wave these goods genially on and keep out of the country the rather more explosive items of equipment (Marxism, feminism, Freudianism) which have arrived with them. Anything unlikely to prove distasteful in the middle-class suburbs is supplied with a work permit; less well-heeled ideas are packed back on the next boat. Some of this criticism has in fact been sharp, subtle and useful: it has represented a significant advance in England on what existed before, and at its best displays an intellectual adventurousness which has not been greatly in evidence since the days of *Scrutiny*. Its individual readings of texts have often been remarkably cogent and rigorous, and French structuralism has been combined with a more English 'feel for language' in valuable ways. It is simply the extreme selectivity of its approach to structuralism, one not always acknowledged, which needs to be highlighted.

The point of this judicious importation of structuralist concepts is to keep literary criticism in a job. It has been evident for some time that it is a little short on ideas, lacking in 'long perspectives', embarrassingly blind both to new theories and to the implications of its own. Just as the EC can help Britain out in economic matters, then, so structuralism can do in intellectual ones. Structuralism has functioned as a kind of aid scheme for intellectually underdeveloped nations, supplying them with the heavy plant which might revive a failing domestic industry. It promises to put the whole literary academic enterprise on a firmer footing, thus permitting it to surmount the so-called 'crisis in the humanities'. It provides a new answer to the question: What is it that we are teaching/studying? The old answer – Literature – is not, as we have seen, wholly satisfactory: roughly speaking, it involves too much subjectivism. But if what we are teaching and studying is not so much 'literary works' but the 'literary system' – the whole system of codes, genres and conventions by which we identify and interpret literary works in the first place – then we seem to have unearthed a rather more solid object of investigation. Literary criticism can become a kind of *meta*criticism: its role is not primarily to make interpretative or evaluative statements but to step back and examine the logic of such statements, to analyse what we are up to, what codes and models we are applying, when we make them. 'To engage in the study of literature,' Jonathan Culler has argued, 'is not to produce yet another interpretation of *King Lear* but to advance one's understanding of the conventions and operations of an institution, a mode of discourse.'[14] Structuralism is a way of refurbishing the literary institution, providing it with a *raison d'être* more respectable and compelling than gush about sunsets.

The point, however, may not be to understand the institution but to change it. Culler seems to assume that an investigation of how literary discourse works is an end in itself, requiring no further justification; but there is no reason to suppose that the 'conventions and operations' of an institution are less to be criticized than gush about sunsets, and enquiring into them without such a critical attitude will certainly mean reinforcing the power of the institution itself. All such conventions and operations, as this book tries to show, are the ideological products of a particular history, crystallizing ways of seeing (and not just of 'literary' seeing) which are far from uncontroversial. Whole social ideologies may be implicit in an apparently neutral critical method; and unless studying such methods takes account of this, it is likely to result in little more than servility to the institution itself. Structuralism has demonstrated that there is nothing innocent about codes; but there is nothing innocent in taking them as the object of one's study either. What is the point of doing this anyway? Whose interests is it likely to serve? Is it likely to give students of literature the impression that the existing corpus of conventions and operations is radically questionable, or will it rather intimate that they constitute some neutral technical wisdom which any student of literature needs to acquire? What is meant by the 'competent' reader? Is there only one kind of competence, and by whose and what criteria is competence to be measured? One could imagine a dazzlingly suggestive interpretation of a poem being produced by someone who entirely lacked 'literary competence' as conventionally defined – someone who produced such a reading not by following the received hermeneutical procedures but by flouting them. A reading is not necessarily 'incompetent' because it ignores a conventional critical mode of operation: many readings are in a different sense incompetent because they follow such conventions all too faithfully. Still less is it easy to assess 'competence' when we consider the way literary interpretation engages values, beliefs and assumptions which are not confined to the literary realm. It is no good the literary critic claiming that he is prepared to be tolerant about beliefs but not about technical procedures: the two are far too closely bound together for that.

Some structuralist arguments would appear to assume that the critic identifies the 'appropriate' codes for deciphering the text and then applies them, so that the codes of the text and the codes of the reader gradually converge into a unitary knowledge. But this is surely too simple-minded a conception of what reading actually involves. In applying a code to the text, we may find that it undergoes revision and transformation in the reading process; continuing to read with this same code, we discover that it now produces a 'different' text, which in turn modifies the code by which we are reading it, and so on. This dialectical process is in principle infinite; and if this is so then it undermines any assumption that once we have identified the proper codes for the text our task is finished. Literary texts are 'code-productive' and 'code-transgressive' as well as 'code-confirming': they may teach us new ways of reading, not just reinforce the ones with which we come equipped. The 'ideal' or 'competent' reader is a static conception: it tends to suppress the truth that all judgements of 'competence' are culturally and ideologically relative, and that all reading involves the mobilizing of extra-literary assumptions for the measuring of which 'competence' is an absurdly inadequate model.

Even at the technical level, however, the concept of competence is a limited one. The competent reader is one who can apply to the text certain rules; but what are the rules for applying rules? The rule seems to indicate to us the way to go, like a pointing finger; but your finger only 'points' within a certain interpretation I make of what you are doing, one which leads me to look at the object indicated rather than up your arm. Pointing is not an 'obvious' activity, and neither do rules carry their applications on their faces: they would not be 'rules' at all if they inexorably determined the way we were to apply them. Rule-following involves creative interpretation, and it is often not at all easy to say whether I am applying a rule in the way that you are, or even whether we are applying the same rule at all. The way you apply a rule is not just a technical affair: it is bound up with wider interpretations of reality, with commitments and predilections which are not themselves reducible to conformity to a rule. The rule may be to trace parallelisms in the poem, but what is to count as a parallelism? If you disagree with what counts for me as a parallelism, you have not broken any rule: I can only settle the argument by appealing to the authority of the literary institution, saying: '*This* is what we mean by a parallelism.' If you ask why we should follow this particular rule in the first place, I can only once more appeal to the authority of the literary institution and say: 'This is the kind of thing we do.' To which you can always reply: 'Well, do something else.' An appeal to the rules which define competence will not allow me to counter this, and neither will an appeal to the text: there are thousands of things one can do with a text. It is not that you are being 'anarchistic': an anarchist, in the loose, popular sense of the word, is not someone who breaks rules but someone who makes a *point* of breaking rules, who breaks rules as a rule. You are simply challenging what the literary institution does, and although I might ward this off on various grounds, I certainly cannot do so by an appeal to 'competence', which is precisely what is in question. Structuralism may examine and appeal to existing practice; but what is its answer to those who say: 'Do something else'?

4

Post-Structuralism

Saussure, as the reader will remember, argues that meaning in language is just a matter of difference. 'Cat' is 'cat' because it is not 'cap' or 'bat'. But how far is one to press this process of difference? 'Cat' is also what it is because it is not 'cad' or 'mat', and 'mat' is what it is because it is not 'map' or 'hat'. Where is one supposed to stop? It would seem that this process of difference in language can be traced round infinitely: but if this is so, what has become of Saussure's idea that language forms a closed, stable system? If every sign is what it is because it is not all the other signs, every sign would seem to be made up of a potentially infinite tissue of differences. Defining a sign would therefore appear to be a more tricky business than one might have thought. Saussure's *langue* suggests a *delimited* structure of meaning; but where in language *do* you draw the line?

Another way of putting Saussure's point about the differential nature of meaning is to say that meaning is always the result of a division or 'articulation' of signs. The signifier 'boat' gives us the concept or signified 'boat' because it divides itself from the signifier 'moat'. The signified, that is to say, is the product of the difference between two signifiers. But it is also the product of the difference between a lot of other signifiers: 'coat', 'boar', 'bolt' and so on. This questions Saussure's view of the sign as a neat symmetrical unity between one signifier and one signified. For the signified 'boat' is really the product of a complex interaction of signifiers, which has no obvious end-point. Meaning is the spin-off of a potentially endless play of signifiers, rather than a concept tied firmly to the tail of a particular signifier. The signifier does not yield us up a signified directly, as a mirror yields up an image: there is no harmonious one-to-one set of correspondences between the level of the signifiers and the level of the signifieds in language. To complicate matters even further, there is no fixed distinction between signifiers and signifieds either. If you want to know the meaning (or signified) of a signifier, you can look it up in the dictionary; but all you will find will be yet more signifiers, whose signifieds you can in turn look up, and so on. The process we are discussing is not only in theory infinite but somehow circular: signifiers keep transforming into signifieds and vice versa, and you will never arrive at a final signified which is not a signifier in itself. If structuralism divided the sign from the referent, this kind of thinking – often known as 'post-structuralism' – goes a step further: it divides the signifier from the signified.

Another way of putting what we have just said is that meaning is not immediately *present* in a sign. Since the meaning of a sign is a matter of what the sign is *not*, its meaning is always in some sense absent from it too. Meaning, if you like, is scattered or dispersed along the whole chain of signifiers: it cannot be easily nailed down, it is never fully present in any one sign alone, but is rather a kind of constant flickering of presence and absence together. Reading a text is more like tracing this process of constant flickering than it is like counting the beads on a necklace. There is also another sense in which we can never quite close our fists over meaning, which arises from the fact that language is a temporal process. When I read a sentence, the meaning of it is always somehow suspended, something deferred or still to come: one signifier relays me to another, and that to another, earlier meanings are modified by later ones, and although the sentence may come to an end the process of language itself does not. There is always more meaning where that came from. I do not grasp the sense of the sentence just by mechanically piling one word on the other: for the words to compose some relatively coherent meaning at all, each one of them must, so to speak, contain the trace of the ones which have gone before, and hold itself open to the trace of those which are coming after. Each sign in the chain of meaning is somehow scored over or traced through with all the others, to form a complex tissue which is never exhaustible; and to this extent no sign is ever 'pure' or 'fully meaningful'. At the same time as this is happening, I can detect in each sign, even if only unconsciously, traces of the other words which it has excluded in order to be itself. 'Cat' is what it is only by fending off 'cap' and 'bat', but these other possible signs, because they are actually constitutive of its identity, still somehow inhere within it.

Meaning, we might say, is thus never identical with itself. It is the result of a process of division or articulation, of signs being themselves only because they are not some other sign. It is also something suspended, held over, still to come. Another sense in which meaning is never identical with itself is that signs must always be repeatable or reproducible. We would not call a 'sign' a mark which only occurred once. The fact that a sign can be reproduced is therefore part of its identity; but it is also what divides its identity, because it can always be reproduced in a different context which changes its meaning. It is difficult to know what a sign 'originally' means, what its 'original' context was: we simply encounter it in many different situations, and although it must maintain a certain consistency across those situations in order to be an identifiable sign at all, because its context is always different it is never *absolutely* the same, never quite identical with itself. 'Cat' may mean a furry four-legged creature, a malicious person, a knotted whip, an American, a horizontal beam for raising a ship's anchor, a six-legged tripod, a short tapered stick, and so on. But even when it just means a furry four-legged animal, this meaning will never quite stay the same from context to context: the signified will be altered by the various chains of signifiers in which it is entangled.

The implication of all this is that language is a much less stable affair than the classical structuralists had considered. Instead of being a well-defined, clearly demarcated structure containing symmetrical units of signifiers and signifieds, it now begins to look much more like a sprawling limitless web where there is a constant interchange and circulation of elements, where none of the elements is absolutely definable and where everything is caught up and traced through by everything else. If this is so, then it strikes a serious blow at certain traditional theories of meaning. For such theories, it was the function of signs to reflect inward experiences or objects in the real world, to 'make present' one's thoughts and feelings or to describe how reality was. We have already seen some of the problems with this idea of 'representation' in our previous discussion of structuralism, but now even more difficulties emerge. For on the theory I have just outlined, nothing is ever fully present in signs: it is an illusion for me to believe that I can ever be fully present to you in what I say or write, because to use signs at all entails that my meaning is always somehow dispersed, divided and never quite at one with itself. Not only my meaning, indeed, but *me*: since language is something I am made out of, rather than merely a convenient tool I use, the whole idea that I am a stable, unified entity must also be a fiction. Not only can I never be fully present to you, but I can never be fully present to myself either. I still need to use signs when I look into my mind or search my soul, and this means that I will never experience any 'full communion' with myself. It is not that I can have a pure, unblemished meaning, intention or experience which then gets distorted and refracted by the flawed medium of language: because language is the very air I breathe, I can never have a pure, unblemished meaning or experience at all.

One way in which I might persuade myself that this is possible is by listening to my own voice when I speak, rather than writing my thoughts down on paper. For in the act of speaking I seem to 'coincide' with myself in a way quite different from what happens when I write. My spoken words seem immediately present to my consciousness, and my voice becomes their intimate, spontaneous medium. In writing, by contrast, my meanings threaten to escape from my control: I commit my thoughts to the impersonal medium of print, and since a printed text has a durable, material existence it can always be circulated, reproduced, cited, used in ways which I did not foresee or intend. Writing seems to rob me of my being: it is a second-hand mode of communication, a pallid, mechanical transcript of speech, and so always at one remove from my consciousness. It is for this reason that the Western philosophical tradition, all the way from Plato to Lévi-Strauss, has consistently vilified writing as a mere lifeless, alienated form of expression, and consistently celebrated the living voice. Behind this prejudice lies a particular view of 'man': man is able spontaneously to create and express his own meanings, to be in full possession of himself, and to dominate language as a transparent medium of his inmost being. What this theory fails to see is that the 'living voice' is in fact quite as material as print; and that since spoken signs, like written ones, work only by a process of difference and division, speaking could be just as much said to be a form of writing as writing is said to be a second-hand form of speaking.

Just as Western philosophy has been 'phonocentric', centred on the 'living voice' and deeply suspicious of script, so also it has been in a broader sense 'logocentric', committed to a belief in some ultimate 'word', presence, essence, truth or reality which will act as the foundation of all our thought, language and experience. It has yearned for the sign which will give meaning to all others – the 'transcendental signifier' – and for the anchoring, unquestionable meaning to which all our signs can be seen to point (the 'transcendental signified'). A great number of candidates for this role – God, the Idea, the World Spirit, the Self, substance, matter and so on – have thrust themselves forward from time to time. Since each of these concepts hopes to *found* our whole system of thought and language, it must itself be beyond that system, untainted by its play of linguistic differences. It cannot be implicated in the very languages which it attempts to order and anchor: it must be somehow anterior to these discourses, must have existed before they did. It must be a meaning, but not like any other meaning just a product of a play of difference. It must figure rather as the meaning of meanings, the lynchpin or fulcrum of a whole thought-system, the sign around which all others revolve and which all others obediently reflect.

That any such transcendental meaning is a fiction – though perhaps a necessary fiction – is one consequence of the theory of language I have outlined. There is no concept which is not embroiled in an open-ended play of signification, shot through with the traces and fragments of other ideas. It is just that, out of this play of signifiers, certain meanings are elevated by social ideologies to a privileged position, or made the centres around which other meanings are forced to turn. Consider, in our own society, Freedom, the Family, Democracy, Independence, Authority, Order and so on. Sometimes such meanings are seen as the *origin* of all the others, the source from which they flow; but this, as we have seen, is a curious way of thinking, because for this meaning ever to have been possible other signs must already have existed. It is difficult to think of an origin without wanting to go back beyond it. At other times such meanings may be seen not as the origin but as the *goal*, towards which all other meanings are or should be steadily marching. 'Teleology', thinking of life, language and history in terms of its orientation to a *telos* or end, is a way of ordering and ranking meanings in a hierarchy of significance, creating a pecking order among them in the light of an ultimate purpose. But any such theory of history or language as a simple linear evolution misses the web-like complexity of signs which I have been describing, the back and forth, present and absent, forward and sideways movement of language in its actual processes. It is that web-like complexity, indeed, which post-structuralism designates by the word 'text'.

Jacques Derrida, the French philosopher whose views I have been expounding over the last few pages, labels as 'metaphysical' any such thought-system which depends on an unassailable foundation, a first principle or unimpeachable ground upon which a whole hierarchy of meanings may be constructed. It is not that he believes that we can merely rid ourselves of the urge to forge such first principles, for such an impulse is deeply embedded in our history, and cannot – at least as yet – be eradicated or ignored. Derrida would see his own work as inescapably 'contaminated' by such metaphysical thought, much as he strives to give it the slip. But if you examine such first principles closely, you can see that they may always be 'deconstructed': they can be shown to be products of a particular system of meaning, rather than what props it up from the outside. First principles of this kind are commonly defined by what they exclude: they are part of the sort of 'binary opposition' beloved of structuralism. Thus, for male-dominated society, man is the founding principle and woman the excluded opposite of this; and as long as such a distinction is tightly held in place the whole system can function effectively. 'Deconstruction' is the name given to the critical operation by which such oppositions can be partly undermined, or by which they can be shown partly to undermine each other in the process of textual meaning. Woman is the opposite, the 'other' of man: she is non-man, defective man, assigned a chiefly negative value in relation to the male first principle. But equally man is what he is only by virtue of ceaselessly shutting out this other or opposite, defining himself in antithesis to it, and his whole identity is therefore caught up and put at risk in the very gesture by which he seeks to assert his unique, autonomous existence. Woman is not just an other in the sense of something beyond his ken, but an other intimately related to him as the image of what he is not, and therefore as an essential reminder of what he is. Man therefore needs this other even as he spurns it, is constrained to give a positive identity to what he regards as no-thing. Not only is his own being parasitically dependent upon the woman, and upon the act of excluding and subordinating her, but one reason why such exclusion is necessary is because she may not be quite so other after all. Perhaps she stands as a sign of something in man himself which he needs to repress, expel beyond his own being, relegate to a securely alien region beyond his own definitive limits. Perhaps what is outside is also somehow inside, what is alien also intimate – so that man needs to police the absolute frontier between the two realms as vigilantly as he does just because it may always be transgressed, has always been transgressed already, and is much less absolute than it appears.

Deconstruction, that is to say, has grasped the point that the binary oppositions with which classical structuralism tends to work represent a way of seeing typical of ideologies. Ideologies like to draw rigid boundaries between what is acceptable and what is not, between self and non-self, truth and falsity, sense and nonsense, reason and madness, central and marginal, surface and depth. Such metaphysical thinking, as I have said, cannot be simply eluded: we cannot catapult ourselves beyond this binary habit of thought into an ultra-metaphysical realm. But by a certain way of operating upon texts – whether 'literary' or 'philosophical' – we may begin to unravel these oppositions a little, demonstrate how one term of an antithesis secretly inheres within the other. Structuralism was generally satisfied if it could carve up a text into binary oppositions (high/low, light/dark, Nature/ Culture and so on) and expose the logic of their working. Deconstruction tries to show how such oppositions, in order to hold themselves in place, are sometimes betrayed into inverting or collapsing themselves, or need to banish to the text's margins certain niggling details which can be made to return and plague them. Derrida's own typical habit of reading is to seize on some apparently peripheral fragment in the work – a footnote, a recurrent minor term or image, a casual allusion – and work it tenaciously through to the point where it threatens to dismantle the oppositions which govern the text as a whole. The tactic of deconstructive criticism, that is to say, is to show how texts come to embarrass their own ruling systems of logic; and deconstruction shows this by fastening on the 'symptomatic' points, the *aporia* or impasses of meaning, where texts get into trouble, come unstuck, offer to contradict themselves.

This is not just an empirical observation about certain kinds of writing: it is a universal proposition about the nature of writing itself. For if the theory of signification with which I began this chapter is at all valid, then there is something in *writing itself* which finally evades all systems and logics. There is a continual flickering, spilling and defusing of meaning – what Derrida calls 'dissemination' – which cannot be easily contained with the categories of the text's structure, or within the categories of a conventional critical approach to it. Writing, like any process of language, works by difference; but difference is not itself a *concept*, is not something that can be *thought*. A text may 'show' us something about the nature of meaning and signification which it is not able to formulate as a proposition. All language, for Derrida, displays this 'surplus' over exact meaning, is always threatening to outrun and escape the sense which tries to contain it. 'Literary' discourse is the place where this is most evident, but it is also true of all other writing; deconstruction rejects the literary/non-literary opposition as any absolute distinction. The advent of the concept of *writing*, then, is a challenge to the very idea of structure: for a structure always presumes a centre, a fixed principle, a hierarchy of meanings and a solid foundation, and it is just these notions which the endless differing and deferring of writing throws into question. We have moved, in other words, from the era of structuralism to the reign of post-structuralism, a style of thought which embraces the deconstructive operations of Derrida, the work of the French historian Michel Foucault, the writings of the French psychoanalyst Jacques Lacan and of the feminist philosopher and critic Julia Kristeva. I have not discussed Foucault's work explicitly in this book; but my Conclusion would have been impossible without it, as its influence there is pervasive.

A way of charting that development is to look briefly at the work of the French critic Roland Barthes. In early works such as *Mythologies* (1957), *On Racine* (1963), *Elements of Semiology* (1964) and *Système de la mode* (1967),

Barthes is a 'high' structuralist, analysing the signifying systems of fashion, striptease, Racinian tragedy and steak and chips with effortless brio. An important essay of 1966, 'Introduction to the Structural Analysis of Narrative', is in the Jakobsonian and Lévi-Straussian mode, breaking down the structure of narrative into distinct units, functions and 'indices' (indicators of character psychology, 'atmosphere' and so on). Though such units follow each other sequentially in narrative itself, the task of the critic is to subsume them into an atemporal frame of explanation. Even at this relatively early point, however, Barthes's structuralism is tempered by other theories – hints of phenomenology in *Michelet par lui-même* (1954), of psychoanalysis in *On Racine* – and qualified above all by his literary style. The *chic*, playful, neologistic prose style of Barthes signifies a kind of 'excess' of writing over the rigours of structuralist enquiry: it is an area of freedom where he can sport, partially released from the tyranny of meaning. His work *Sade, Fourier, Loyola* (1971) is an interesting blend of the earlier structuralism and the later erotic play, seeing in Sade's writing a ceaseless systematic permutation of erotic positions.

Language is Barthes's theme from beginning to end, and in particular the Saussurean insight that the sign is always a matter of historical and cultural convention. The 'healthy' sign, for Barthes, is one which draws attention to its own arbitrariness – which does not try to palm itself off as 'natural' but which, in the very moment of conveying a meaning, communicates something of its own relative, artificial status as well. The impulse behind this belief in the earlier work is a political one: signs which pass themselves off as natural, which offer themselves as the only conceivable way of viewing the world, are by that token authoritarian and ideological. It is one of the functions of ideology to 'naturalize' social reality, to make it seem as innocent and unchangeable as Nature itself. Ideology seeks to convert culture into Nature, and the 'natural' sign is one of its weapons. Saluting a flag, or agreeing that Western democracy represents the true meaning of the word 'freedom', become the most obvious, spontaneous responses in the world. Ideology, in this sense, is a kind of contemporary mythology, a realm which has purged itself of ambiguity and alternative possibility.

In Barthes's view, there is a literary ideology which corresponds to this 'natural attitude', and its name is realism. Realist literature tends to conceal the socially relative or constructed nature of language: it helps to confirm the prejudice that there is a form of 'ordinary' language which is somehow natural. This natural language gives us reality 'as it is': it does not – like Romanticism or Symbolism – distort it into subjective shapes, but represents the world to us as God himself might know it. The sign is not seen as a changeable entity determined by the rules of a particular changeable sign-system: it is seen rather as a translucent window on to the object, or on to the mind. It is quite neutral and colourless in itself: its only job is to represent something else, become the vehicle of a meaning conceived quite independently of itself, and it must interfere with what it mediates as little as possible. In the ideology of realism or representation, words are felt to link up with their thoughts or objects in essentially right and uncontrovertible ways: the word becomes the only proper way of viewing this object or expressing this thought.

The realist or representational sign, then, is for Barthes essentially unhealthy. It effaces its own status as a sign, in order to foster the illusion that we are perceiving reality without its intervention. The sign as 'reflection', 'expression' or 'representation' denies the *productive* character of language: it suppresses the fact that we only have a 'world' at all because we have language to signify it, and that what we count as 'real' is bound up with what alterable structures of signification we live within. Barthes's 'double' sign – the sign which gestures to its own material existence at the same time as it conveys a meaning – is the grandchild of the 'estranged' language of the Formalists and Czech structuralists, of the Jakobsonian 'poetic' word which flaunts its own palpable linguistic being. I say 'grandchild' rather than 'child', because the more direct offspring of the Formalists were the socialist artists of the German Weimar Republic – Bertolt Brecht among them – who employed such 'estrangement effects' to political ends. In their hands, the estranging devices of Shklovsky and Jakobson became more than verbal functions: they became poetic, cinematic and theatrical instruments for 'denaturalizing' and 'defamiliarizing' political society, showing just how deeply questionable what everyone took for granted as 'obvious' actually was. These artists were also the inheritors of the Bolshevik Futurists and other Russian *avant-gardistes*, of Mayakovsky, the 'Left Front in Art' and the cultural revolutionists of the Soviet 1920s. Barthes has an enthusiastic essay on Brecht's theatre in his *Critical Essays* (1964), and was an early champion of that theatre in France.

The early structuralist Barthes still trusts to the possibility of a 'science' of literature, though this, as he comments, could only be a science of 'forms' rather than of 'contents'. Such a scientific criticism would in some sense aim to know its object 'as it really was'; but does this not run counter to Barthes's hostility to the neutral sign? The critic, after all, has to use language too, in order to analyse the literary text, and there is no reason to believe that this language will escape the strictures which Barthes has made about representational discourse in general. What is the relation between the discourse of criticism and the discourse of the literary text? For the structuralist, criticism is a form of 'metalanguage' – a language about another language – which rises above its object to a point from which it can peer down and disinterestedly examine it. But as Barthes recognizes in *Système de la mode*, there can be no ultimate metalanguage: another critic can always come along and take your criticism as his object of study, and so on in an infinite regress. In his *Critical Essays*, Barthes speaks of criticism as 'cover[ing the text] as completely as possible by its own language'; in *Critique et vérité* (1966), critical discourse is seen as a 'second language' which 'floats above the primary language of the work'. The same essay begins to characterize literary language itself in what are now recognizably post-structuralist terms: it is a language 'without bottom', something like a 'pure ambiguity' supported by an 'empty meaning'. If this is so, then it is doubtful that the methods of classical structuralism can cope with it at all.

The 'work of the break' is Barthes's astonishing study of Balzac's story *Sarrasine*, *S/Z* (1970). The literary work is now no longer treated as a stable object or delimited structure, and the language of the critic has disowned all pretensions to scientific objectivity. The most intriguing texts for criticism are not those which can be *read*, but those which are 'writable' (*scriptible*) – texts which encourage the critic to carve them up, transpose them into different discourses, produce his or her semi-arbitrary play of meaning athwart the work itself. The reader or critic shifts from the role of consumer to that of producer. It is not exactly as though 'anything goes' in interpretation, for Barthes is careful to remark that the work cannot be got to mean anything at all; but literature is now less an object to which criticism must conform than a free space in which it can sport. The 'writable' text, usually a modernist one, has no determinate meaning, no settled signifieds, but is plural and diffuse, an inexhaustible tissue or galaxy of signifiers, a seamless weave of codes and fragments of codes, through which the critic may cut his own errant path. There are no beginnings and no ends, no sequences which cannot be reversed, no hierarchy of textual 'levels' to tell you what is more or less significant. All literary texts are woven out of other literary texts, not in the conventional sense that they bear the traces of 'influence' but in the more radical sense that every word, phrase or segment is a reworking of other writings which precede or surround the individual work. There is no such thing as literary 'originality', no such thing as the 'first' literary work: all literature is 'intertextual'. A specific piece of writing thus has no clearly defined boundaries: it spills over constantly into the works clustered around it, generating a hundred different perspectives which dwindle to vanishing point. The work cannot be sprung shut, rendered determinate, by an appeal to the author, for the 'death of the author' is a slogan that modern criticism is now confidently able to proclaim.[1] The biography of the author is, after all, merely another text, which need not be ascribed any special privilege: this text too can be deconstructed. It is language which speaks in literature, in all its swarming 'polysemic' plurality, not the author himself. If there is any place where this seething multiplicity of the text is momentarily focused, it is not the author but the *reader*.

When post-structuralists speak of 'writing' or 'textuality', it is usually these particular senses of writing and text that they have in mind. The movement from structuralism to post-structuralism is in part, as Barthes himself has phrased it, a movement from 'work' to 'text'.[2] It is a shift from seeing the poem or novel as a closed entity, equipped with definite meanings which it is the critic's task to decipher, to seeing it as irreducibly plural, an endless play of signifiers which can never be finally nailed down to a single centre, essence or meaning. This obviously makes for a radical difference in the practice of criticism itself, as *S/Z* makes clear. Barthes's method in the book is to divide the Balzac story into a number of small units or 'lexies', and to apply to them five codes: the 'proiaretic' (or narrative) code, a 'hermeneutic' code concerned with the tale's unfolding enigmas, a 'cultural' code which examines the stock of social knowledge on which the work draws, a 'semic' code dealing with the connotations of persons, places and objects, and a 'symbolic' code charting the sexual and psychoanalytical relations set up in the text. None of this so far may seem to diverge much from standard structuralist practice. But the division of the text into units is more or less arbitrary; the five codes are simply five selected from an indefinite possible number; they are ranked in no sort of hierarchy, but applied, sometimes three to the same lexie, in a pluralist way; and they refrain from finally 'totalizing' the work into any kind of coherent sense. Rather, they demonstrate its dispersal and fragmentation. The text, Barthes argues, is less a 'structure' than an open-ended process of 'structuration', and it is criticism which does this structurating. Balzac's novella appears to be a realist work, not at all obviously amenable to the kind of semiotic violence which Barthes wreaks upon it: his critical account does not 're-create' its object, but drastically rewrites and reorganizes it out of all conventional recognition. What is thereby revealed, however, is a dimension of the work which has hitherto remained unnoticed. *Sarrasine* is exposed as a 'limit text' for literary realism, a work in which its ruling assumptions are shown to be secretly in trouble: the narrative revolves upon a frustrated act of narrating, sexual castration, the mysterious sources of capitalist wealth, and a profound confusion of fixed sexual roles. In a *coup de grâce*, Barthes is able to claim that the very 'contents' of the novella are related to his own method of analysis:

the story concerns a crisis in literary representation, sexual relations and economic exchange. In all of these instances, the bourgeois ideology of the sign as 'representational' is beginning to be called into question; and in this sense, by a certain interpretative violence and *bravura*, Balzac's narrative can be read as peering beyond its own historical moment in the early nineteenth century to Barthes's own modernist period.

It is, in fact, the literary movement of modernism which brought structuralist and post-structuralist criticism to birth in the first place. Some of the later works of Barthes and Derrida are modernist literary texts in themselves, experimental, enigmatic and richly ambiguous. There is no clear division for post-structuralism between 'criticism' and 'creation': both modes are subsumed into 'writing' as such. Structuralism began to happen when language became an obsessive preoccupation of intellectuals; and this happened in turn because in the late nineteenth and twentieth centuries, language in Western Europe was felt to be in the throes of deep crisis. How was one to write, in an industrial society where discourse had become degraded to a mere instrument of science, commerce, advertising and bureaucracy? What audience was one to write for in any case, given the saturation of the reading public by a 'mass', profit-hungry, anodyne culture? Could a literary work be at once an artefact and a commodity on the open market? Could we any longer share the confident rationalist or empiricist trust of the mid-nineteenth-century middle class that language did indeed hook itself on to the world? How was writing possible without the existence of a framework of collective belief shared with one's audience, and how, in the ideological turmoil of the twentieth century, could such a shared framework possibly be reinvented?

It was questions such as these, rooted in the real historical conditions of modern writing, which 'foregrounded' the problem of language so dramatically. The Formalist, Futurist and structuralist preoccupation with the estrangement and renewal of the word, with restoring to an alienated language the richness of which it had been robbed, were all in their different ways responses to this same historical dilemma. But it was also possible to set up language itself as an alternative to the social problems which plagued you – to renounce, gloomily or triumphantly, the traditional notion that one wrote *about* something *for* somebody, and to make language itself one's cherished object. In his masterly early essay *Writing Degree Zero* (1953), Barthes maps something of the historical development by which writing for the French nineteenth-century Symbolist poets becomes an 'intransitive' act: not writing for a particular purpose on a specific topic, as in the age of 'classical' literature, but writing as an end and a passion in itself. If objects and events in the real world are experienced as lifeless and alienated, if history seems to have lost direction and lapsed into chaos, it is always possible to put all of this 'in brackets', 'suspend the referent' and take words as your object instead. Writing turns in on itself in a profound act of narcissism, but always troubled and overshadowed by the social guilt of its own uselessness. Unavoidably complicit with those who have reduced it to an unwanted commodity, it nevertheless strains to free itself from the contamination of social meaning, either by pressing towards the purity of silence, as with the Symbolists, or by seeking an austere neutrality, a 'degree zero of writing' which would hope to appear innocent but which is in reality, as Hemingway exemplifies, just as much a literary style as any other. There is no doubt that the 'guilt' of which Barthes speaks is the guilt of the institution of Literature itself – an institution which, as he comments, testifies to the division of languages and the division of classes. To write in a 'literary' way, in modern society, is inevitably to collude with such divisiveness.

Structuralism is best seen as both symptom of and reaction to the social and linguistic crisis I have outlined. It flees from history to language – an ironic action, since as Barthes sees few moves could be more historically significant. But in holding history and the referent at bay, it also seeks to restore a sense of the 'unnaturalness' of the signs by which men and women live, and so open up a radical awareness of their historical mutability. In this way it may rejoin the very history which it began by abandoning. Whether it does so or not, however, depends on whether the referent is suspended provisionally, or for good and all. With the advent of post-structuralism, what seemed reactionary about structuralism was not this refusal of history, but nothing less than the very concept of structure itself. For the Barthes of *The Pleasure of the Text* (1973), all theory, ideology, determinate meaning, social commitment have become, it appears, inherently terroristic, and 'writing' is the answer to them all. Writing, or reading-as-writing, is the last uncolonized enclave in which the intellectual can play, savouring the sumptuousness of the signifier in heady disregard of whatever might be going on in the Elysée palace or the Renault factories. In writing, the tyranny of structural meaning could be momentarily ruptured and dislocated by a free play of language; and the writing/reading subject could be released from the straitjacket of a single identity into an ecstatically diffused self. The text, Barthes announces, 'is [. . .] that uninhibited person who shows his behind to the Political Father'. We have come a long way from Matthew Arnold.

That reference to the Political Father is not fortuitous. *The Pleasure of the*

Text was published five years after a social eruption which rocked France's political fathers to their roots. In 1968 the student movement had swept across Europe, striking against the authoritarianism of the educational institutions and in France briefly threatening the capitalist state itself. For a dramatic moment, that state teetered on the brink of ruin: its police and army fought in the streets with students who were struggling to forge solidarity with the working class. Unable to provide a coherent political leadership, plunged into a confused mêlée of socialism, anarchism and infantile behind-baring, the student movement was rolled back and dissipated; betrayed by their supine Stalinist leaders, the working-class movement was unable to assume power. Charles de Gaulle returned from a hasty exile, and the French state regrouped its forces in the name of patriotism, law and order.

Post-structuralism was a product of that blend of euphoria and disillusionment, liberation and dissipation, carnival and catastrophe, which was 1968. Unable to break the structures of state power, post-structuralism found it possible instead to subvert the structures of language. Nobody, at least, was likely to beat you over the head for doing so. The student movement was flushed off the streets and driven underground into discourse. Its enemies, as for the later Barthes, became coherent belief-systems of any kind – in particular all forms of political theory and organization which sought to analyse, and act upon, the structures of society as a whole. For it was precisely such politics which seemed to have failed: the system had proved too powerful for them, and the 'total' critique offered of it by a heavily Stalinized Marxism had been exposed as part of the problem, not as the solution. All such total systematic thought was now suspect as terroristic: conceptual meaning itself, as opposed to libidinal gesture and anarchist spontaneity, was feared as repressive. Reading for the later Barthes is not cognition but erotic play. The only forms of political action now felt to be acceptable were of a local, diffused, strategic kind: work with prisoners and other marginalized social groups, particular projects in culture and education. The women's movement, hostile to the classical forms of left-wing organization, developed libertarian, 'decentred' alternatives and in some quarters rejected systematic theory as male. For many post-structuralists, the worst error was to believe that such local projects and particular engagements should be brought together within an overall understanding of the working of monopoly capitalism, which could only be as oppressively 'total' as the very system it opposed. Power was everywhere, a fluid, quicksilver force which seeped through every pore of society, but it did not have a centre any more than did the literary text. The 'system as a whole' could not be combatted, because there was in fact no 'system as a whole'. You could thus intervene in social and political life at any point you liked, as Barthes could chop *S/Z* into an arbitrary play of codes. It was not entirely clear how one *knew* that there was no system as a whole, if general concepts were taboo; nor was it clear that such a viewpoint was as viable in other parts of the world as it was in Paris. In the so-called Third World, men and women sought to liberate their countries from the political and economic dominance of Europe and the USA under the guidance of some general grasp of the logic of imperialism. They were seeking to do so in Vietnam at the time of the European student movements, and despite their 'general theories' were to prove a few years later rather more successful than the Parisian students had been. Back in Europe, however, such theories were rapidly becoming *passé*. Just as the older forms of 'total' politics had dogmatically proclaimed that more local concerns were of merely passing relevance, so the new politics of the fragments was also prone to dogmatize that any more global engagement was a dangerous illusion.

Such a position, as I have argued, was born of a specific political defeat and disillusion. The 'total structure' which it identified as the enemy was an historically particular one: the armed, repressive state of late monopoly capitalism, and the Stalinist politics which pretended to confront it but were deeply complicit with its rule. Long before the emergence of post-structuralism, generations of socialists had been fighting both of these monoliths. But they had overlooked the possibility that the erotic *frissons* of reading, or even work confined to those labelled criminally insane, were an adequate solution, and so had the guerrilla fighters of Guatemala.

In one of its developments, post-structuralism became a convenient way of evading such political questions altogether. The work of Derrida and others had cast grave doubt upon the classical notions of truth, reality, meaning and knowledge, all of which could be exposed as resting on a naively representational theory of language. If meaning, the signified, was a passing product of words or signifiers, always shifting and unstable, part-present and part-absent, how could there be any determinate truth or meaning at all? If reality was constructed by our discourse rather than reflected by it, how could we ever know reality itself, rather than merely knowing our own discourse? Was all talk just talk about our talk? Did it make sense to claim that one interpretation of reality, history or the literary text was 'better' than another? Hermeneutics had devoted itself to sympathetically understanding the meaning of the past; but was there really any past to be known at all, other than as a mere function of present discourse?

Whether all this was or was not what the founding fathers of post-structuralism actually held, such scepticism rapidly became a fashionable style in Left academic circles. To employ words like 'truth', 'certainty' and the 'real' was in some quarters to be instantly denounced as a metaphysician. If you demurred at the dogma that we could never know anything at all, then this was because you clung nostalgically to notions of absolute truth, and to a megalomaniac conviction that you, along with some of the smarter natural scientists, could see reality 'just as it was'. The fact that nowadays one encounters extremely few believers in such doctrines, not least among philosophers of science, did not seem to deter the sceptics. The model of science frequently derided by post-structuralism is usually a positivist one – some version of the nineteenth-century rationalistic claim to a transcendental, value-free knowledge of 'the facts'. This model is actually a straw target. It does not exhaust the term 'science', and nothing is to be gained by this caricature of scientific self-reflection. To say that there are no absolute grounds for the use of such words as truth, certainty, reality and so on is not to say that these words lack meaning or are ineffectual. Whoever thought such absolute grounds existed, and what would they look like if they did?

One advantage of the dogma that we are the prisoners of our own discourse, unable to advance reasonably certain truth-claims because such claims are merely relative to our language, is that it allows you to drive a coach and horses through everybody else's beliefs while not saddling you with the inconvenience of having to adopt any yourself. It is, in effect, an invulnerable position, and the fact that it is also purely empty is simply the price one has to pay for this. The view that the most significant aspect of any piece of language is that it does not know what it is talking about smacks of a jaded resignation to the impossibility of truth which is by no means unrelated to post-1968 historical disillusion. But it also frees you at a stroke from having to assume a position on important issues, since what you say of such things will be no more than a passing product of the signifier and so in no sense to be taken as 'true' or 'serious'. A further benefit of this stance is that it is mischievously radical in respect of everyone else's opinions, able to unmask the most solemn declarations as mere dishevelled plays of signs, while utterly conservative in every other way. Since it commits you to affirming nothing, it is as injurious as blank ammunition.

Deconstruction in the Anglo-American world has tended on the whole to take this path. Of the so-called Yale school of deconstruction – Paul de Man, J. Hillis Miller, Geoffrey Hartman and in some respects Harold Bloom – de Man's criticism in particular is devoted to demonstrating that literary language constantly undermines its own meaning. Indeed de Man discovers in this operation nothing less than a new way of defining the 'essence' of literature itself. All language, as de Man rightly perceives, is ineradicably metaphorical, working by tropes and figures; it is a mistake to believe that any language is *literally* literal. Philosophy, law, political theory work by metaphor just as poems do, and so are just as fictional. Since metaphors are essentially 'groundless', mere substitutions of one set of signs for another, language tends to betray its own fictive and arbitrary nature at just those points where it is offering to be most intensively persuasive. 'Literature' is that realm in which this ambiguity is most evident – in which the reader finds herself suspended between a 'literal' and a figurative meaning, unable to choose between the two, and thus cast dizzyingly into a bottomless linguistic abyss by a text which has become 'unreadable'. Literary works, however, are in a sense less deluded than other forms of discourse, because they implicitly acknowledge their own rhetorical status – the fact that what they say is different from what they do, that all their claims to knowledge work through figurative structures which render them ambiguous and inde-terminate. They are, one might say, ironic in nature. Other forms of writing are just as figurative and ambiguous, but pass themselves off as unquestion-able truth. For de Man, as for his colleague Hillis Miller, literature does not need to be deconstructed by the critic: it can be shown to deconstruct itself, and moreover is actually 'about' this very operation.

The textual ambiguities of the Yale critics differ from the poetic ambival-ences of New Criticism. Reading is not a matter of fusing two different but determinate meanings, as it was for the New Critics: it is a matter of being caught on the hop between two meanings which can be neither reconciled nor refused. Literary criticism thus becomes an ironic, uneasy business, an unsettling venture into the inner void of the text which lays bare the illus-oriness of meaning, the impossibility of truth and the deceitful guiles of all discourse. In another sense, however, such Anglo-American deconstruction is no more than the return of the old New Critical formalism. Indeed it returns in intensified form, because whereas for New Criticism the poem did in some indirect way discourse about extra-poetic reality, literature for the deconstructionists testifies to the impossibility of language's ever doing more than talk about its own failure, like some barroom bore. Literature is the ruin of all reference, the cemetery of communication.[3] New Criticism saw the literary text as a blessed suspension of doctrinal belief in an increas-ingly ideological world; deconstruction sees social reality less as oppressively determinate than as yet more shimmering webs of undecidability stretching to the horizon. Literature is not content, as with New Criticism, to offer a cloistered alternative to material history: it now reaches out and colonizes that history, rewriting it in its own image, viewing famines, revolutions, soccer matches and sherry trifle as yet more undecidable 'text'. Since prudent men and women are not prone to take action in situations whose significance is not reasonably clear, this viewpoint is not without its implications for one's style of social and political life. Yet since literature is the privileged paradigm of all such indeterminacy, the New Critical *retreat* into the literary text can be reproduced at the same time as criticism reaches out a revenging hand over the world and strikes it empty of meaning. Whereas for earlier literary theories it was *experience* which was elusive, evanescent, richly ambiguous, now it is language. The terms have altered; much of the world-view has remained remarkably unchanged.

But it is not, as with Bakhtin, language as 'discourse'; Jacques Derrida's work is strikingly indifferent to such concerns. It is largely because of this that the doctrinal obsession with 'undecidability' arises. Meaning may well be ultimately undecidable if we view language contemplatively, as a chain of signifiers on a page; it becomes 'decidable', and words like 'truth', 'reality', 'knowledge' and 'certainty' have something of their force restored to them, when we think of language rather as something we *do*, as indissociably interwoven with our practical forms of life. It is not of course that language then becomes fixed and luminous: on the contrary, it becomes even more fraught and conflictual than the most 'deconstructed' literary text. It is just that we are then able to see, in a practical rather than academicist way, what would *count* as deciding, determining, persuading, certainty, being truthful, falsifying and the rest – and see, moreover, what beyond language itself is *involved* in such definitions. Anglo-American deconstruction largely ignores this real sphere of struggle, and continues to churn out its closed critical texts. Such texts are closed precisely because they are empty: there is little to be done with them beyond admiring the relentlessness with which all positive particles of textual meaning have been dissolved away. Such dissolution is an imperative in the academic game of deconstruction: for you can be sure that if your own critical account of someone else's critical account of a text has left the tiniest grains of 'positive' meaning within its folds, somebody else will come along and deconstruct you in turn. Such deconstruction is a power-game, a mirror-image of orthodox academic competition. It is just that now, in a religious twist to the old ideology, victory is achieved by *kenosis* or self-emptying: the winner is the one who has managed to get rid of all his cards and sit with empty hands.

If Anglo-American deconstruction would seem to signal the latest stage of a liberal scepticism familiar in the modern histories of both societies, the story in Europe is somewhat more complex. As the 1960s gave way to the

1970s, as the carnivalesque memories of 1968 faded and world capitalism stumbled into economic crisis, some of the French post-structuralists originally associated with the avant-garde literary journal *Tel Quel* moved from a militant Maoism to a strident anti-Communism. Post-structuralism in France has been able with a good conscience to praise the Iranian mullahs, celebrate the USA as the one remaining oasis of freedom and pluralism in a regimented world, and recommend various brands of portentous mysticism as the solution to human ills. If Saussure could have foreseen what he started he might well have stuck to the genitive case in Sanskrit.

Like all stories, however, the narrative of post-structuralism has another side. If the American deconstructionists considered that their textual enterprise was faithful to the spirit of Jacques Derrida, one of those who did not was Jacques Derrida. Certain American uses of deconstruction, Derrida has observed, work to ensure 'an institutional closure' which serves the dominant political and economic interests of American society.[4] Derrida is clearly out to do more than develop new techniques of reading: deconstruction is for him an ultimately *political* practice, an attempt to dismantle the logic by which a particular system of thought, and behind that a whole system of political structures and social institutions, maintains its force. He is not seeking, absurdly, to deny the existence of relatively determinate truths, meanings, identities, intentions, historical continuities; he is seeking rather to see such things as the effects of a wider and deeper history – of language, of the unconscious, of social institutions and practices. That his own work has been grossly unhistorical, politically evasive and in practice oblivious to language as 'discourse' is not to be denied: no neat binary opposition can be drawn up between an 'authentic' Derrida and the abuses of his acolytes. But the widespread opinion that deconstruction denies the existence of anything but discourse, or affirms a realm of pure difference in which all meaning and identity dissolves, is a travesty of Derrida's own work and of the most productive work which has followed from it.

Nor will it do to dismiss post-structuralism as a simple anarchism or hedonism, much in evidence though such motifs have been. Post-structuralism was right to upbraid the orthodox Left politics of its time with having failed: in the late 1960s and early 1970s, new political forms began to emerge before which the traditional Left stood mesmerized and indecisive. Its immediate response was either to belittle them, or to try to absorb them as subordinate parts of its own programme. But the new political presence which would respond to neither tactic was the resurgent women's movement of Europe and the United States. The women's movement rejected the narrowly economic focus of much classical Marxist thought, a focus which was clearly incapable of explaining the particular conditions of women as an oppressed social group, or of contributing significantly to their transformation. For though the oppression of women is indeed a material reality, a matter of motherhood, domestic labour, job discrimination and unequal wages, it cannot be reduced to these factors: it is also a question of sexual ideology, of the ways men and women image themselves and each other in male-dominated society, of perceptions and behaviour which range from the brutally explicit to the deeply unconscious. Any politics which failed to place such issues at the heart of its theory and practice was likely to find itself consigned to the dustheap of history. Because sexism and gender roles are questions which engage the deepest personal dimensions of human life, a politics which was blind to the experience of the human subject was crippled from the outset. The movement from structuralism to post-structuralism was in part a response to these political demands. Of course it is untrue that the women's movement has a monopoly of 'experience', as is sometimes implied: what else has socialism been but the bitter hopes and desires of many millions of men and women over the generations, who lived and sometimes died in the name of something rather more than a 'doctrine of the totality' or the primacy of the economic? Nor is it adequate to *identify* the personal and political: that the personal is political is profoundly true, but there is an important sense in which the personal is also personal and the political political. Political struggle cannot be *reduced* to the personal, or vice versa. The women's movement rightly rejected certain rigid organizational forms and certain 'over-totalizing' political theories; but in doing so it often enough advanced the personal, the spontaneous and the experiential as though these provided an adequate political strategy, rejected 'theory' in ways almost indistinguishable from commonplace anti-intellectualism, and in some of its sectors seemed as indifferent to the sufferings of anybody but women, and to the question of their political resolution, as some Marxists had seemed indifferent to the oppression of anybody but the working class.

There are other relations between feminism and post-structuralism. For of all the binary oppositions which post-structuralism sought to undo, the hierarchical opposition between men and women was perhaps the most virulent. Certainly it seemed the most perdurable: there was no time in history at which a good half of the human race had not been banished and subjected as a defective being, an alien inferior. This staggering fact could not of course be put right by a new theoretical technique; but it became possible to see how, though historically speaking the conflict between men and women could not have been more real, the ideology of this antagonism involved a metaphysical illusion. If it was held in place by the material and psychical benefits which accrued to men from it, it was also held in place by a complex structure of fear, desire, aggression, masochism and anxiety which urgently needed to be examined. Feminism was not an isolatable issue, a particular 'campaign' alongside other political projects, but a dimension which informed and interrogated every facet of personal, social and political life. The message of the women's movement, as interpreted by some of those outside it, is not just that women should have equality of power and status with men; it is a questioning of all such power and status. It is not that the world will be better off with more female participation in it; it is that without the 'feminization' of human history, the world is unlikely to survive.

With post-structuralism, we have brought the story of modern literary theory up to the present time. Within post-structuralism as a 'whole', real conflicts and differences exist whose future history cannot be predicted. There are forms of post-structuralism which represent a hedonist withdrawal from history, a cult of ambiguity or irresponsible anarchism; there are other forms, as with the formidably rich researches of the French historian Michel Foucault, which while not without their severe problems point in a more positive direction. There are modes of 'radical' feminism which emphasize plurality, difference and sexual separatism; there are also forms of socialist feminism which, while refusing to view the women's struggle as a mere element or sub-sector of a movement which might then dominate and engulf it, hold that the liberation of other oppressed groups and classes in society is not only a moral and political imperative in itself, but a necessary (though by no means sufficient) condition for the emancipation of women.

We have travelled, at any rate, from Saussure's difference between signs to the oldest difference in the world; and it is this which we can now explore further.

5

Psychoanalysis

In the previous few chapters I have suggested a relationship between developments in modern literary theory and the political and ideological turmoil of the twentieth century. But such turmoil is never only a matter of wars, economic slumps and revolutions: it is also experienced by those caught up in it in the most intimately personal ways. It is a crisis of human relationships, and of the human personality, as well as a social convulsion. This is not of course to argue that anxiety, fear of persecution and the fragmentation of the self are experiences peculiar to the era from Matthew Arnold to Paul de Man: they can be found throughout recorded history. What *is* perhaps significant is that in this period such experiences become constituted in a new way as a systematic field of knowledge. That field of knowledge is known as psychoanalysis, developed by Sigmund Freud in late nineteenth-century Vienna; and it is Freud's doctrines that I now want briefly to summarize.

'The motive of human society is in the last resort an economic one.' It was Freud, not Karl Marx, who made this statement, in his *Introductory Lectures on Psychoanalysis*. What has dominated human history to date is the need to labour; and for Freud that harsh necessity means that we must repress some of our tendencies to pleasure and gratification. If we were not called upon to work in order to survive, we might simply lie around all day doing nothing. Every human being has to undergo this repression of what Freud named the 'pleasure principle' by the 'reality principle', but for some of us, and arguably for whole societies, the repression may become excessive and make us ill. We are sometimes willing to forgo gratification to an heroic extent, but usually in the canny trust that by deferring an immediate pleasure we will recoup it in the end, perhaps in richer form. We are prepared to put up with repression as long as we see that there is something in it for us; if too much is demanded of us, however, we are likely to fall sick. This form of sickness is known as neurosis; and since, as I have said, all human beings must be repressed to some degree, it is possible to speak of the human race, in the words of one of Freud's commentators, as the 'neurotic animal'. It is important to see that such neurosis is involved with what is creative about us as a race, as well as with the causes of our unhappiness. One way in which we cope with desires we cannot fulfil is by 'sublimating' them, by which Freud means directing them towards a more socially valued end. We might find an unconscious outlet for sexual frustration in building bridges or cathedrals. For Freud, it is by virtue of such sublimation that civilization itself comes about: by switching and harnessing our instincts to these higher goals, cultural history itself is created.

If Marx looked at the consequences of our need to labour in terms of the social relations, social classes and forms of politics which it entailed, Freud looks at its implications for the psychical life. The paradox or contradiction on which his work rests is that we come to be what we are only by a massive repression of the elements which have gone into our making. We are not of course conscious of this, any more than for Marx men and women are generally conscious of the social processes which determine their lives. Indeed we could not be by definition conscious of this fact, since the place to which we relegate the desires we are unable to fulfil is known as the unconscious. One question which immediately arises, however, is why it is human beings who should be the neurotic animal, rather than snails or tortoises. It is possible that this is merely a Romantic idealization of such creatures and that they are secretly a good deal more neurotic than we think; but they seem well-adjusted enough to an outsider, even though there may be one or two cases of hysterical paralysis on record.

One feature which distinguishes human beings from the other animals is that for evolutionary reasons we are born almost entirely helpless and are wholly reliant for our survival on the care of the more mature members of the species, usually our parents. We are all born 'prematurely'. Without such immediate, unceasing care we would die very quickly. This unusually prolonged dependence on our parents is first of all a purely material matter, a question of being fed and kept from harm: it is a matter of the satisfaction of what may be called our 'instincts', by which is meant the biologically fixed needs human beings have for nourishment, warmth and so on. (Such self-preservative instincts are, as we shall see, a good deal more immutable than 'drives', which very often alter their nature.) But our dependence on our parents for these services does not stop at the biological. The small baby will suck its mother's breast for milk, but will discover in doing so that this biologically essential activity is also pleasurable; and this, for Freud, is the first dawning of sexuality. The baby's mouth becomes not only an organ of its physical survival but an 'erotogenic zone', which the child might reactivate a few years later by sucking its thumb, and a few years later than that by kissing. The relation to the mother has taken on a new, libidinal dimension: sexuality has been born, as a kind of drive which was at first inseparable from biological instinct but which has now separated itself out from it and attained a certain autonomy. Sexuality for Freud is itself a 'perversion' – a 'swerving away' of a natural self-preservative instinct towards another goal.

As the infant grows, other erotogenic zones come into play. The oral stage, as Freud calls it, is the first phase of sexual life, and is associated with the drive to incorporate objects. In the anal stage, the anus becomes an erotogenic zone, and with the child's pleasure in defecation a new contrast between activity and passivity, unknown in the oral stage, comes to light. The anal stage is sadistic, in that the child derives erotic pleasure from expulsion and destruction; but it is also connected with the desire for retention and possessive control, as the child learns a new form of mastery and a manipulation of the wishes of others through the 'granting' or withholding of the faeces. The ensuing 'phallic' stage begins to focus the child's libido (or sexual drive) on the genitals, but is called 'phallic' rather than 'genital' because according to Freud only the male organ is recognized at this point. The little girl in Freud's view has to be content with the clitoris, the 'equivalent' of the penis, rather than with the vagina.

What is happening in this process – though the stages overlap, and should not be seen as a strict sequence – is a gradual organization of the libidinal drives, but one still centred on the child's own body. The drives themselves are extremely flexible, in no sense fixed like biological instinct: their objects are contingent and replaceable, and one sexual drive can substitute itself for another. What we can imagine in the early years of the child's life, then, is not a unified subject confronting and desiring a stable object, but a complex shifting field of force in which the subject (the child itself) is caught up and dispersed, in which it has as yet no centre of identity and in which the boundaries between itself and the external world are indeterminate. Within this field of libidinal force, objects and part-objects emerge and disappear again, shift places kaleidoscopically, and prominent among such objects is the child's body as the play of drives laps across it. One can speak of this also as an 'auto-eroticism', within which Freud sometimes includes the whole of infantile sexuality: the child takes erotic delight in its own body, but without as yet being able to view its body as a complete object. Auto-eroticism must thus be distinguished from what Freud will call 'narcissism', a state in which one's body or ego as a whole is 'cathected', or taken as an object of desire.

It is clear that the child in this state is not even prospectively a citizen who could be relied upon to do a hard day's work. It is anarchic, sadistic, aggressive, self-involved and remorselessly pleasure-seeking, under the sway of what Freud calls the pleasure principle; nor does it have any respect for differences of gender. It is not yet what we might call a 'gendered subject': it surges with sexual drives, but this libidinal energy recognizes no distinction between masculine and feminine. If the child is to succeed in life at all, it obviously has to be taken in hand; and the mechanism by which this happens is what Freud famously terms the Oedipus complex. The child who emerges from the pre-Oedipal stages we have been following is not only anarchic and sadistic but incestuous to boot: the boy's close involvement with his mother's body leads him to an unconscious desire for sexual union with her, whereas the girl, who has been similarly bound up with the mother and whose first desire is therefore always homosexual, begins to turn her libido towards the father. The early 'dyadic' or two-term relationship between infant and mother, that is to say, has now opened up into a triangle consisting of child and both parents; and for the child, the parent of the same sex will come to figure as a rival in its affections for the parent of the opposite sex.

What persuades the boy-child to abandon his incestuous desire for the mother is the father's threat of castration. This threat need not necessarily be spoken; but the boy, in perceiving that the girl is herself 'castrated', begins to imagine this as a punishment which might be visited upon himself. He thus represses his incestuous desire in anxious resignation, adjusts himself to the 'reality principle', submits to the father, detaches himself from the mother, and comforts himself with the unconscious consolation that though he cannot *now* hope to oust his father and possess his mother, his father symbolizes a place, a possibility, which he himself will be able to take up and realize in the furture. If he is not a patriarch now, he will be later. The boy makes peace with his father, identifies with him, and is thus introduced into the symbolic role of manhood. He has become a gendered subject, surmounting his Oedipus complex; but in doing so he has, so to speak, driven his forbidden desire underground, repressed it into the place we call the unconscious. This is not a place that was ready and waiting to receive such a desire: it is produced, opened up, by this act of primary repression. As a man in the making, the boy will now grow up within those images and practices which his society happens to define as 'masculine'. He will one day become a father himself, thus sustaining this society by contributing to the business of sexual reproduction. His earlier diffuse libido has become organized through the Oedipus complex in a way which centres it upon genital sexuality. If the boy is unable successfully to overcome the Oedipus complex, he may be sexually incapacitated for such a role: he may privilege the image of his mother above all other women, which for Freud may lead to homosexuality; or the recognition that women are 'castrated' may have traumatized him so deeply that he is unable to enjoy satisfying sexual relationships with them.

The story of the little girl's passage through the Oedipus complex is a good deal less straightforward. It should be said right away that Freud was nowhere more typical of his own male-dominated society than in his bafflement in the face of female sexuality – the 'dark continent', as he once called it. We shall have occasion to comment later on the demeaning, prejudiced attitudes towards women which disfigure his work, and his account of the girl's process of oedipalization is by no means easily separable from this sexism. The little girl, perceiving that she is inferior because 'castrated', turns in disillusionment from her similarly 'castrated' mother to the project of seducing her father; but since this project is doomed, she must finally turn back reluctantly to the mother, effect an identification with her, assume her feminine gender role, and unconsciously substitute for the penis which she envies but can never possess a baby, which she desires to receive from the father. There is no obvious reason why the girl should abandon this desire, since being 'castrated' already she cannot be threatened with castration; and it is therefore difficult to see by what mechanism her Oedipus complex is dissolved. 'Castration', far from prohibiting her incestuous desire as with the boy, is what makes it possible in the first place. Moreover the girl, to enter into the Oedipus complex, must change her 'love-object' from mother to father, whereas the boy has merely to carry on loving the mother; and since a change of love-objects is a more complex, difficult affair, this too raises a problem about female oedipalization.

Before leaving the question of the Oedipus complex, its utter centrality to Freud's work should be emphasized. It is not just another complex: it is the structure of relations by which we come to be the men and women that we are. It is the point at which we are produced and constituted as subjects; and one problem for us is that it is always in some sense a partial, defective mechanism. It signals the transition from the pleasure principle to the reality principle; from the enclosure of the family to society at large, since we turn from incest to extra-familial relations; and from Nature to Culture, since we can see the infant's relation to the mother as somehow 'natural', and the post-Oedipal child as one who is in the process of assuming a position within the cultural order as a whole. (To see the mother–child relationship as 'natural', however, is in one sense highly dubious: it does not matter in the least to the infant who the provider actually is.) Moreover, the Oedipus complex is for Freud the beginnings of morality, conscience, law and all forms of social and religious authority. The father's real or imagined prohibition of incest is symbolic of all the higher authority to be later encountered; and in 'introjecting' (making its own) this patriarchal law, the child begins to form what Freud calls its 'superego', the awesome, punitive voice of conscience within it.

All, then, would now seem in place for gender roles to be reinforced, satisfactions to be postponed, authority to be accepted and the family and society to be reproduced. But we have forgotten about the unruly, insubordinate unconscious. The child has now developed an ego or individual identity, a particular place in the sexual, familial and social networks; but it can do this only by, so to speak, splitting off its guilty desires, repressing them into the unconscious. The human subject who emerges from the Oedipal process is a *split* subject, torn precariously between conscious and unconscious; and the unconscious can always return to plague it. In popular English speech, the word 'subconscious' rather than 'unconscious' is often used; but this is to underestimate the radical *otherness* of the unconscious, imagining it as a place just within reach below the surface. It underestimates the extreme strangeness of the unconscious, which is a place and a non-place, which is completely indifferent to reality, which knows no logic or negation or causality or contradiction, wholly given over as it is to the instinctual play of the drives and the search for pleasure.

The 'royal road' to the unconscious is dreams. Dreams allow us one of our few privileged glimpses of it at work. Dreams for Freud are essentially symbolic fulfilments of unconscious wishes; and they are cast in symbolic form because if this material were expressed directly then it might be shocking and disturbing enough to wake us up. In order that we should get some sleep, the unconscious charitably conceals, softens and distorts its meanings, so that our dreams become symbolic texts which need to be deciphered. The watchful ego is still at work even within our dreaming, censoring an image here or scrambling a message there; and the unconscious itself adds to this obscurity by its peculiar modes of functioning. With the economy of the indolent, it will condense together a whole set of images into a single 'statement'; or it will 'displace' the meaning of one object on to another somehow associated with it, so that in my dream I am venting on a crab an aggression I feel towards somebody with that surname. This constant condensation and displacement of meaning corresponds to what Roman Jakobson identified as the two primary operations of human language: metaphor (condensing meanings together), and metonymy (displacing one on to another). It was this which moved the French psychoanalyst Jacques Lacan to comment that 'the unconscious is structured like a language'. Dream-texts are also cryptic because the unconscious is rather poor in techniques for representing what it has to say, being largely confined to visual images, and so must often craftily translate a verbal significance into a visual one: it might seize upon the image of a tennis *racket* to make a point about some shady dealing. At any rate, dreams are enough to demonstrate that the unconscious has the admirable resourcefulness of a lazy, ill-supplied chef, who slings together the most diverse ingredients into a cobbled-together stew, substituting one spice for another which he is out of, making do with whatever has arrived in the market that morning as a dream will draw opportunistically on the 'day's residues', mixing in events which took place during the day or sensations felt during sleep with images drawn deep from our childhood.

Dreams provide our main, but not our only, access to the unconscious. There are also what Freud calls 'parapraxes', unaccountable slips of the tongue, failures of memory, bunglings, misreadings and mislayings which can be traced to unconscious wishes and intentions. The presence of the unconscious is also betrayed in jokes, which for Freud have a largely libidinal, anxious or aggressive content. Where the unconscious is most damagingly at work, however, is in psychological disturbance of one form or another. We may have certain unconscious desires which will not be denied, but which dare not find practical outlet either; in this situation, the desire forces its way in from the unconscious, the ego blocks it off defensively, and the result of this internal conflict is what we call neurosis. The patient begins to develop symptoms which, in compromising fashion, at once protect against the unconscious desire and covertly express it. Such neuroses may be obsessional (having to touch every lamp-post in the street), hysterical (developing a paralysed arm for no good organic reason), or phobic (being unreasonably afraid of open spaces or certain animals). Behind these neuroses, psychoanalysis discerns unresolved conflicts whose roots run back to the individual's early development, and which are likely to be focused in the Oedipal moment; indeed Freud calls the Oedipus complex the 'nucleus of the neuroses'. There will usually be a relation between the kind of neurosis a patient displays, and the point in the pre-Oedipal stage at which his or her psychical development became arrested or 'fixated'. The aim of psychoanalysis is to uncover the hidden causes of the neurosis in order to relieve the patient of his or her conflicts, so dissolving the distressing symptoms.

Much more difficult to cope with, however, is the condition of psychosis, in which the ego, unable as in neurosis partly to repress the unconscious desire, actually comes under its sway. If this happens, the link between the ego and the external world is ruptured, and the unconscious begins to build up an alternative, delusional reality. The psychotic, in other words, has lost contact with reality at key points, as in paranoia and schizophrenia: if the neurotic may develop a paralysed arm, the psychotic may believe that his arm has turned into an elephant's trunk. 'Paranoia' refers to a more or less systematized state of delusion, under which Freud includes not only delusions of persecution but delusional jealousy and delusions of grandeur. The root of such paranoia he locates in an unconscious defence against homosexuality: the mind denies this desire by converting the love-object into a rival or persecutor, systematically reorganizing and reinterpreting reality to confirm this suspicion. Schizophrenia involves a detachment from reality and a turning in on the self, with an excessive but loosely systematized production of fantasies: it is as though the 'id', or unconscious desire, has surged up and flooded the conscious mind with its illogicality, riddling associations and affective rather than conceptual links between ideas. Schizophrenic language has in this sense an interesting resemblance to poetry.

Psychoanalysis is not only a theory of the human mind, but a practice for curing those who are considered mentally ill or disturbed. Such cures, for Freud, are not achieved just by explaining to the patient what is wrong with him, revealing to him his unconscious motivations. This is a part of psychoanalytical practice, but it will not cure anybody in itself. Freud is not in this sense a rationalist, believing that if only we understand ourselves or the world we can take appropriate action. The nub of the cure for Freudian theory is what is known as 'transference', a concept sometimes popularly confused with what Freud calls 'projection', or the ascribing to others of feelings and wishes which are actually our own. In the course of treatment, the analysand (or patient) may begin unconsciously to 'transfer' on to the figure of the analyst the psychical conflicts from which he or she suffers. If he has had difficulties with his father, for example, he may unconsciously cast the analyst in that role. This poses a problem for the analyst, since such 'repetition' or ritual re-enactment of the original conflict is one of the patient's unconscious ways of avoiding having to come to terms with it. We repeat, sometimes compulsively, what we cannot properly remember, and we cannot remember it because it is unpleasant. But transference also provides the analyst with a peculiarly privileged insight into the patient's psychical life, in a controlled situation in which he or she can intervene. (One of the several reasons why psychoanalysts must themselves undergo analysis in training is so that they can become reasonably aware of their own unconscious processes, thus resisting as far as possible the danger of 'counter-transferring' their own problems to their patients.) By virtue of this drama of transference, and the insights and interventions which it permits the analyst, the patient's problems are gradually redefined in terms of the analytic situation itself. In this sense, paradoxically, the problems which are handled in the consulting room are never quite at one with the real-life problems of the patient: they have, perhaps, something of the 'fictional' relation to those real-life problems which a literary text has to the real-life materials it transforms. Nobody leaves the consulting room cured of exactly the problems with which he walked in. The patient is likely to resist the analyst's access to her unconscious by a number of familiar techniques, but if all goes well the transferential process will allow her problems to be 'worked through' into consciousness, and by dissolving the transference relation at the right moment the analyst will hope to relieve her of them. Another way of describing this process is to say that the patient becomes able to recollect portions of her life which she has repressed: she is able to recount a new, more complete narrative about herself, one which will interpret and make sense of the disturbances from which she suffers. The 'talking cure', as it is called, will have taken effect.

The work of psychoanalysis can perhaps best be summarized in one of Freud's own slogans: 'Where id was, there shall ego be.' Where men and women were in the paralysing grip of forces which they could not comprehend, there reason and self-mastery shall reign. Such a slogan makes Freud sound rather more of a rationalist than he actually was. Though he once commented that nothing in the end could withstand reason and experience, he was about as far from underestimating the cunning and obstinacy of the mind as it is possible to be. His estimate of human capacities is on the whole conservative and pessimistic: we are dominated by a desire for gratification and an aversion to anything which might frustrate it. In his later work, he comes to see the human race as languishing in the grip of a terrifying death drive, a primary masochism which the ego unleashes on itself. The final goal of life is death, a return to that blissful inanimate state where the ego cannot be injured. Eros, or sexual energy, is the force which builds up history, but it is locked in tragic contradiction with Thanatos or the death drive. We strive onwards only to be constantly driven backwards, struggling to return to a state before we were even conscious. The ego is a pitiable, precarious entity, battered by the external world, scourged by the cruel upbraidings of the superego, plagued by the greedy, insatiable demands of the id. Freud's compassion for the ego is a compassion for the human race, labouring under the almost intolerable demands placed upon it by a civilization built upon the repression of desire and the deferment of gratification. He was scornful of all utopian proposals for changing this condition; but though many of his social views were conventional and authoritarian, he nevertheless looked with a certain favour upon attempts to abolish or at least reform the institutions of private property and the nation state. He did so because he was deeply convinced that modern society had become tyrannical in its repressiveness. As he argued in *The Future of an Illusion*, if a society has not developed beyond a point at which the satisfaction of one group of its members depends upon the suppression of another, it is understandable that those suppressed should develop an intense hostility towards a culture whose existence their labour has made possible, but in whose riches they have too small a share. 'It goes without saying,' Freud declares, 'that a civilization which leaves so large a number of its participants unsatisfied and drives them into revolt neither has nor deserves the prospect of a lasting existence.'

Any theory as complex and original as Freud's is bound to be a source of fierce contention. Freudianism has been attacked on a great number of grounds, and should in no way be taken as unproblematical. There are problems, for instance, about how it would test its doctrines, about what would count as evidence for or against its claims; as one American behaviourist psychologist remarked in conversation: 'The trouble with Freud's work is that it just isn't *testicle!*' It all depends, of course, on what you mean by 'testable'; but it would seem true that Freud sometimes invokes a nineteenth-century concept of science which is no longer really acceptable. Disinterested and objective though it strives to be, his work is shot through with what might be called 'counter-transference', shaped by his own unconscious desires and sometimes distorted by his conscious ideological beliefs. The sexist values we have touched on already are a case in point. Freud was probably no more patriarchal in attitude than most other nineteenth-century Viennese males, but his view of women as passive, narcissistic, masochistic and penis-envying, less morally conscientious than men, has been searchingly criticized by feminists.[1] One has only to compare the tone of Freud's case study of a young women (Dora) with the tone of his analysis of a small boy (little Hans) to catch the difference of sexual attitude:

brisk, suspicious and at times grotesquely off-target in the case of Dora; genial, avuncular and admiring towards that proto-Freudian philosopher little Hans.

Equally serious is the complaint that psychoanalysis as a medical practice is a form of oppressive social control, labelling individuals and forcing them to conform to arbitrary definitions of 'normality'. This charge is in fact more usually aimed against psychiatric medicine as a whole: as far as Freud's own views on 'normality' are concerned, the accusation is largely misdirected. Freud's work showed, scandalously, just how 'plastic' and variable in its choice of objects libido really is, how so-called sexual perversions form part of what passes as normal sexuality, and how heterosexuality is by no means a natural or self-evident fact. It is true that Freudian psychoanalysis does usually work with some concept of a sexual 'norm'; but this is in no sense given by Nature.

There are other familiar criticisms of Freud, which are not easy to substantiate. One is a merely commonsensical impatience: how could a little girl possibly desire her father's baby? Whether this is true or not, it is not 'common sense' which will allow us to decide. One should remember the sheer bizarreness of the unconscious as it manifests itself in dreams, its distance from the daylight world of the ego, before rushing to dismiss Freud on such intuitive grounds. Another common criticism is that Freud 'brings everything down to sex' – that he is, in the technical term, a 'pan-sexualist'. This is certainly untenable: Freud was a radically dualistic thinker, no doubt excessively so, and always counterposed to the sexual drives such non-sexual forces as the 'ego-instincts' of self-perservation. The seed of truth in the pan-sexualist charge is that Freud regarded sexuality as central enough to human life to provide a *component* of all our activities; but that is not a sexual reductionism.

One criticism of Freud still sometimes heard on the political Left is that his thinking is individualist – that he substitutes 'private' psychological causes and explanations for social and historical ones. This accusation reflects a radical misunderstanding of Freudian theory. There is indeed a real problem about how social and historical factors are *related* to the unconscious; but one point of Freud's work is that it makes it possible for us to think of the development of the human individual in social and historical terms. What Freud produces, indeed, is nothing less than a materialist theory of the making of the human subject. We come to be what we are by an interrelation of bodies – by the complex transactions which take place during infancy between our bodies and those which surround us. This is not a biological reductionism: Freud does not of course believe that we are nothing *but* our bodies, or that our minds are mere reflexes of them. Nor is it an asocial model of life, since the bodies which surround us, and our relations with them, are always socially specific. The roles of parents, the practices of child care, the images and beliefs associated with all of this are cultural matters which can vary considerably from one society or one point in history to another. 'Childhood' is a recent historical invention, and the range of different historical set-ups encompassed by the word 'family' makes the word itself of limited value. One belief which has apparently not varied in these institutions is the assumption that girls and women are inferior to boys and men: this prejudice would seem to unite all known societies. Since it is a prejudice with deep roots in our early sexual and familial development, psychoanalysis has become of major importance to some feminists.

One Freudian theorist to whom such feminists have had recourse for this purpose is the French psychoanalyst Jacques Lacan. It is not that Lacan is a pro-feminist thinker: on the contrary, his attitudes to the women's movement are in the main arrogant and contemptuous. But Lacan's work is a strikingly original attempt to 'rewrite' Freudianism in ways relevant to all those concerned with the question of the human subject, its place in society, and above all its relationship to language. This last concern is why Lacan is also of interest to literary theorists. What Lacan seeks to do in his *Ecrits* is to reinterpret Freud in the light of structuralist and post-structuralist theories of discourse; and while this leads to a sometimes bafflingly opaque, enigmatic body of work, it is nevertheless one that we must now briefly consider if we are to see how post-structuralism and psychoanalysis are interrelated.

I have described how for Freud, at an early point in the infant's development, no clear distinction between subject and object, itself and the external world, is yet possible. It is this state of being which Lacan names the 'imaginary', by which he means a condition in which we lack any defined centre of self, in which what 'self' we have seems to pass into objects, and objects into it, in a ceaseless closed exchange. In the pre-Oedipal state, the child lives a 'symbiotic' relation with its mother's body which blurs any sharp boundary between the two: it is dependent for its life on this body, but we can equally imagine the child as experiencing what it knows of the external world as dependent upon itself. This merging of identities is not quite as blissful as it might sound, according to the Freudian theorist Melanie Klein: at a very early age the infant will harbour murderously aggressive instincts towards its mother's body, entertain fantasies of tearing it to bits and suffer paranoid delusions that this body will in turn destroy it.[2]

If we imagine a small child contemplating itself in a mirror – Lacan's so-called 'mirror stage' – we can see how, from within this 'imaginary' state of being, the child's first development of an ego, of an integrated self-image, begins to happen. The child, who is still physically uncoordinated, finds reflected back to itself in the mirror a gratifyingly unified image of itself; and although its relation to this image is still of an 'imaginary' kind – the image in the mirror both is and is not itself, a blurring of subject and object still obtains – it has begun the process of constructing a centre of self. This self, as the mirror situation suggests, is essentially narcissistic: we arrive at a sense of an 'I' by finding that 'I' reflected back to ourselves by some object or person in the world. This object is at once somehow part of ourselves – we *identify* with it – and yet not ourselves, something alien. The image which the small child sees in the mirror is in this sense an 'alienated' one: the child 'misrecognizes' itself in it, finds in the image a pleasing unity which it does not actually experience in its own body. The imaginary for Lacan is precisely this realm of *images* in which we make identifications, but in the very act of doing so are led to misperceive and misrecognize ourselves. As the child grows up, it will continue to make such imaginary identifications with objects, and this is how its ego will be built up. For Lacan, the ego is just this narcissistic process whereby we bolster up a fictive sense of unitary selfhood by finding something in the world with which we can identify.

In discussing the pre-Oedipal or imaginary phase, we are considering a register of being in which there are really no more than two terms: the child itself and the other body, which at this point is usually the mother, and which represents external reality for the child. But as we have seen in our account of the Oedipus complex, this 'dyadic' structure is destined to give way to a 'triadic' one: and this happens when the father enters upon and disrupts this harmonious scene. The father signifies what Lacan calls the Law, which is in the first place the social taboo on incest: the child is disturbed in its libidinal relation with the mother, and must begin to recognize in the figure of the father that a wider familial and social network exists of which it is only part. Not only is the child merely a part of this network, but the role it must play there is already predetermined, laid down for it by the practices of the society into which it has been born. The appearance of the father divides the child from the mother's body, and in doing so, as we have seen, drives its desire underground into the unconscious. In this sense the first appearance of the Law, and the opening up of unconscious desire, occur at the same moment: it is only when the child acknowledges the taboo or prohibition which the father symbolizes that it represses its guilty desire, and that desire just *is* what is called the unconscious.

For the drama of the Oedipus complex to come about at all, the child must of course have become dimly aware of sexual difference. It is the entry of the father which signifies this sexual difference; and one of the key-terms in Lacan's work, the phallus, denotes this signification of sexual distinction. It is only by accepting the necessity of sexual difference, of distinct gender roles, that the child, who has previously been unaware of such problems, can become properly 'socialized'. Lacan's originality is to rewrite this process, which we have already seen in Freud's account of the Oedipus complex, in terms of language. We can think of the small child contemplating itself before the mirror as a kind of 'signifier' – something capable of bestowing meaning – and of the image it sees in the mirror as a kind of 'signified'. The image the child sees is somehow the 'meaning' of itself. Here, signifier and signified are as harmoniously united as they are in Saussure's sign. Alternatively, we could read the mirror situation as a kind of metaphor: one item (the child) discovers a likeness of itself in another (the reflection). This, for Lacan, is an appropriate image of the imaginary as a whole: in this mode of being, objects ceaselessly reflect themselves in each other in a sealed circuit, and no real differences or divisions are yet apparent. It is a world of *plenitude*, with no lacks or exclusions of any kind: standing before the mirror, the 'signifier' (the child) finds a 'fullness', a whole and unblemished identity, in the signified of its reflection. No gap has yet opened up between signifier and signified, subject and world. The infant is so far happily unplagued by the problems of post-structuralism – by the fact that, as we have seen, language and reality are not so smoothly synchronized as this situation would suggest.

With the entry of the father, the child is plunged into post-structuralist anxiety. It now has to grasp Saussure's point that identities come about only as a result of difference – that one term or subject is what it is only by excluding another. Significantly, the child's first discovery of sexual differ-ence occurs at about the same time that it is discovering language itself. The baby's cry is not really a sign but a signal: it indicates that it is cold, hungry or whatever. In gaining access to language, the small child unconsciously learns that a sign has meaning only by dint of its difference from other signs, and learns also that a sign presupposes the *absence* of the object it signifies. Our language 'stands in' for objects: all language is in a way 'metaphorical', in that it substitutes itself for some direct, wordless possession of the object itself. It saves us from the inconvenience of Swift's Laputans, who carry on their back a sack full of all the objects they might need in conversation, and simply hold these objects up to each other as a way of talking. But just as the child is unconsciously learning these lessons in the sphere of language, it is also unconsciously learning them in the world of sexuality. The presence of the father, symbolized by the phallus, teaches the child that it must take up a place in the family which is defined by sexual difference, by exclusion (it cannot be its parent's lover) and by absence (it must relinquish its earlier bonds to the mother's body). Its identity as a subject, it comes to perceive, is constituted by its relations of difference and similarity to the other subjects around it. In accepting all of this, the child moves from the imaginary register into what Lacan calls the 'symbolic order': the pre-given structure of social and sexual roles and relations which make up the family and society. In Freud's own terms, it has successfully negotiated the painful passage through the Oedipus complex.

All, however, is not entirely well. For as we have seen, in Freud the subject who emerges from this process is a 'split' one, radically divided between the conscious life of the ego and the unconscious, or repressed desire. It is this primary repression of desire which makes us what we are. The child must now resign itself to the fact that it can never have any *direct* access to reality, in particular to the now prohibited body of the mother. It has been banished from this 'full', imaginary possession into the 'empty' world of language. Language is 'empty' because it is just an endless process of difference and absence: instead of being able to possess anything in its fullness, the child will now simply move from one signifier to another, along a linguistic chain which is potentially infinite. One signifier implies another, and that another, and so on *ad infinitum*: the 'metaphorical' world of the mirror has yielded ground to the 'metonymic' world of language. Along this metonymic chain of signifiers, meanings, or signifieds, will be produced; but no object or person can ever be fully 'present' in this chain, because as we have seen with Derrida its effect is to divide and differentiate all identities.

This potentially endless movement from one signifier to another is what Lacan means by desire. All desire springs from a lack, which it strives continually to fill. Human language works by such lack: the absence of the real objects which signs designate, the fact that words have meaning only by virtue of the absence and exclusion of others. To enter language, then, is to become a prey to desire: language, Lacan remarks, is 'what hollows being into desire'. Language divides up – *articulates* – the fullness of the imaginary: we will now never be able to find rest in the single object, the final meaning, which will make sense of all the others. To enter language is to be severed from what Lacan calls the 'real', that inaccessible realm which is always beyond the reach of signification, always outside the symbolic order. In particular, we are severed from the mother's body: after the Oedipus crisis, we will never again be able to attain this precious object, even though we will spend all of our lives hunting for it. We have to make do instead with substitute objects, what Lacan calls the 'object little *a*', with which we try vainly to plug the gap at the very centre of our being. We move among substitutes for substitutes, metaphors of metaphors, never able to recover the pure (if fictive) self-identity and self-completion which we knew in the imaginary. There is no 'transcendental' meaning or object which will ground this endless yearning – or if there is such a transcendental reality, it is the phallus itself, the 'transcendental signifier' as Lacan calls it. But this is not in fact an object or reality, not the actual male sexual organ: it is merely an empty marker of difference, a sign of what divides us from the imaginary and inserts us into our predestined place within the symbolic order.

Lacan, as we have seen in our discussion of Freud, regards the unconscious as structured like a language. This is not only because it works by metaphor and metonymy: it is also because, like language itself for the poststructuralists, it is composed less of *signs* – stable meanings – than of *signifiers*. If you dream of a horse, it is not immediately obvious what this signifies: it may have many contradictory meanings, may be just one of a whole chain of signifiers with equally multiple meanings. The image of the horse, that is to say, is not a sign in Saussure's sense – it does not have one determined signified tied neatly to its tail – but is a signifier which may be attached to many different signifieds, and which may itself bear the traces of the other signifiers which surround it. (I was not aware, when I wrote the above sentence, of the word-play involved in 'horse' and 'tail': one signifier interacted with another against my conscious intention.) The unconscious is just a continual movement and activity of signifiers, whose signifieds are often inaccessible to us because they are *repressed*. This is why Lacan speaks of the unconscious as a 'sliding of the signified beneath the signifier', as a constant fading and evaporation of meaning, a bizarre 'modernist' text which is almost unreadable and which will certainly never yield up its final secrets to interpretation.

If this constant sliding and hiding of meaning were true of conscious life, then we would of course never be able to speak coherently at all. If the whole of language were present to me when I spoke, then I would not be able to articulate anything at all. The ego, or consciousness, can therefore only work by repressing this turbulent activity, provisionally nailing down words on to meanings. Every now and then a word from the unconscious which I do not want insinuates itself into my discourse, and this is the famous Freudian slip of the tongue or parapraxis. But for Lacan all our discourse is in a sense a slip of the tongue: if the process of language is as slippery and ambiguous as he suggests, we can never mean precisely what we say and never say precisely what we mean. Meaning is always in some sense an approximation, a near-miss, a part-failure, mixing non-sense and non-communication into sense and dialogue. We can certainly never articulate the truth in some 'pure', unmediated way: Lacan's own notoriously sybilline style, a language of the unconscious all in itself, is meant to suggest that language of the unconscious all in itself, is meant to suggest that any attempt to convey a whole, unblemished meaning in speech or script is a pre-Freudian illusion. In conscious life, we achieve some sense of ourselves as reasonably unified, coherent selves, and without this action would be impossible. But all this is merely at the 'imaginary' level of the ego, which is no more than the tip of the iceberg of the human subject known to psychoanalysis. The ego is function or effect of a subject which is always dispersed, never identical with itself, strung out along the chains of the discourses which constitute it. There is a radical split between these two levels of being – a gap most dramatically exemplified by the act of referring to myself in a sentence. When I say 'Tomorrow I will mow the lawn,' the 'I' which I pronounce is an immediately intelligible, fairly stable point of reference which belies the murky depths of the 'I' which does the pronouncing. The former 'I' is known to linguistic theory as the 'subject of the enunciation', the topic designated by my sentence; the latter 'I', the one who speaks the sentence, is the 'subject of the enunciating', the subject of the actual act of speaking. In the process of speaking and writing, these two 'I's seem to achieve a rough sort of unity; but this unity is of an imaginary kind. The 'subject of the enunciating', the actual speaking, writing human person, can never represent himself or herself fully in what is said: there is no sign which will, so to speak, sum up my entire being. I can only *designate* myself in language by a convenient pronoun. The pronoun 'I' *stands in* for the ever-elusive subject, which will always slip through the nets of any particular piece of language; and this is equivalent to saying that I cannot 'mean' and 'be' simultaneously. To make this point, Lacan boldly rewrites Descartes's 'I think, therefore I am' as: 'I am not where I think, and I think where I am not.'

There is an interesting analogy between what we have just described and those 'acts of enunciation' known as literature. In some literary works, in particular realist fiction, our attention as readers is drawn not to the 'act of enunciating', to *how* something is said, from what kind of position and with what end in view, but simply to *what* is said, to the enunciation itself. Any such 'anonymous' enunciation is likely to have more authority, to engage our assent more readily, than one which draws attention to how the enunciation is actually constructed. The language of a legal document or scientific textbook may impress or even intimidate us because we do not see how the language got there in the first place. The text does not allow the reader to see how the facts it contains were selected, what was excluded, why these facts were organized in this particular way, what assumptions governed this process, what forms of work went into the making of the text, and how all of this might have been different. Part of the power of such texts thus lies in their suppression of what might be called their modes of production, how they got to be what they are; in this sense, they have a curious resemblance to the life of the human ego, which thrives by repressing the process of its own making. Many modernist literary works, by contrast, make the 'act of enunciating', the process of their own production, part of their actual 'content'. They do not try to pass themselves off as unquestionable, like Barthes's 'natural' sign, but as the Formalists would say 'lay bare the device' of their own composition. They do this so that they will not be mistaken for absolute truth – so that the reader will be encouraged to reflect critically on the partial, particular ways they construct reality, and so to recognize how it might all have happened differently. The finest example of such literature is perhaps the drama of Bertolt Brecht; but many other instances are available in the modern arts, not least in film. Think on the one hand of a typical Hollywood film which simply uses the camera as a kind of 'window' or second eye through which the viewer contemplates reality – which holds the camera steady and allows it simply to 'record' what is happening. Watching such a film, we tend to forget that 'what is happening' is not in fact just 'happening', but is a highly complex *construct*, involving the actions and assumptions of a great many people. Think then on the other hand of a cinematic sequence in which the camera darts restlessly, nervously from object to object, focusing first on one and then discarding it to pick out another, probing these objects compulsively from several different angles before trailing away, disconsolately as it were, to frame something else. This would not be a particularly avant-garde procedure; but even this highlights how, in contrast to the first type of film, the *activity* of the camera, the way of mounting the episode, is being 'foregrounded', so that we cannot as spectators simply stare through this obtrusive operation to the objects themselves.[3] The 'content' of the sequence can be grasped as the *product* of a specific set of technical devices, not as a 'natural' or given reality which the camera is simply there to reflect. The 'signified' – the 'meaning' of the sequence – is a product of the 'signifier' – the cinematic techniques – rather than something which preceded it.

In order to pursue further the implications of Lacan's thought for the human subject, we shall have to take a brief detour through a famous essay written under Lacan's influence by the French Marxist philosopher Louis Althusser. In 'Ideology and Ideological State Apparatuses', contained in his book *Lenin and Philosophy* (1971), Althusser tries to illuminate, with the implicit aid of Lacanian psychoanalytic theory, the working of ideology in society. How is it, the essay asks, that human subjects very often come to submit themselves to the dominant ideologies of their societies – ideologies which Althusser sees as vital to maintaining the power of a ruling class? By what mechanisms does this come about? Althusser has sometimes been seen as a 'structuralist' Marxist, in that for him human individuals are the product of many different social determinants, and thus have no essential unity. As far as a science of human societies goes, such individuals can be studied simply as the functions, or effects, of this or that social structure – as occupying a place in a mode of production, as a member of a specific social class, and so on. But this of course is not at all the way we actually experience ourselves. We tend to see ourselves rather as free, unified, autonomous, self-generating individuals; and unless we did so we would be incapable of playing our parts in social life. For Althusser, what allows us to experience ourselves in this way is ideology. How is this to be understood?

As far as society is concerned, I as an individual am utterly dispensable. No doubt someone has to fulfil the functions I carry out (writing, teaching, lecturing and so on), since education has a crucial role to play in the reproduction of this kind of social system, but there is no particular reason why this individual should be myself. One reason why this thought does not lead me to join a circus or take an overdose is that this is not usually the way that I experience my own identity, not the way I actually 'live out' my life. I do not *feel* myself to be a mere function of a social structure which could get along without me, true though this appears when I *analyse* the situation, but as somebody with a significant *relation* to society and the world at large, a relation which gives me enough sense of meaning and value to enable me to act purposefully. It is as though society were not just an impersonal structure to me, but a 'subject' which 'addresses' me personally – which recognizes me, tells me that I am valued, and so makes me by that very act of recognition into a free, autonomous subject. I come to feel, not exactly as though the world exists for me alone, but as though it is significantly 'centred' on me, and I in turn am significantly 'centred' on it. Ideology, for Althusser, is the set of beliefs and practices which does this centring. It is far more subtle, pervasive and unconscious than a set of explicit doctrines: it is the very medium in which I 'live out' my relation to society, the realm of signs and social practices which binds me to the social structure and lends me a sense of coherent purpose and identity. Ideology in this sense may include the act of going to church, of casting a vote, of letting women pass first through doors; it may encompass not only such conscious predilections

as my deep devotion to the monarchy but the way I dress and the kind of car
I drive, my deeply unconscious images of others and of myself.

What Althusser does, in other words, is to rethink the concept of ideology
in terms of Lacan's 'imaginary'. For the relation of an individual subject to
society as a whole in Althusser's theory is rather like the relation of the small
child to his or her mirror-image in Lacan's. In both cases, the human subject
is supplied with a satisfyingly unified image of selfhood by identifying with
an object which reflects this image back to it in a closed, narcissistic circle.
In both cases, too, this image involves a *mis*recognition, since it idealizes the
subject's real situation. The child is not actually as integrated as its image in
the mirror suggests; I am not actually the coherent, autonomous, self-
generating subject I know myself to be in the ideological sphere, but the
'decentred' function of several social determinants. Duly enthralled by the
image of myself I receive, I subject myself to it; and it is through this
'subjection' that I become a subject.

Most commentators would now agree that Althusser's suggestive essay is
seriously flawed. It seems to assume, for example, that ideology is little more
than an oppressive force which subjugates us, without allowing sufficient
space for the realities of ideological *struggle*; and it involves some rather
serious misinterpretations of Lacan. Nevertheless, it is one attempt to show
the relevance of Lacanian theory to issues beyond the consulting room:
it sees, rightly, that such a body of work has deep-seated implications
for several fields beyond psychoanalysis itself. Indeed, by reinterpreting
Freudianism in terms of language, a pre-eminently social activity, Lacan
permits us to explore the relations between the unconscious and human
society. One way of describing his work is to say that he makes us recognize
that the unconscious is not some kind of seething, tumultuous, private
region 'inside' us, but an effect of our relations with one another. The
unconscious is, so to speak, 'outside' rather than 'within' us – or rather it
exists 'between' us, as our relationships do. It is elusive not so much because
it is buried deep within our minds, but because it is a kind of vast, tangled
network which surrounds us and weaves itself through us, and which can
therefore never be pinned down. The best image for such a network, which
is both beyond us and yet is the very stuff of which we are made, is language
itself; and indeed for Lacan the unconscious is a particular effect of language, a process of desire set in motion by difference. When we enter the
symbolic order, we enter into language itself; yet this language, for Lacan as
for the structuralists, is never something entirely within our individual
control. On the contrary, as we have seen, language is what internally *divides*
us, rather than an instrument we are confidently able to manipulate. Lan-

guage always pre-exists us: it is always already 'in place', waiting to assign us *our* places within it. It is ready and waiting for us rather as our parents are; and we shall never wholly dominate it or subdue it to our own ends, just as we shall never be able entirely to shake off the dominant role which our parents play in our constitution. Language, the unconscious, the parents, the symbolic order: these terms in Lacan are not exactly synonymous, but they are intimately allied. They are sometimes spoken of by him as the 'Other' – as that which like language is always anterior to us and will always escape us, that which brought us into being as subjects in the first place but which always outruns our grasp. We have seen that for Lacan our unconscious desire is directed towards this Other, in the shape of some ultimately gratifying reality which we can never have; but it is also true for Lacan that our desire is in some way always *received* from the Other too. We desire what others – our parents, for instance – unconsciously desire for us; and desire can only happen because we are caught up in linguistic, sexual and social relations – the whole field of the 'Other' – which generate it.

Lacan himself is not much interested in the social relevance of his theories, and he certainly does not 'solve' the problem of the relation between society and the unconscious. Freudianism as a whole, however, does enable us to pose this question; and I want now to examine it in terms of a concrete literary example, D. H. Lawrence's novel *Sons and Lovers*. Even conservative critics, who suspect such phrases as the 'Oedipus complex' as alien jargon, sometimes admit that there is something at work in this text which looks remarkably like Freud's famous drama. (It is interesting, incidentally, how conventionally-minded critics seem quite content to employ such jargon as 'symbol', 'dramatic irony' and 'densely textured', while remaining oddly resistant to terms such as 'signifier' and 'decentring'.) At the time of writing *Sons and Lovers*, Lawrence, as far as we know, knew something of Freud's work at second hand from his German wife Frieda; but there seems no evidence that he had any direct or detailed acquaintance with it, a fact which might be taken as striking independent confirmation of Freud's doctrine. For it is surely the case that *Sons and Lovers*, without appearing to be at all aware of it, is a profoundly Oedipal novel: the young Paul Morel who sleeps in the same bed as his mother, treats her with the tenderness of a lover and feels strong animosity towards his father, grows up to be the man Morel, unable to sustain a fulfilling relationship with a woman, and in the end achieving possible release from this condition by killing his mother in an ambiguous act of love, revenge and self-liberation. Mrs Morel, for her part, is jealous of Paul's relationship with Miriam, behaving like a rival mistress. Paul rejects Miriam for his mother; but in rejecting Miriam he is also unconsciously rejecting his mother *in* her, in what he feels to be Miriam's stifling spiritual possessiveness.

Paul's psychological development, however, does not take place in a social void. His father, Walter Morel, is a miner, while his mother is of a slightly higher social class. Mrs Morel is concerned that Paul should not follow his father into the pit, and wants him to take a clerical job instead. She herself remains at home as a housewife: the family set-up of the Morels is part of what is known as the 'sexual division of labour', which in capitalist society takes the form of the male parent being used as labour-power in the productive process while the female parent is left to provide the material and emotional 'maintenance' of him and the labour-force of the future (the children). Mr Morel's estrangement from the intense emotional life of the home is due in part to this social division – one which alienates him from his own children, and brings them emotionally closer to the mother. If, as with Walter Morel, the father's work is especially exhausting and oppressive, his role in the family is likely to be further diminished: Morel is reduced to establishing human contact with his children through his practical skills about the house. His lack of education, moreover, makes it difficult for him to articulate his feelings, a fact which further increases the distance between himself and his family. The fatiguing, harshly disciplined nature of the work process helps to create in him a domestic irritability and violence which drives the children deeper into their mother's arms, and which spurs on her jealous possessiveness of them. To compensate for his inferior status at work, the father struggles to assert a traditional male authority at home, thus estranging his children from him still further.

In the case of the Morels, these social factors are further complicated by the class-distinction between them. Morel has what the novel takes to be a characteristically proletarian inarticulateness, physicality and passivity: *Sons and Lovers* portrays the miners as creatures of the underworld who live the life of the body rather than the mind. This is a curious portraiture, since in 1912, the year in which Lawrence finished the book, the miners launched the biggest strike which Britain had ever seen. One year later, the year of the novel's publication, the worst mining disaster for a century resulted in a paltry fine for a seriously negligent management, and class-warfare was everywhere in the air throughout the British coalfields. These developments, with all their acute political awareness and complex organization, were not the actions of mindless hulks. Mrs Morel (it is perhaps significant that we do not feel inclined to use her first name) is of lower-middle-class origin, reasonably well-educated, articulate and determined. She therefore symbolizes what the young, sensitive and artistic Paul may hope to achieve:

his emotional turning to her from the father is, inseparably, a turning from the impoverished, exploitative world of the colliery towards the life of emancipated consciousness. The potentially tragic tension in which Paul then finds himself trapped, and almost destroyed, springs from the fact that his mother – the very source of the energy which pushes him ambitiously beyond home and pit – is at the same time the powerful emotional force which draws him back.

A psychoanalytical reading of the novel, then, need not be an alternative to a social interpretation of it. We are speaking rather of two sides or aspects of a single human situation. We can discuss Paul's 'weak' image of his father and 'strong' image of his mother in both Oedipal and class terms; we can see how the human relationships between an absent, violent father, an ambitious, emotionally demanding mother and a sensitive child are understandable both in terms of unconscious processes and in terms of certain social forces and relations. (Some critics, of course, would find neither kind of approach acceptable, and opt for a 'human' reading of the novel instead. It is not easy to know what this 'human' is, which excludes the characters' concrete life-situations, their jobs and histories, the deeper significance of their personal relationships and identities, their sexuality and so on.) All of this, however, is still confined to what may be called 'content analysis', looking at what is said rather than how it is said, at 'theme' rather than 'form'. But we can carry these considerations into 'form' itself – into such matters as how the novel delivers and structures its narrative, how it delineates character, what narrative point of view it adopts. It seems evident, for example, that the text itself largely, though by no means entirely, identifies with and endorses Paul's own viewpoint: since the narrative is seen chiefly through his eyes, we have no real source of testimony other than him. As Paul moves into the foreground of the story, his father recedes into the background. The novel is also in general more 'inward' in its treatment of Mrs Morel than it is of her husband; indeed we might argue that it is organized in a way which tends to highlight her and obscure him, a formal device which reinforces the protagonist's own attitudes. The very way in which the narrative is structured, in other words, to some extent conspires with Paul's own unconscious: it is not clear to us, for example, that Miriam as she is presented in the text, very much from Paul's own viewpoint, actually merits the irritable impatience which she evokes in him, and many readers have had the uneasy sense that the novel is in some way 'unjust' to her. (The real-life Miriam, Jessie Chambers, hotly shared this opinion, but this for our present purposes is neither here nor there.) But how are we to validate this sense of injustice, when Paul's own viewpoint is consistently 'foregrounded' as our source of supposedly reliable evidence?

On the other hand, there are aspects of the novel which would seem to run counter to this 'angled' presentation. As H. M. Daleski has perceptively put it: 'The weight of hostile comment which Lawrence directs against Morel is balanced by the unconscious sympathy with which he is presented dramatically, while the overt celebration of Mrs Morel is challenged by the harshness of her character in action.'[4] In the terms we have used about Lacan, the novel does not exactly say what it means or mean what it says. This itself can partly be accounted for in psychoanalytical terms: the boy's Oedipal relation to his father is an ambiguous one, for the father is loved as well as unconsciously hated as a rival, and the child will seek to protect the father from his own unconscious aggression towards him. Another reason for this ambiguity, however, is that on one level the novel sees very well that though Paul must reject the narrowed, violent world of the miners for his venture into middle-class consciousness, such consciousness is by no means wholly to be admired. There is much that is dominative and life-denying as well as valuable in it, as we can see in the character of Mrs Morel. It is Walter Morel, so the text tells us, who has 'denied the god in him'; but it is hard to feel that this heavy authorial interpolation, solemn and obtrusive as it is, really earns its keep. For the very novel which *tells* us this also *shows* us the opposite. It shows us the ways in which Morel is indeed still alive; it cannot stop us from seeing how the diminishing of him has much to do with its own narrative organization, turning as it does from him to his son; and it also shows us, intentionally or not, that even if Morel *has* 'denied the god in him' then the blame is ultimately to be laid not on him but on the predatory capitalism which can find no better use for him than as a cog in the wheel of production. Paul himself, intent as he is on extricating himself from the father's world, cannot afford to confront these truths, and neither, explicitly, does the novel: in writing *Sons and Lovers* Lawrence was not just writing about the working class but writing his way out of it. But in such telling incidents as the final reunion of Baxter Dawes (in some ways a parallel figure to Morel) with his estranged wife Clara, the novel 'unconsciously' makes reparation for its upgrading of Paul (whom this incident shows in a much more negative light) at the expense of his father. Lawrence's final reparation for Morel will be Mellors, the 'feminine' yet powerful male protagonist of *Lady Chatterley's Lover*. Paul is never allowed by the novel to voice the kind of full, bitter criticism of his mother's possessiveness which some of the 'objective' evidence would seem to warrant; yet the way in which the relationship between mother and son is actually dramatized allows *us* to see why this should be so.

In reading *Sons and Lovers* with an eye to these aspects of the novel, we are constructing what may be called a 'sub-text' for the work – a text which runs within it, visible at certain 'symptomatic' points of ambiguity, evasion or overemphasis, and which we as readers are able to 'write' even if the novel itself does not. All literary works contain one or more such sub-texts, and there is a sense in which they may be spoken of as the 'unconscious' of the work itself. The work's insights, as with all writing, are deeply related to its blindnesses: what it does not say, and *how* it does not say it, may be as important as what it articulates; what seems absent, marginal or ambivalent about it may provide a central clue to its meanings. We are not simply rejecting or inverting 'what the novel says', arguing, for example, that Morel is the real hero and his wife the villain. Paul's viewpoint is not simply invalid: his mother is indeed an incomparably richer source of sympathy than his father. We are looking rather at what such statements must inevitably silence or suppress, examining the ways in which the novel is not quite identical with itself. Psychoanalytical criticism, in other words, can do more than hunt for phallic symbols: it can tell us something about how literary texts are actually formed, and reveal something of the meaning of that formation.

Psychoanalytical literary criticism can be broadly divided into four kinds, depending on what it takes as its object of attention. It can attend to the *author* of the work; to the work's *contents*; to its *formal construction*; or to the *reader*. Most psychoanalytical criticism has been of the first two kinds, which are in fact the most limited and problematical. Psychoanalysing the author is a speculative business, and runs into just the same kind of problems we examined when discussing the relevance of authorial 'intention' to works of literature. The psychoanalysis of 'content' – commenting on the unconscious motivations of characters, or on the psychoanalytical significance of objects or events in the text – has a limited value, but, in the manner of the notorious hunt for the phallic symbol, is too often reductive. Freud's own sporadic ventures into the field of art and literature were mainly in these two modes. He wrote a fascinating monograph on Leonardo da Vinci, an essay on Michelangelo's statue 'Moses' and some literary analyses, notably of a short novel by the German writer Wilhelm Jensen entitled *Gradiva*. These essays either offer a psychoanalytical account of the author himself as he reveals himself in his work, or examine symptoms of the unconscious in art as one would in life. In either case, the 'materiality' of the artefact itself, its specific formal constitution, tends to be overlooked.

Equally inadequate is Freud's best-remembered opinion of art: his comparison of it to neurosis.[5] What he meant by this is that the artist, like the neurotic, is oppressed by unusually powerful instinctual needs which lead him to turn away from reality to fantasy. Unlike other fantasists, however, the artist knows how to work over, shape and soften his own day-dreams in ways which make them acceptable to others – for, envious egoists that we are, we tend in Freud's opinion to find others' day-dreams repulsive. Crucial to this shaping and softening is the power of artistic form, which affords the reader or viewer what Freud calls 'fore-pleasure', relaxes his defences against others' wish-fulfilments and so enables him to lift his repression for a brief moment and take forbidden pleasure in his own unconscious processes. The same is roughly true of Freud's theory of jokes, in *Jokes and their Relation to the Unconscious* (1905): jokes express a normally censored aggressive or libidinal impulse, but this is made socially acceptable by the joke's 'form', its wit and word-play.

Questions of form, then, do enter into Freud's reflections on art; but the image of the artist as neurotic is surely much too simple, the solid citizen's caricature of the distraught, moonstruck Romantic. Much more suggestive for a psychoanalytical literary theory is Freud's commentary in his masterpiece, *The Interpretation of Dreams* (1900), on the nature of dreaming. Literary works of course involve conscious labour, while dreams do not: in this sense they resemble dreams less than they resemble jokes. But with this reservation in mind, what Freud argues in his book is highly significant. The 'raw materials' of a dream, what Freud calls its 'latent content', are unconscious wishes, bodily stimuli while sleeping, images reaped from the previous day's experiences; but the dream itself is the product of an intensive transformation of these materials, known as the 'dream-work'. The mechanisms of the dream-work we have looked at already: they are the unconscious's techniques of condensing and displacing its materials, together with finding intelligible ways of representing it. The dream which is produced by this labour, the dream we actually remember, is termed by Freud the 'manifest content'. The dream, then, is not just the 'expression' or 'reproduction' of the unconscious: between the unconscious and the dream we have, a process of 'production' or transformation has intervened. The 'essence' of the dream, Freud considers, is not the raw materials or 'latent content', but the dream-work itself: it is this 'practice' which is the object of his analysis.

One stage of the dream-work, known as 'secondary revision', consists in the reorganization of the dream so as to present it in the form of a relatively consistent and comprehensible narrative. Secondary revision systematizes the dream, fills in its gaps and smooths over its contradictions, reorders its chaotic elements into a more coherent fable.

Most of the literary theory we have examined so far in this book could be considered a form of 'secondary revision' of the literary text. In its obsessive pursuit of 'harmony', 'coherence', 'deep structure' or 'essential meaning', such theory fills in the text's gaps and smooths over its contradictions, domesticating its disparate aspects and defusing its conflicts. It does this so that the text may be, so to speak, more easily 'consumed' – so that the path is made straight for the reader, who will not be ruffled by any unexplained irregularities. Much literary scholarship in particular is resolutely devoted to this end, briskly 'resolving' ambiguities and staking the text down for the reader's untroubled inspection. An extreme example of such secondary revision, although one not altogether untypical of much critical interpretation, is the kind of account of T. S. Eliot's *The Waste Land* which reads the poem as the story of a little girl who went on a sledge-ride with her uncle the Archduke, changed sex a few times in London, got caught up in a hunt for the Holy Grail and ended up fishing glumly on the edge of an arid plain. The diverse, divided materials of Eliot's poem are tamed to a coherent narrative, the shattered human subjects of the work unified to a single ego.

Much of the literary theory we have looked at also tends to view the literary work as an 'expression' or 'reflection' of reality: it enacts human experience, or embodies an author's intention, or its structures reproduce the structures of the human mind. Freud's account of the dream, by contrast, enables us to see the work of literature not as a reflection but as a form of production. Like the dream, the work takes certain 'raw materials' – language, other literary texts, ways of perceiving the world – and transforms them by certain techniques into a product. The techniques by which this production is carried out are the various devices we know as 'literary form'. In working on its raw materials, the literary text will tend to submit them to its own form of secondary revision: unless it is a 'revolutionary' text like *Finnegans Wake*, it will try to organize them into a reasonably coherent, consumable whole, even if, as with *Sons and Lovers*, it will not be always successful. But just as the dream-text can be analysed, deciphered, decomposed in ways which show up something of the processes by which it was produced, so too can the literary work. A 'naive' reading of literature might stop short at the textual product itself, as I might listen to your gripping account of a dream without bothering to probe it further. Psychoanalysis, on the other hand, is in the phrase of one of its interpreters a 'hermeneutic of suspicion': its concern is not just to 'read the text' of the unconscious, but to uncover the processes, the dream-work, by which that text was produced. To do this, it focuses in particular on what have been called 'symptomatic' places in the dream-text – distortions, ambiguities, absence and elisions which may provide a specially valuable mode of access to the 'latent content', or unconscious drives, which have gone into its making. Literary criticism, as we saw in the case of Lawrence's novel, can do something similar: by attending to what may seem like evasions, ambivalences and points of intensity in the narrative – words which do not get spoken, words which are spoken with unusual frequency, doublings and slidings of language – it can begin to probe through the layers of secondary revision and expose something of the 'sub-text' which, like an unconscious wish, the work both conceals and reveals. It can attend, in other words, not only to what the text says, but to how it *works*.[6]

Some Freudian literary criticism has pursued this project to a certain extent. In his *The Dynamics of Literary Response* (1968), the American critic Norman N. Holland, following Freud, sees works of literature as setting in motion in the reader an interplay of unconscious fantasies and conscious defences against them. The work is enjoyable because by devious formal means it transforms our deepest anxieties and desires into socially acceptable meanings. If it did not 'soften' these desires by its form and language, allowing us sufficient mastery of and defence against them, it would prove unacceptable; but so would it if it merely reinforced our repressions. This, in effect, is little more than a restatement in Freudian guise of the old Romantic opposition between turbulent content and harmonizing form. Literary form for the American critic Simon Lesser, in his *Fiction and the Unconscious* (1957), has a 'reassuring influence', combating anxiety and celebrating our commitment to life, love and order. Through it, according to Lesser, we 'pay homage to the superego'. But what of modernist forms which pulverize order, subvert meaning and explode our self-assurance? Is literature just a sort of therapy? Holland's later work would suggest that he thinks so: *Five Readers Reading* (1975) examines the unconscious responses of readers to literary texts in order to see how these readers come to adapt their identities in the process of interpretation, yet thereby discover a reassuring unity in themselves. Holland's belief that it is possible to abstract from an individual's life an 'unchanging essence' of personal identity aligns his work with so-called American 'ego-psychology' – a domesticated version of Freudianism which diverts attention from the 'split subject' of classical psychoanalysis and projects it instead on to the unity of the ego. It is a psychology concerned with how the ego adapts to social life: by therapeutic techniques, the individual is 'fitted' into his natural, healthy role as an aspiring executive with the appropriate make of automobile, and any distressing personality traits which might deviate from this norm are 'treated'. With this brand of psychology, the Freudianism which began as scandal and affront to middle-class society becomes a way of underwriting its values.

Two very different American critics indebted to Freud are Kenneth Burke, who eclectically blends Freud, Marx and linguistics to produce his own suggestive view of the literary work as a form of symbolic action, and Harold Bloom, who has used the work of Freud to launch one of the most daringly original literary theories of the past decade. What Bloom does, in effect, is to rewrite literary history in terms of the Oedipus complex. Poets live anxiously in the shadow of a 'strong' poet who came before them, as sons are oppressed by their fathers; and any particular poem can be read as an attempt to escape this 'anxiety of influence' by its systematic remoulding of a previous poem. The poet, locked in Oedipal rivalry with his castrating 'precursor', will seek to disarm that strength by entering it from within, writing in a way which revises, displaces and recasts the precursor poem; in this sense all poems can be read as rewritings of other poems, and as 'misreadings' or 'misprisions' of them, attempts to fend off their overwhelming force so that the poet can clear a space for his own imaginative originality. Every poet is 'belated', the last in a tradition; the strong poet is the one with the courage to acknowledge this belatedness and set about undermining the precursor's power. Any poem, indeed, is nothing *but* such an undermining – a series of devices, which can be seen both as rhetorical strategies and psychoanalytic defence mechanisms, for undoing and outdoing another poem. The meaning of a poem is another poem.

Bloom's literary theory represents an impassioned, defiant return to the Protestant Romantic 'tradition' from Spenser and Milton to Blake, Shelley and Yeats, a tradition ousted by the conservative Anglo-Catholic lineage (Donne, Herbert, Pope, Johnson, Hopkins) mapped out by Eliot, Leavis and their followers. Bloom is the prophetic spokesman for the creative imagination in the modern age, reading literary history as an heroic battle of giants or mighty psychic drama, trusting to the 'will to expression' of the strong poet in his struggle for self-origination. Such doughty Romantic individualism is fiercely at odds with the sceptical, anti-humanist *ethos* of a deconstructive age, and indeed Bloom has defended the value of individual poetic 'voice' and genius against his Derridean colleagues (Hartman, de Man, Hillis Miller) at Yale. His hope is that he may snatch from the jaws of a deconstructive criticism he in some ways respects a Romantic humanism which will reinstate author, intention and the power of the imagination.

Such a humanism will wage war with the 'serene linguistic nihilism' which Bloom rightly discerns in much American deconstruction, turning from the mere endless undoing of determinate meaning to a vision of poetry as human will and affirmation. The strenuous, embattled, apocalyptic tone of much of his own writing, with its outlandish spawning of esoteric terms, is witness to the strain and desperateness of this enterprise. Bloom's criticism starkly exposes the dilemma of the modern liberal or Romantic humanist – the fact that on the one hand no reversion to a serene, optimistic human faith is possible after Marx, Freud and post-structuralism, but that on the other hand any humanism which like Bloom's has taken the agonizing pressures of such doctrines is bound to be fatally compromised and contaminated by them. Bloom's epical battles of poetic giants retain the psychic splendour of a pre-Freudian age, but have lost its innocence: they are domestic rows, scenes of guilt, envy, anxiety and aggression. No humanistic literary theory which overlooked such realities could offer itself as reputably 'modern' at all; but any such theory which takes them on board is bound to be sobered and soured by them to the point where its own capacity to affirm becomes almost maniacally wilful. Bloom advances far enough down the primrose path of American deconstruction to be able to scramble back to the heroically human only by a Nietzschean appeal to the 'will to power' and 'will to persuasion' of the individual imagination which is bound to remain arbitrary and gestural. In this exclusively patriarchal world of fathers and sons, everything comes to centre with increasing rhetorical stridency on power, struggle, strength of will; criticism itself for Bloom is just as much a form of poetry as poems are implicit literary criticism of other poems, and whether a critical reading 'succeeds' is in the end not at all a question of its truth-value but of the rhetorical force of the critic himself. It is humanism on the extreme edge, grounded in nothing but its own assertive faith, stranded between a discredited rationalism on the one hand and an intolerable scepticism on the other.

Watching his grandson playing in his pram one day, Freud observed him throwing a toy out of the pram and exclaiming *fort!* (gone away), then hauling it in again on a string to the cry of *da!* (here). This, the famous *fort-da* game, Freud interpreted in *Beyond the Pleasure Principle* (1920) as the infant's symbolic mastery of its mother's absence; but it can also be read as the first glimmerings of narrative. *Fort-da* is perhaps the shortest story we can imagine: an object is lost, and then recovered. But even the most complex narratives can be read as variants on this model: the pattern of classical narrative is that an original settlement is disrupted and ultimately restored. From this viewpoint, narrative is a source of consolation: lost objects are a cause of anxiety to us, symbolizing certain deeper unconscious losses (of birth, the faeces, the mother), and it is always pleasurable to find them put securely back in place. In Lacanian theory, it is an original lost object – the mother's body – which drives forward the narrative of our lives, impelling us to pursue substitutes for this lost paradise in the endless metonymic movement of desire. For Freud, it is a desire to scramble back to a place where we cannot be harmed, the inorganic existence which precedes all conscious life, which keeps us struggling forward: our restless attachments (Eros) are in thrall to the death drive (Thanatos). Something must be lost or absent in any narrative for it to unfold: if everything stayed in place there would be no story to tell. This loss is distressing, but exciting as well: desire is stimulated by what we cannot quite possess, and this is one source of narrative satisfaction. If we could *never* possess it, however, our excitation might become intolerable and turn into unpleasure; so we must know that the object will be finally restored to us, that Tom Jones will return to Paradise Hall and Hercule Poirot will track down the murderer. Our excitation is gratifyingly released: our energies have been cunningly 'bound' by the suspenses and repetitions of the narrative only as a preparation for their pleasurable expenditure.[7] We have been able to tolerate the disappearance of the object because our unsettling suspense was all the time shot through by the secret knowledge that it would finally come home. *Fort* has meaning only in relation to *da*.

But, of course, vice versa too. Once installed within the symbolic order, we cannot contemplate or possess any object without seeing it unconsciously in the light of its possible absence, knowing that its presence is in some way arbitrary and provisional. If the mother goes away then this is merely preparatory to her return, but when she is with us again we cannot forget the fact that she might always disappear, and perhaps always not return. Classical narrative of the realist kind is on the whole a 'conservative' form, which slides our anxiety at absence under the comforting sign of presence; many modernist texts, such as those of Brecht and Beckett, remind us that what we are seeing might always have happened differently, or not happened at all. If for psychoanalysis the prototype of all absence is castration – the little boy's fear that he will lose his sexual organ, the little girl's supposed disappointment that she has 'lost' hers – then such texts, post-structuralism would say, have accepted the reality of castration, the ineluctability of loss, absence and difference in human life. Reading them, we too are brought to encounter these realities – to prise ourselves loose from the 'imaginary', where loss and difference are unthinkable, and where it seemed that the world was made for us and we for the world. There is no death in the imaginary, since the world's continuing existence depends upon my life just as much as my life depends upon it; it is only by entering the symbolic order that we confront the truth that we can die, since the world's existence does not in fact depend upon us. As long as we remain in an imaginary realm of being we misrecognize our own identities, seeing them as fixed and rounded, and misrecognize reality as something immutable. We remain, in Althusser's terms, in the grip of ideology, conforming to social reality as 'natural' rather than critically questioning how it, and ourselves, came to be constructed, and so could possibly be transformed.

We have seen in our discussion of Roland Barthes how much literature conspires in its very forms to forestall such critical interrogation. Barthes's 'naturalized' sign is equivalent to Lacan's 'imaginary': in both cases an alienated personal identity is confirmed by a 'given', inevitable world. This is not to say that literature written in such a mode is necessarily conservative in what it *says*; but the radicalism of its statements may be undermined by the forms in which they are held. Raymond Williams has pointed to the interesting contradiction between the social radicalism of much naturalistic theatre (Shaw, for example) and the formal methods of such drama. The discourse of the play may be urging change, criticism, rebellion; but the dramatic forms – itemize the furniture and aim for an exact 'verisimilitude' – inevitably enforce upon us a sense of the unalterable solidity of this social world, all the way down to the colour of the maid's stockings.[8] For the drama to break with these ways of seeing, it would need to move beyond naturalism altogether into some more experimental mode – as indeed did the later Ibsen and Strindberg. Such transfigured forms might jolt the audience out of the reassurance of recognition – the self-security which springs from contemplating a world which is familiar. We can contrast Shaw in this respect with Bertolt Brecht, who uses certain dramatic techniques (the so-called 'estrangement effect') to render the most taken-for-granted aspects of social reality shockingly unfamiliar, and so to rouse the audience to a new critical awareness of them. Far from being concerned to reinforce the audience's sense of security, Brecht wants, as he says, to 'create contradictions within them' – to unsettle their convictions, dismantle and refashion their received identities, and expose the unity of this selfhood as an ideological illusion.

We can find another meeting-point of political and psychoanalytical theories in the work of the feminist philosopher Julia Kristeva. Kristeva's thinking is much influenced by Lacan; yet for any feminist such influence clearly poses a problem. For the symbolic order of which Lacan writes is in reality the patriarchal sexual and social order of modern class-society, structured around the 'transcendental signifier' of the phallus, dominated by the Law which the father embodies. There is no way, then, in which a feminist or pro-feminist may uncritically celebrate the symbolic order at the expense of the imaginary: on the contrary, the oppressiveness of the actual social and sexual relations of such a system is precisely the target of the feminist critique. In her book *La Révolution du langage poétique* (1974), Kristeva therefore opposes to the symbolic not so much the imaginary, as what she terms the 'semiotic'. She means by this a pattern or play of forces which we can detect inside language, and which represents a sort of residue of the pre-Oedipal phase. The child in the pre-Oedipal phase does not yet have access to language ('infant' means 'speechless'), but we can imagine its body as criss-crossed by a flow of 'pulsions' or drives which are at this point relatively unorganized. This rhythmic pattern can be seen as a form of language, though it is not yet meaningful. For language as such to happen, this heterogeneous flow must be as it were chopped up, articulated into stable terms, so that in entering the symbolic order this 'semiotic' process is repressed. The repression, however, is not total: for the semiotic can still be discerned as a kind of pulsional pressure within language itself, in tone, rhythm, the bodily and material qualities of language, but also in contradiction, meaninglessness, disruption, silence and absence. The semiotic is the 'other' of language which is none the less intimately entwined with it. Because it stems from the pre-Oedipal phase, it is bound up with the child's contact with the mother's body, whereas the symbolic, as we have seen, is associated with the Law of the father. The semiotic is thus closely connected with femininity: but is by no means a language exclusive to women, for it arises from a pre-Oedipal period which recognizes no distinctions of gender.

Kristeva looks to this 'language' of the semiotic as a means of undermining the symbolic order. In the writings of some of the French Symbolist poets and other avant-garde authors, the relatively secure meanings of 'ordinary' language are harassed and disrupted by this flow of signification, which presses the linguistic sign to its extreme limit, values its tonal, rhythmic and material properties, and sets up a play of unconscious drives in the text which threatens to split apart received social meanings. The semiotic is fluid and plural, a kind of pleasurable creative excess over precise meaning, and it takes sadistic delight in destroying or negating such signs. It is opposed to all fixed, transcendental significations; and since the ideologies of modern male-dominated class-society rely on such fixed signs for their power (God, father, state, order, property and so on), such literature becomes a kind of equivalent in the realm of language to revolution in the sphere of politics. The reader of such texts is equally disrupted or 'decentred' by this linguistic force, thrown into contradiction, unable to take up any one, simple 'subject-position' in relation to these polymorphous works. The semiotic throws into confusion all tight divisions between masculine and feminine – it is a 'bisexual' form of writing – and offers to deconstruct all the scrupulous binary oppositions – proper/improper, norm/deviation, sane/ mad, mine/yours, authority/obedience – by which societies such as ours survive.

The English-language writer who perhaps most strikingly exemplifies Kristeva's theories is James Joyce.[9] But aspects of it are also evident in the writings of Virginia Woolf, whose fluid, diffuse, sensuous style offers a resistance to the kind of male metaphysical world symbolized by the philosopher Mr Ramsay in *To the Lighthouse*. Ramsay's world works by abstract truths, sharp divisions and fixed essences: it is a patriarchal world, for the phallus is the symbol of sure, self-identical truth and is not to be challenged. Modern society, as the post-structuralists would say, is 'phallocentric'; it is also, as we have seen, 'logocentric', believing that its discourses can yield us immediate access to the full truth and presence of things. Jacques Derrida has conflated these two terms to the compound 'phallogocentric', which we might roughly translate as 'cocksure'. It is this cocksureness, by which those who wield sexual and social power maintain their grip, that Woolf's 'semiotic' fiction could be seen as challenging.

This raises the vexed question, much debated in feminist literary theory, as to whether there is a specifically feminine mode of writing. Kristeva's 'semiotic' is not, as we have seen, *inherently* feminine: indeed most of the 'revolutionary' writers she discusses are male. But because it is closely related to the mother's body, and because there are complex psychoanalytical reasons for holding that women retain a closer relationship to that body than men do, one might expect such writing to be on the whole more typical of women. Some feminists have sharply rejected this theory, fearing that it simply reinvents some 'female essence' of a non-cultural kind, and perhaps also suspecting that it may be no more than a high-falutin version of the sexist view that women babble. Neither of these beliefs is in my view necessarily implied by Kristeva's theory. It is important to see that the semiotic is not an *alternative* to the symbolic order, a language one could speak instead of 'normal' discourse: it is rather a process *within* our conventional sign-systems, which questions and transgresses their limits. In Lacanian theory, anyone who is unable to enter the symbolic order at all, to symbolize their experience through language, would become psychotic. One might see the semiotic as a kind of internal limit or borderline of the symbolic order; and in this sense the 'feminine' could equally be seen as existing on such a border. For the feminine is at once constructed within the symbolic order, like any gender, and yet is relegated to its margins, judged inferior to masculine power. The woman is both 'inside' and 'outside' male society, both a romantically idealized member of it and a victimized outcast. She is sometimes what stands between man and chaos, and sometimes the embodiment of chaos itself. This is why she troubles the neat categories of such a regime, blurring its well-defined boundaries. Women are represented within male-governed society, fixed by sign, image, meaning, yet because they are also the 'negative' of that social order there is always in them something which is left over, superfluous, unrepresentable, which refuses to be figured there.

On this view, the feminine – which is a mode of being and discourse not necessarily identical with women – signifies a force within society which opposes it. And this has its obvious political implications in the form of the women's movement. The political correlative of Kristeva's own theories – of a semiotic force which disrupts all stable meanings and institutions – would appear to be some kind of anarchism. If such an unending overthrow of all fixed structure is an inadequate response in the political realm, so too in the theoretical sphere is the assumption that a literary text which undermines meaning is *ipso facto* 'revolutionary'. It is quite possible for a text to do this in the name of some right-wing irrationalism, or to do it in the name of nothing much at all. Kristeva's argument is dangerously formalistic and easily caricaturable: will reading Mallarmé bring down the bourgeois state? She does not, of course, claim that it will; but she pays too little attention to the political *content* of a text, the historical conditions in which its overturn-ing of the signified is carried out, and the historical conditions in which all of this is interpreted and used. Nor is the dismantling of the unified subject a revolutionary gesture in itself. Kristeva rightly perceives that bourgeois individualism thrives on such a fetish, but her work tends to halt at the point where the subject has been fractured and thrown into contradiction. For Brecht, by contrast, the dismantling of our given identities through art is inseparable from the practice of producing a new kind of human subject altogether, which would need to know not only internal fragmentation but social solidarity, which would experience not only the gratifications of libid-inal language but the fulfilments of fighting political injustice. The implicit anarchism or libertarianism of Kristeva's suggestive theories is not the only kind of politics which follows from her recognition that women, and certain 'revolutionary' literary works, pose a radical question to existing society precisely because they mark out the frontier beyond which it dare not venture.

There is one simple and evident connection between psychoanalysis and literature which is worth touching on in conclusion. Rightly or wrongly, Freudian theory regards the fundamental motivation of all human behaviour as the avoidance of pain and the gaining of pleasure: it is a form of what is philosophically known as hedonism. The reason why the vast majority of people read poems, novels and plays is because they find them pleasurable. This fact is so obvious that it is hardly ever mentioned in universities. It is, admittedly, difficult to spend some years studying literature in most universities and still find it pleasurable at the end: many university literature courses seem to be constructed to prevent this from happening, and those who emerge still able to enjoy literary works might be considered either heroic or perverse. As we saw earlier in this book, the fact that reading literature is generally an enjoyable pursuit posed a serious problem for those who first established it as an academic 'discipline': it was necessary to make the whole affair rather more intimidating and dispiriting, if 'English' was to earn its keep as a reputable cousin of Classics. Meanwhile, in the world outside, people carried on devouring romances, thrillers and historical novels without the faintest idea that the halls of academia were beset by these anxieties.

It is a symptom of this curious situation that the word 'pleasure' has trivializing overtones; it is certainly a less serious word than 'serious'. To say that we find a poem intensely enjoyable seems somehow a less acceptable critical statement than to claim that we thought it morally profound. It is difficult not to feel that comedy is a more superficial business than tragedy. Between the Cambridge roundheads who speak dauntingly of 'moral seriousness', and the Oxford cavaliers who find George Eliot 'amusing', there seems little space for a more adequate theory of pleasure. But psychoanalysis is among other things precisely this: its bristling intellectual armoury is bent on the exploration of such fundamental matters as what people find gratifying and what they do not, how they can be relieved of their misery and made more happy. If Freudianism is a science, concerned with an impersonal analysis of psychical forces, it is a science committed to the emancipation of human beings from what frustrates their fulfilment and well-being. It is a theory at the service of a transformative practice, and to that extent has parallels with radical politics. It recognizes that pleasure and displeasure are extremely complex issues, unlike the kind of traditional literary critic for whom statements of personal liking or disliking are merely propositions of 'taste' which it is impossible to analyse any further. For such a critic, saying that you enjoyed the poem is the end-point of the argument; for another kind of critic, this may be precisely where the argument begins.

This is not to suggest that psychoanalysis alone can provide the key to problems of literary value and pleasure. We like or dislike certain pieces of language not only because of the unconscious play of drives they induce in us, but because of certain conscious commitments and predilections we share. There is a complex interaction between these two regions, which needs to be demonstrated in the detailed examination of a particular literary text.[10] The problems of literary value and pleasure would seem to lie somewhere at the juncture of psychoanalysis, linguistics and ideology, and little work has been done here as yet. We know enough, however, to suspect that it is a good deal more possible to say why someone enjoys certain arrangements of words than conventional literary criticism has believed.

More importantly, it is possible that by a fuller understanding of the pleasures and displeasures readers reap from literature, a modest but significant light may be cast on some rather more pressing problems of happiness and misery. One of the richest traditions to have emerged from Freud's own writings is one very far removed from the preoccupations of a Lacan: it is a form of political-psychoanalytical work engaged with the question of happiness as it affects whole societies. Prominent in this lineage has been the work of the German psychoanalyst Wilhelm Reich, and the writings of Herbert Marcuse and other members of the so-called Frankfurt school of social enquiry.[11] We live in a society which on the one hand pressurizes us into the pursuit of instant gratification, and on the other hand imposes on whole sectors of the population an endless deferment of fulfilment. The spheres of economic, political and cultural life become 'eroticized', thronged with seductive commodities and flashy images, while the sexual relationships between men and women grow diseased and disturbed. Aggression in such a society is not only a matter of sibling rivalry: it becomes the growing possibility of nuclear self-destruction, the death drive legitimated as a military strategy. The sadistic satisfactions of power are matched by the masochistic conformity of many of the powerless. In such a condition, Freud's title *The Psychopathology of Everyday Life* assumes a new, ominous meaning. One reason why we need to enquire into the dynamics of pleasure and unpleasure is because we need to know how much repression and deferred fulfilment a society is likely to tolerate; how it is that desire can be switched from ends that we would value to ends which trivialize and degrade it; how it comes about that men and women are sometimes prepared to suffer oppression and indignity, and at what points such submission is likely to fail. We can learn from psychoanalytical theory more about why most people prefer John Keats to Leigh Hunt; we can also learn more about the nature of a 'civilization which leaves so large a number of its participants unsatisfied and drives them into revolt, [. . .] neither has nor deserves the prospect of a lasting existence'.

Conclusion: Political Criticism

In the course of this book we have considered a number of problems of literary theory. But the most important question of all has as yet gone unanswered. What is the *point* of literary theory? Why bother with it in the first place? Are there not issues in the world more weighty than codes, signifiers and reading subjects?

Let us consider merely one such issue. As I write, it is estimated that the world contains over 60,000 nuclear warheads, many with a capacity a thousand times greater than the bomb which destroyed Hiroshima. The possibility that these weapons will be used in our lifetime is steadily growing. The approximate cost of these weapons is 500 billion dollars a year, or 1.3 billion dollars a day. Five per cent of this sum – 25 billion dollars – could drastically, fundamentally alleviate the problems of the poverty-stricken Third World. Anyone who believed that literary theory was more important than such matters would no doubt be considered somewhat eccentric, but perhaps only a little less eccentric than those who consider that the two topics might be somehow related. What has international politics to do with literary theory? Why this perverse insistence on dragging politics into the argument?

There is, in fact, no need to drag politics into literary theory: as with South African sport, it has been there from the beginning. I mean by the political no more than the way we organize our social life together, and the power-relations which this involves; and what I have tried to show throughout this book is that the history of modern literary theory is part of the political and ideological history of our epoch. From Percy Bysshe Shelley to Norman N. Holland, literary theory has been indissociably bound up with political beliefs and ideological values. Indeed literary theory is less an object of intellectual enquiry in its own right than a particular perspective in which to view the history of our times. Nor should this be in the least cause for surprise. For any body of theory concerned with human meaning, value, language, feeling and experience will inevitably engage with broader, deeper beliefs about the nature of human individuals and societies, problems of power and sexuality, interpretations of past history, versions of the present and hopes for the future. It is not a matter of *regretting* that this is so – of *blaming* literary theory for being caught up with such questions, as opposed to some 'pure' literary theory which might be absolved from them. Such 'pure' literary theory is an academic myth: some of the theories we have examined in this book are nowhere more clearly ideological than in their attempts to ignore history and politics altogether. Literary theories are not to be upbraided for being political, but for being on the whole covertly or unconsciously so – for the blindness with which they offer as a supposedly 'technical', 'self-evident', 'scientific' or 'universal' truth doctrines which with a little reflection can be seen to relate to and reinforce the particular interests of particular groups of people at particular times. The title of this section, 'Conclusion: Political Criticism', is not intended to mean: 'Finally, a political alternative'; it is intended to mean: 'The conclusion is that the literary theory we have examined is political.'

It is not only, however, a matter of such biases being covert or unconscious. Sometimes, as with Matthew Arnold, they are neither, and at other times, as with T. S. Eliot, they are certainly covert but not in the least unconscious. It is not the fact that literary theory is political which is objectionable, nor just the fact that its frequent obliviousness of this tends to mislead: what is really objectionable is the nature of its politics. That objection can be briefly summarized by stating that the great majority of the literary theories outlined in this book have strengthened rather than challenged the assumptions of the power-system some of whose present-day consequences I have just described. I do not mean by this that Matthew Arnold supported nuclear weapons, or that there are not a good many literary theorists who would not dissent in one way or another from a system in which some grow rich on profits from armaments while others starve in the street. I do not believe that many, perhaps most, literary theorists and critics are not disturbed by a world in which some economies, left stagnant and lopsided by generations of colonial exploitation, are still in fee to Western capitalism through their crippling repayments of debts, or that all literary theorists would genially endorse a society like our own, in which considerable private wealth remains concentrated in the hands of a tiny minority, while the human services of education, health, culture and recreation for the great majority are torn to shreds. It is just that they would not regard literary theory as at all relevant to such matters. My own view, as I have commented, is that literary theory has a most particular relevance to this political system: it has helped, wittingly or not, to sustain and reinforce its assumptions.

Literature, we are told, is vitally engaged with the living situations of men and women: it is concrete rather than abstract, displays life in all its rich variousness, and rejects barren conceptual enquiry for the feel and taste of what it is to be alive. The story of modern literary theory, paradoxically, is the narrative of a flight from such realities into a seemingly endless range of alternatives: the poem itself, the organic society, eternal verities, the imagination, the structure of the human mind, myth, language and so on. Such a flight from real history is in part understandable as a reaction to the antiquarian, historically reductionist criticism which held sway in the nineteenth century; but the extremism of this reaction has been nevertheless striking. It is indeed the *extremism* of literary theory, its obstinate, perverse, endlessly resourceful refusal to countenance social and historical realities, which most strikes a student of its documents, even though 'extremism' is a term more commonly used of those who would seek to call attention to literature's role in actual life. Even in the act of fleeing modern ideologies, however, literary theory reveals its often unconscious complicity with them, betraying its elitism, sexism or individualism in the very 'aesthetic' or 'unpolitical' language it finds natural to use of the literary text. It assumes, in the main, that at the centre of the world is the contemplative individual self, bowed over its book, striving to gain touch with experience, truth, reality, history or tradition. Other things matter too, of course – this individual is in personal relationship with others, and we are always much more than readers – but it is notable how often such individual consciousness, set in its small circle of relationships, ends up as the touchstone of all else. The further we move from the rich inwardness of the personal life, of which literature is the supreme exemplar, the more drab, mechanical and impersonal existence becomes. It is a view equivalent in the literary sphere to what has been called possessive individualism in the social realm, much as the former attitude may shudder at the latter: it reflects the values of a political system which subordinates the sociality of human life to solitary individual enterprise.

I began this book by arguing that literature did not exist. How in that case can literary theory exist either? There are two familiar ways in which any theory can provide itself with a distinct purpose and identity. Either it can

define itself in terms of its particular *methods* of enquiry; or it can define itself
in terms of the particular *object* that is being enquired into. Any attempt to
define literary theory in terms of a distinctive method is doomed to failure.
Literary theory is supposed to reflect on the nature of literature and literary
criticism. But just think of how many methods are involved in literary
criticism. You can discuss the poet's asthmatic childhood, or examine her
peculiar use of syntax; you can detect the rustling of silk in the hissing of
the *s*'s, explore the phenomenology of reading, relate the literary work to
the state of the class-struggle or find out how many copies it sold. These
methods have nothing whatsoever of significance in common. In fact
they have more in common with other 'disciplines' – linguistics, history,
sociology and so on – than they have with each other. Methodologically
speaking, literary criticism is a non-subject. If literary theory is a kind of
'metacriticism', a critical reflection on criticism, then it follows that it too is
a non-subject.

Perhaps, then, the unity of literary studies is to be sought elsewhere.
Perhaps literary criticism and literary theory just mean any kind of talk (of
a certain level of 'competence', clearly enough) about an object named
literature. Perhaps it is the object, not the method, which distinguishes and
delimits the discourse. As long as that object remains relatively stable, we
can move equably from biographical to mythological to semiotic methods
and still know where we are. But as I argued in the Introduction, literature
has no such stability. The unity of the object is as illusory as the unity of the
method. 'Literature', as Roland Barthes once remarked, 'is what gets
taught.'

Maybe this lack of methodological unity in literary studies should not
worry us unduly. After all, it would be a rash person who would define
geography or philosophy, distinguish neatly between sociology and anthropology or advance a snap definition of 'history'. Perhaps we should celebrate
the plurality of critical methods, adopt a tolerantly ecumenical posture and
rejoice in our freedom from the tyranny of any single procedure. Before we
become too euphoric, however, we should notice that there are certain
problems here too. For one thing, not all of these methods are mutually
compatible. However generously liberal-minded we aim to be, trying to
combine structuralism, phenomenology and psychoanalysis is more likely to
lead to a nervous breakdown than to a brilliant literary career. Those critics
who parade their pluralism are usually able to do so because the different
methods they have in mind are not all that different in the end. For another
thing, some of these 'methods' are hardly methods at all. Many literary
critics dislike the whole idea of method and prefer to work by glimmers and

hunches, intuitions and sudden perceptions. It is perhaps fortunate that this way of proceeding has not yet infiltrated medicine or aeronautical engineering; but even so one should not take this modest disowning of method altogether seriously, since what glimmers and hunches you have will depend on a latent structure of assumptions often quite as stubborn as that of any structuralist. It is notable that such 'intuitive' criticism, which relies not on 'method' but on 'intelligent sensitivity', does not often seem to intuit, say, the presence of ideological values in literature. Yet there is no reason, on its own reckoning, why it should not. Some traditional critics would appear to hold that other people subscribe to theories while they prefer to read literature 'straightforwardly'. No theoretical or ideological predilections, in other words, mediate between themselves and the text: to describe George Eliot's later world as one of 'mature resignation' is not ideological, whereas to claim that it reveals evasion and compromise is. It is therefore difficult to engage such critics in debate about ideological preconceptions, since the power of ideology over them is nowhere more marked than in their honest belief that their readings are 'innocent'. It was Leavis who was being 'doctrinal' in attacking Milton, not C. S. Lewis in defending him; it is feminist critics who insist on confusing literature with politics by examining fictional images of gender, not conventional critics who are being political by arguing that Richardson's Clarissa is largely responsible for her own rape.

Even so, the fact that some critical methods are less methodical than others proves something of an embarrassment to the pluralists who believe that there is a little truth in everything. (This theoretical pluralism also has its political correlative: seeking to understand everybody's point of view quite often suggests that you yourself are disinterestedly up on high or in the middle, and trying to resolve conflicting viewpoints into a consensus implies a refusal of the truth that some conflicts can be resolved on one side alone.) Literary criticism is rather like a laboratory in which some of the staff are seated in white coats at control panels, while others are throwing sticks in the air or spinning coins. Genteel amateurs jostle with hard-nosed professionals, and after a century or so of 'English' they have still not decided to which camp the subject really belongs. This dilemma is the product of the peculiar history of English, and it cannot really be settled because what is at stake is much more than a mere conflict over methods or the lack of them. The true reason why the pluralists are wishful thinkers is that what is at issue in the contention between different literary theories or 'non-theories' are competing ideological strategies related to the very destiny of English studies in modern society. The problem with literary theory is that it can neither beat nor join the dominant ideologies of late industrial capitalism. Liberal humanism seeks to oppose or at least modify such ideologies with its distaste for the technocratic and its nurturing of spiritual wholeness in a hostile world; certain brands of formalism and structuralism try to take over the technocratic rationality of such a society and thus incorporate themselves into it. Northrop Frye and the New Critics thought that they had pulled off a synthesis of the two, but how many students of literature today read them? Liberal humanism has dwindled to the impotent conscience of bourgeois society, gentle, sensitive and ineffectual; structuralism has already more or less vanished into the literary museum.

The impotence of liberal humanism is a symptom of its essentially contradictory relationship to modern capitalism. For although it forms part of the 'official' ideology of such society, and the 'humanities' exist to reproduce it, the social order within which it exists has in one sense very little time for it at all. Who is concerned with the uniqueness of the individual, the imperishable truths of the human condition or the sensuous textures of lived experience in the Foreign Office or the boardroom of Standard Oil? Capitalism's reverential hat-tipping to the arts is obvious hypocrisy, except when it can hang them on its walls as a sound investment. Yet capitalist states have continued to direct funds into higher education humanities departments, and though such departments are usually the first in line for savage cutting when capitalism enters on one of its periodic crises, it is doubtful that it is only hypocrisy, a fear of appearing in its true philistine colours, which compels this grudging support. The truth is that liberal humanism is at once largely ineffectual, and the best ideology of the 'human' that present bourgeois society can muster. The 'unique individual' is indeed important when it comes to defending the business entrepreneur's right to make profit while throwing men and women out of work; the individual must at all costs have the 'right to choose', provided this means the right to buy one's child an expensive private education while other children are deprived of their school meals, rather than the rights of women to decide whether to have children in the first place. The 'imperishable truths of the human condition' include such verities as freedom and democracy, the essences of which are embodied in our particular way of life. The 'sensuous textures of lived experience' can be roughly translated as reacting from the gut – judging according to habit, prejudice and 'common sense', rather than according to some inconvenient, 'aridly theoretical' set of debatable ideas. There is, after all, room for the humanities yet, much as those who guarantee our freedom and democracy despise them.

Departments of literature in higher education, then, are part of the ideological apparatus of the modern capitalist state. They are not wholly reliable apparatuses, since for one thing the humanities contain many values, meanings and traditions which are antithetical to that state's social priorities, which are rich in kinds of wisdom and experience beyond its comprehension. For another thing, if you allow a lot of young people to do nothing for a few years but read books and talk to each other then it is possible that, given certain wider historical circumstances, they will not only begin to question some of the values transmitted to them but begin to interrogate the authority by which they are transmitted. There is of course no harm in students questioning the values conveyed to them: indeed it is part of the very meaning of higher education that they should do so. Independent thought, critical dissent and reasoned dialectic are part of the very stuff of a humane education; hardly anyone, as I commented earlier, will demand that your essay on Chaucer or Baudelaire arrives inexorably at certain pre-set conclusions. All that is being demanded is that you manipulate a particular language in acceptable ways. Becoming certificated by the state as proficient in literary studies is a matter of being able to talk and write in certain ways. It is this which is being taught, examined and certificated, not what you personally think or believe, though what is thinkable will of course be constrained by the language itself. You can think or believe what you want, as long as you can speak this particular language. Nobody is especially concerned about what you say, with what extreme, moderate, radical or conservative positions you adopt, provided that they are compatible with, and can be articulated within, a specific form of discourse. It is just that certain meanings and positions will not be articulable within it. Literary studies, in other words, are a question of the signifier, not of the signified. Those employed to teach you this form of discourse will remember whether or not you were able to speak it proficiently long after they have forgotten what you said.

Literary theorists, critics and teachers, then, are not so much purveyors of doctrine as custodians of a discourse. Their task is to preserve this discourse, extend and elaborate it as necessary, defend it from other forms of discourse, initiate newcomers into it and determine whether or not they have successfully mastered it. The discourse itself has no definite signified, which is not to say that it embodies no assumptions: it is rather a network of signifiers able to envelop a whole field of meanings, objects and practices. Certain pieces of writing are selected as being more amenable to this discourse than others, and these are what is known as literature or the 'literary canon'. The fact that this canon is usually regarded as fairly fixed, even at times as eternal and immutable, is in a sense ironic, because since literary critical discourse has no definite signified it can, if it wants to, turn its attention to more or less any kind of writing. Some of those hottest in their defence of the canon have from time to time demonstrated how the discourse can be made to operate on 'non-literary' writing. This, indeed, is the embarrassment of literary criticism, that it defines for itself a special object, literature, while existing as a set of discursive techniques which have no reason to stop short at that object at all. If you have nothing better to do at a party you can always try on a literary critical analysis of it, speak of its styles and genres, discriminate its significant nuances or formalize its sign-systems. Such a 'text' can prove quite as rich as one of the canonical works, and critical dissections of it quite as ingenious as those of Shakespeare. So either literary criticism confesses that it can handle parties just as well as it can Shakespeare, in which case it is in danger of losing its identity along with its object; or it agrees that parties may be interestingly analysed provided that this is called something else: ethnomethodology or hermeneutical phenomenology, perhaps. Its own concern is with literature, because literature is more valuable and rewarding than any of the other texts on which the critical discourse might operate. The disadvantage of this claim is that it is plainly untrue: many films and works of philosophy are considerably more valuable than much that is included in the 'literary canon'. It is not that they are valuable in different ways: they could present objects of value in the sense that criticism defines that term. Their exclusion from what is studied is not because they are not 'amenable' to the discourse: it is a question of the arbitrary authority of the literary institution.

Another reason why literary criticism cannot justify its self-limiting to certain works by an appeal to their 'value' is that criticism is part of a literary institution which constitutes these works as valuable in the first place. It is not only parties that need to be *made* into worthwhile literary objects by being treated in specific ways, but also Shakespeare. Shakespeare was not great literature lying conveniently to hand, which the literary institution then happily discovered: he is great literature because the institution constitutes him as such. This does not mean that he is not 'really' great literature – that it is just a matter of people's opinions about him – because there is no such thing as literature which is 'really' great, or 'really' anything, independently of the ways in which that writing is treated within specific forms of social and institutional life. There are an indefinite number of ways of discussing Shakespeare, but not all of them count as literary critical. Perhaps Shakespeare himself, his friends and actors, did not talk about his plays in ways which we would regard as literary critical. Perhaps some of the most interesting statements which could be made about Shakespearian drama would also not count as belonging to literary criticism. Literary criticism selects, processes, corrects and rewrites texts in accordance with certain institutionalized norms of the 'literary' – norms which are at any given time arguable, and always historically variable. For though I have said that critical discourse has no determinate signified, there are certainly a great many ways of talking about literature which it excludes, and a great many discursive moves and strategies which it disqualifies as invalid, illicit, non-critical, nonsense. Its apparent generosity at the level of the signified is matched only by its sectarian intolerance at the level of the signifier. Regional dialects of the discourse, so to speak, are acknowledged and sometimes tolerated, but you must not sound as though you are speaking another language altogether. To do so is to recognize in the sharpest way that critical discourse is power. To be on the inside of the discourse itself is to be blind to this power, for what is more natural and non-dominative than to speak one's own tongue?

The power of critical discourse moves on several levels. It is the power of 'policing' language – of determining that certain statements must be excluded because they do not conform to what is acceptably sayable. It is the power of policing writing itself, classifying it into the 'literary' and 'non-literary', the enduringly great and the ephemerally popular. It is the power of authority *vis-à-vis* others – the power-relations between those who define and preserve the discourse, and those who are selectively admitted to it. It is the power of certificating or non-certificating those who have been judged to speak the discourse better or worse. Finally, it is a question of the power-relations between the literary-academic institution, where all of this occurs, and the ruling power-interests of society at large, whose ideological needs will be served and whose personnel will be reproduced by the preservation and controlled extension of the discourse in question.

I have argued that the theoretically limitless extendibility of critical discourse, the fact that it is only arbitrarily confined to 'literature', is or should be a source of embarrassment to the custodians of the canon. The objects of criticism, like those of the Freudian drive, are in a certain sense contingent and replaceable. Ironically, criticism only really became aware of this fact when, sensing that its own liberal humanism was running out of steam, it turned for aid to more ambitious or rigorous critical methods. It thought that by adding a judicious pinch of historical analysis here or swallowing a non-addictive dose of structuralism there, it could exploit these otherwise alien approaches to eke out its own dwindling spiritual capital. The boot, however, might well prove to be on the other foot. For you cannot engage in an historical analysis of literature without recognizing that literature itself is a recent historical invention; you cannot apply structuralist tools to *Paradise*

Lost without acknowledging that just the same tools can be applied to the *Daily Mirror*. Criticism can thus prop itself up only at the risk of losing its defining object; it has the unenviable choice of stifling or suffocating. If literary theory presses its own implications too far, then it has argued itself out of existence.

This, I would suggest, is the best possible thing for it to do. The final logical move in a process which began by recognizing that literature is an illusion is to recognize that literary theory is an illusion too. It is not of course an illusion in the sense that I have invented the various people I have discussed in this book: Northrop Frye really did exist, and so did F. R. Leavis. It is an illusion first in the sense that literary theory, as I hope to have shown, is really no more than a branch of social ideologies, utterly without any unity or identity which would adequately distinguish it from philosophy, linguistics, psychology, cultural and sociological thought; and secondly in the sense that the one hope it has of distinguishing itself – clinging to an object named literature – is misplaced. We must conclude, then, that this book is less an introduction than an obituary, and that we have ended by burying the object we sought to unearth.

My intention, in other words, is not to counter the literary theories I have critically examined in this book with a literary theory of my own, which would claim to be more politically acceptable. Any reader who has been expectantly waiting for a Marxist theory has obviously not been reading this book with due attention. There are indeed Marxist and feminist theories of literature, which in my opinion are more valuable than any of the theories discussed here, and to which the reader may like to refer in the bibliography. But this is not exactly the point. The point is whether it is possible to speak of 'literary theory' without perpetuating the illusion that literature exists as a distinct, bounded object of knowledge, or whether it is not preferable to draw the practical consequences of the fact that literary theory can handle Bob Dylan just as well as John Milton. My own view is that it is most useful to see 'literature' as a name which people give from time to time for different reasons to certain kinds of writing within a whole field of what Michel Foucault has called 'discursive practices', and the if anything is to be an object of study it is this whole field of practices rather than just those sometimes rather obscurely labelled 'literature'. I am countering the theories set out in this book not with a *literary* theory, but with a different kind of discourse – whether one calls it of 'culture', 'signifying practices' or whatever is not of first importance – which would include the objects ('literature') with which these other theories deal, but which would transform them by setting them in a wider context.

But is this not to extend the boundaries of literary theory to a point where any kind of particularity is lost? Would not a 'theory of discourse' run into just the same problems of methodology and object of study which we have seen in the case of literary studies? After all, there are any number of discourses and any number of ways of studying them. What would be specific to the kind of study I have in mind, however, would be its concern for the kinds of *effects* which discourses produce, and how they produce them. Reading a zoology textbook to find out about giraffes is part of studying zoology, but reading it to see how its discourse is structured and organized, and examining what kind of effects these forms and devices produce in particular readers in actual situations, is a different kind of project. It is, in fact, probably the oldest form of 'literary criticism' in the world, known as rhetoric. Rhetoric, which was the received form of critical analysis all the way from ancient society to the eighteenth century, examined the way discourses are constructed in order to achieve certain effects. It was not worried about whether its objects of enquiry were speaking or writing, poetry or philosophy, fiction or historiography: its horizon was nothing less than the field of discursive practices in society as a whole, and its particular interest lay in grasping such practices as forms of power and performance. This is not to say that it ignored the truth-value of the discourses in question, since this could often be crucially relevant to the kinds of effect they produced in their readers and listeners. Rhetoric in its major phase was neither a 'humanism', concerned in some intuitive way with people's experience of language, nor a 'formalism', preoccupied simply with analysing linguistic devices. It looked at such devices in terms of concrete performance – they were means of pleading, persuading, inciting and so on – and at people's responses to discourse in terms of linguistic structures and the material situations in which they functioned. It saw speaking and writing not merely as textual objects, to be aesthetically contemplated or endlessly deconstructed, but as forms of *activity* inseparable from the wider social relations between writers and readers, orators and audiences, and as largely unintelligible outside the social purposes and conditions in which they were embedded.[1]

Like all the best radical positions, then, mine is a thoroughly traditionalist one. I wish to recall literary criticism from certain fashionable, new-fangled ways of thinking it has been seduced by – 'literature' as a specially privileged object, the 'aesthetic' as separable from social determinants, and so on – and return it to the ancient paths which it has abandoned. Although my case is thus reactionary, I do not mean that we should revive the whole range of ancient rhetorical terms and substitute these for modern critical language.

We do not need to do this, since there are enough concepts contained in the literary theories examined in this book to allow us at least to make a start. Rhetoric, or discourse theory, shares with Formalism, structuralism and semiotics an interest in the formal devices of language, but like reception theory is also concerned with how these devices are actually effective at the point of 'consumption'; its preoccupation with discourse as a form of power and desire can learn much from deconstruction and psychoanalytical theory, and its belief that discourse can be a humanly transformative affair shares a good deal with liberal humanism. The fact that 'literary theory' is an illusion does not mean that we cannot retrieve from it many valuable concepts for a different kind of discursive practice altogether.

There was, of course, a reason why rhetoric bothered to analyse discourses. It did not analyse them just because they were there, any more than most forms of literary criticism today examine literature just for the sake of it. Rhetoric wanted to find out the most effective ways of pleading, persuading and debating, and rhetoricians studied such devices in other people's language in order to use them more productively in their own. It was, as we would say today, a 'creative' as well as a 'critical' activity: the word 'rhetoric' covers both the practice of effective discourse and the science of it. Similarly, there must be a reason why we would consider it worthwhile to develop a form of study which would look at the various sign-systems and signifying practices in our own society, all the way from *Moby Dick* to the Muppet show, from Dryden and Jean-Luc Godard to the portrayal of women in advertisements and the rhetorical techniques of government reports. All theory and knowledge, as I have argued previously, is 'interested', in the sense that you can always ask why one should bother to develop it in the first place. One striking weakness of most formalist and structuralist criticism is that it is unable to answer this question. The structuralist really does examine sign-systems because they happen to be there, or if this seems indefensible is forced into some rationale – studying our modes of sense-making will deepen our critical self-awareness – which is not much different from the standard line of the liberal humanists. The strength of the liberal humanist case, by contrast, is that it is able to say why dealing with literature is worth while. Its answer, as we have seen, is roughly that it makes you a better person. This is also the weakness of the liberal humanist case.

The liberal humanist response, however, is not weak because it believes that literature can be transformative. It is weak because it usually grossly overestimates this transformative power, considers it in isolation from any determining social context, and can formulate what it means by a 'better person' only in the most narrow and abstract of terms. They are terms which generally ignore the fact that to be a person in the Western society of the late twentieth century is to be bound up with, and in some sense responsible for, the kinds of political conditions which I began this Conclusion by outlining. Liberal humanism is a suburban moral ideology, limited in practice to largely interpersonal matters. It is stronger on adultery than on armaments, and its valuable concern with freedom, democracy and individual rights are simply not concrete enough. Its view of democracy, for example, is the abstract one of the ballot box, rather than a specific, living and practical democracy which might also somehow concern the operations of the Foreign Office and Standard Oil. Its view of individual freedom is similarly abstract: the freedom of any particular individual is crippled and parasitic as long as it depends on the futile labour and active oppression of others. Literature may protest against such conditions or it may not, but it is only possible in the first place because of them. As the German critic Walter Benjamin put it: 'There is no cultural document that is not at the same time a record of barbarism.'[2] Socialists are those who wish to draw the full, concrete, practical applications of the abstract notions of freedom and democracy to which liberal humanism subscribes, taking them at their word when they draw attention to the 'vividly particular'. It is for this reason that many Western socialists are restless with the liberal humanist opinion of the tyrannies in Eastern Europe, feeling that these opinions simply do not go far enough: what would be necessary to bring down such tyrannies would not be just more free speech, but a workers' revolution against the state.

What it means to be a 'better person', then, must be concrete and practical – that is to say, concerned with people's political situations as a whole – rather than narrowly abstract, concerned only with the immediate interpersonal relations which can be abstracted from this concrete whole. It must be a question of political and not only of 'moral' argument: that is to say, it must be *genuine* moral argument, which sees the relations between individual qualities and values and our whole material conditions of existence. Political argument is not an alternative to moral preoccupations: it is those preoccupations taken seriously in their full implications. But the liberal humanists are right to see that there is a *point* in studying literature, and that this point is not itself, in the end, a literary one. What they are arguing, although this way of putting it would grate harshly on their ears, is that literature has a *use*. Few words are more offensive to literary ears than 'use', evoking as it does paperclips and hair-dryers. The Romantic opposition to the utilitarian ideology of capitalism has made 'use' an unusable word: for the aesthetes, the glory of art is its utter uselessness. Yet few of us nowadays would be prepared to subscribe to *that*: every reading of a work is surely in some sense a use of it. We may not use *Moby Dick* to learn how to hunt whales, but we 'get something out of it' even so. Every literary theory presupposes a certain use of literature, even if what you get out of it is its utter uselessness. Liberal humanist criticism is not wrong to use literature, but wrong to deceive itself that it does not. It uses it to further certain moral values, which as I hope to have shown are in fact indissociable from certain ideological ones, and in the end imply a particular form of politics. It is not that it reads the texts 'disinterestedly' and then places what it has read in the service of its values: the values govern the actual reading process itself, inform what sense criticism makes of the works it studies. I am not going to argue, then, for a 'political criticism' which would read literary texts in the light of certain values which are related to political beliefs and actions; all criticism does this. The idea that there are 'non-political' forms of criticism is simply a myth which furthers certain political uses of literature all the more effectively. The difference between a 'political' and 'non-political' criticism is just the difference between the prime minister and the monarch: the latter furthers certain political ends by pretending not to, while the former makes no bones about it. It is always better to be honest in these matters. The difference between a conventional critic who speaks of the 'chaos of experience' in Conrad or Woolf, and the feminist who examines those writers' images of gender, is not a distinction between non-political and political criticism. It is a distinction between different forms of politics – between those who subscribe to the doctrine that history, society and human reality as a whole are fragmentary, arbitrary and directionless, and those who have other interests which imply alternative views about the way the world is. There is no way of settling the question of which politics is preferable in literary critical terms. You simply have to argue about politics. It is not a question of debating whether 'literature' should be related to 'history' or not: it is a question of different readings of history itself.

The feminist critic is not studying representations of gender simply because she believes that this will further her political ends. She also believes that gender and sexuality are central themes in literature and other sorts of discourse, and that any critical account which suppresses them is seriously defective. Similarly, the socialist critic does not see literature in terms of ideology or class-struggle because these happen to be his or her political interests, arbitrarily projected on to literary works. He or she would hold that such matters are the very stuff of history, and that in so far as literature is an historical phenomenon, they are the very stuff of literature too. What would be strange would be if the feminist or socialist critic thought analysing questions of gender or class was merely a matter of academic interest –

merely a question of achieving a more satisfyingly complete account of literature. For why should it be worth doing this? Liberal humanist critics are not merely out for a more complete account of literature: they wish to discuss literature in ways which will deepen, enrich and extend our lives. Socialist and feminist critics are quite at one with them on this: it is just that they wish to point out that such deepening and enriching entails the transformation of a society divided by class and gender. They would like the liberal humanist to draw the full implications of his or her position. If the liberal humanist disagrees, then this is a political argument, not an argument about whether one is 'using' literature or not.

I argued earlier that any attempt to define the study of literature in terms of either its method or its object is bound to fail. But we have now begun to discuss another way of conceiving what distinguishes one kind of discourse from another, which is neither ontological or methodological but *strategic*. This means asking first not *what* the object is or *how* we should approach it, but *why* we should want to engage with it in the first place. The liberal humanist response to this question, I have suggested, is at once perfectly reasonable and, as it stands, entirely useless. Let us try to concretize it a little by asking how the reinvention of rhetoric that I have proposed (though it might equally as well be called 'discourse theory' or 'cultural studies' or whatever) might contribute to making us all better people. Discourses, signsystems and signifying practices of all kinds, from film and television to fiction and the languages of natural science, produce effects, shape forms of consciousness and unconsciousness, which are closely related to the maintenance or transformation of our existing systems of power. They are thus closely related to what it means to be a person. Indeed 'ideology' can be taken to indicate no more than this connection – the link or nexus between discourses and power. Once we have seen this, then the questions of theory and method may be allowed to appear in a new light. It is not a matter of starting from certain theoretical or methodological problems: it is a matter of starting from what we want to *do*, and then seeing which methods and theories will best help us to achieve these ends. Deciding on your strategy will not predetermine which methods and objects of study are most valuable. As far as the object of study goes, what you decide to examine depends very much on the practical situation. It may seem best to look at Proust and *King Lear*, or at children's television programmes or popular romances or avant-garde films. A radical critic is quite liberal on these questions: he rejects the dogmatism which would insist that Proust is always more worthy of study than television advertisements. It all depends on what you are trying to do, in what situation. Radical critics are also open-minded about questions of theory and method: they tend to be pluralists in this respect. Any method or theory which will contribute to the strategic goal of human emancipation, the production of 'better people' through the socialist transformation of society, is acceptable. Structuralism, semiotics, psychoanalysis, deconstruction, reception theory and so on: all of these approaches, and others, have their valuable insights which may be put to use. Not all literary theories, however, are likely to prove amenable to the strategic goals in question: there are several examined in this book which seem to me highly unlikely to do so. What you choose and reject theoretically, then, depends upon what you are practically trying to do. This has always been the case with literary criticism: it is simply that it is often very reluctant to realize the fact. In any academic study we select the objects and methods of procedure which we believe the most important, and our assessment of their importance is governed by frames of interest deeply rooted in our practical forms of social life. Radical critics are no different in this respect: it is just that they have a set of social priorities with which most people at present tend to disagree. This is why they are commonly dismissed as 'ideological', because 'ideology' is always a way of describing other people's interests rather than one's own.

No theory or method, in any case, will have merely one strategic use. They can be mobilized in a variety of different strategies for a variety of ends. But not all methods will be equally amenable to particular ends. It is a matter of finding out, not of assuming from the start that a single method or theory will do. One reason why I have not ended this book with an account of socialist or feminist literary theory is that I believe such a move might encourage the reader to make what the philosophers call a 'category mistake'. It might mislead people into thinking that 'political criticism' was another sort of critical approach from those I have discussed, different in its assumptions but essentially the same kind of thing. Since I have made clear my view that all criticism is in some sense political, and since people tend to give the word 'political' to criticism whose politics disagrees with their own, this cannot be so. Socialist and feminist criticism are, of course, concerned with developing theories and methods appropriate to their aims: they consider questions of the relations between writing and sexuality, or of text and ideology, as other theories in general do not. They will also want to claim that these theories are more powerfully explanatory than others, for if they were not there would be no point in advancing them as theories. But it would be a mistake to see the particularity of such forms of criticism as consisting in the offering of alternative theories of methods. These forms of criticism differ from others because they define the object of analysis differently, have different values, beliefs and goals, and thus offer different kinds of strategy for the realizing of these goals.

I say 'goals', because it should not be thought that this form of criticism has only one. There are many goals to be achieved, and many ways of achieving them. In some situations the most productive procedure may be to explore how the signifying systems of a 'literary' text produce certain ideological effects; or it may be a matter of doing the same with a Hollywood film. Such projects may prove particularly important in teaching cultural studies to children; but it may also be valuable to use literature to foster in them a sense of linguistic potential denied to them by their social conditions. There are 'utopian' uses of literature of this kind, and a rich tradition of such utopian thought which should not be airily dismissed as 'idealist'. The active enjoyment of cultural artefacts should not, however, be relegated to the primary school, leaving older students with the grimmer business of analysis. Pleasure, enjoyment, the potentially transformative effects of discourse is quite as 'proper' a topic for 'higher' study as is the setting of puritan tracts in the discursive formations of the seventeenth century. On other occasions what might prove more useful will not be the criticism or enjoyment of other people's discourse but the production of one's own. Here, as with the rhetorical tradition, studying what other people have done may help. You may want to stage your own signifying practices to enrich, combat, modify or transform the effects which others' practices produce.

Within all of this varied activity, the study of what is currently termed 'literature' will have its place. But it should not be taken as an *a priori* assumption that what is currently termed 'literature' will always and everywhere be the most important focus of attention. Such dogmatism has no place in the field of cultural study. Nor are the texts now dubbed 'literature' likely to be perceived and defined as they are now, once they are returned to the broader and deeper discursive formations of which they are part. They will be inevitably 'rewritten', recycled, put to different uses, inserted into different relations and practices. They always have been, of course; but one effect of the word 'literature' is to prevent us from recognizing this fact.

Such a strategy obviously has far-reaching institutional implications. It would mean, for example, that departments of literature as we presently know them in higher education would cease to exist. Since the government, as I write, seems on the point of achieving this end more quickly and effectively than I could myself, it is necessary to add that the first political priority for those who have doubts about the ideological implications of such departmental organizations is to defend them unconditionally against government assaults. But this priority cannot mean refusing to contemplate how we might better organize literary studies in the longer term. The ideological effects of such departments lie not only in the particular values they disseminate, but in their implicit and actual dislocation of 'literature' from other cultural and social practices. The churlish admission of such practices as literary 'background' need not detain us: 'background', with its static, distancing connotations, tells its own story. Whatever would in the long term replace such departments – and the proposal is a modest one, for such experiments are already under way in certain areas of higher education – would centrally involve education in the various theories and methods of cultural analysis. The fact that such education is not routinely provided by many existing departments of literature, or is provided 'optionally' or marginally, is one of their most scandalous and farcical features. (Perhaps their other most scandalous and farcical feature is the largely wasted energy which postgraduate students are required to pour into obscure, often spurious research topics in order to produce dissertations which are frequently no more than sterile academic exercises, and which few others will ever read.) The genteel amateurism which regards criticism as some spontaneous sixth sense has not only thrown many students of literature into understandable confusion for many decades, but serves to consolidate the authority of those in power. If criticism is no more than a knack, like being able to whistle and hum different tunes simultaneously, then it is at once rare enough to be preserved in the hands of an elite, while 'ordinary' enough to require no stringent theoretical justification. Exactly the same pincer movement is at work in English 'ordinary language' philosophy. But the answer is not to replace such dishevelled amateurism with a well-groomed professionalism intent on justifying itself to the disgusted taxpayer. Such professionalism, as we have seen, is equally bereft of any social validation of its activities, since it cannot say why it should bother with literature at all other than to tidy it up, drop texts into their appropriate categories and then move over into marine biology. If the point of criticism is not to interpret literary works but to master in some disinterested spirit the underlying sign-systems which generate them, what is criticism to do once it has achieved this mastery, which will hardly take a lifetime and probably not much more than a few years?

The present crisis in the field of literary studies is at root a crisis in the definition of the subject itself. That it should prove difficult to provide such a definition is, as I hope to have shown in this book, hardly surprising. Nobody is likely to be dismissed from an academic job for trying on a little semiotic analysis of Edmund Spenser; they are likely to be shown the door, or refused entry through it in the first place, if they question whether the 'tradition' from Spenser to Shakespeare and Milton is the best or only way of carving up discourse into a syllabus. It is at this point that the canon is trundled out to blast offenders out of the literary arena.

Those who work in the field of cultural practices are unlikely to mistake their activity as utterly central. Men and women do not live by culture alone, the vast majority of them throughout history have been deprived of the chance of living by it at all, and those few who are fortunate enough to live by it now are able to do so because of the labour of those who do not. Any cultural or critical theory which does not begin from this single most important fact, and hold it steadily in mind in its activities, is in my view unlikely to be worth very much. There is no document of culture which is not also a record of barbarism. But even in societies which, like our own as Marx reminded us, have no time for culture, there are times and places when it suddenly becomes newly relevant, charged with a significance beyond itself. Four such major moments are evident in our own world. Culture, in the lives of nations struggling for their independence from imperialism, has a meaning quite remote from the review pages of the Sunday newspapers. Imperialism is not only the exploitation of cheap labour-power, raw materials and easy markets but the uprooting of languages and customs – not just the imposition of foreign armies, but of alien ways of experiencing. It manifests itself not only in company balance-sheets and in airbases, but can be tracked to the most intimate roots of speech and signification. In such situations, which are not all a thousand miles from our own doorstep, culture is so vitally bound up with one's common identity that there is no need to argue for its relation to political struggle. It is arguing against it which would seem incomprehensible.

The second area where cultural and political action have become closely united is in the women's movement. It is in the nature of feminist politics that signs and images, written and dramatized experience, should be of especial significance. Discourse in all its forms is an obvious concern for feminists, either as places where women's oppression can be deciphered, or as places where it can be challenged. In any politics which puts identity and relationship centrally at stake, renewing attention to lived experience and the discourse of the body, culture does not need to argue its way to political relevance. Indeed one of the achievements of the women's movement has been to redeem such phrases as 'lived experience' and 'the discourse of the body' from the empiricist connotations with which much literary theory has invested them. 'Experience' need now no longer signify an appeal away from

power-systems and social relations to the privileged certainties of the private, for feminism recognizes no such distinction between questions of the
human subject and questions of political struggle. The discourse of the body
is not a matter of Lawrentian ganglions and suave loins of darkness, but a
politics of the body, a rediscovery of its sociality through an awareness of the
forces which control and subordinate it.

The third area in question is the 'culture industry'. While literary critics
have been cultivating sensibility in a minority, large segments of the media
have been busy trying to devastate it in the majority; yet it is still presumed
that studying, say, Gray and Collins is inherently more important than
examining television or the popular press. Such a project differs from the
two I have outlined already in its essentially defensive character: it represents a critical reaction to someone else's cultural ideology rather than an
appropriation of culture for one's own ends. Yet is is a vital project nevertheless, which must not be surrendered to a melancholic Left or Right mythology of the media as impregnably monolithic. We know that people do not
after all believe all that they see and read; but we also need to know much
more than we do about the role such effects play in their general consciousness, even though such critical study should be seen, politically, as no more
than a holding operation. The democratic control of these ideological apparatuses, along with popular alternatives to them, must be high on the agenda
of any future socialist programme.[3]

The fourth and final area is that of the strongly emergent movement of
working-class writing. Silenced for generations, taught to regard literature
as a coterie activity beyond their grasp, working people over the past decade
in Britain have been actively organizing to find their own literary styles and
voices.[4] The worker writers' movement is almost unknown to academia,
and has not been exactly encouraged by the cultural organs of the state;
but it is one sign of a significant break from the dominant relations of
literary production. Community and cooperative publishing enterprises are
associated projects, concerned not simply with a literature wedded to
alternative social values, but with one which challenges and changes the
existing social relations between writers, publishers, readers and other
literary workers. It is because such ventures interrogate the ruling *definitions*
of literature that they cannot so easily be incorporated by a literary institution quite happy to welcome *Sons and Lovers*, and even, from time to time,
Robert Tressell.

These areas are not alternatives to the study of Shakespeare and Proust. If
the study of such writers could become as charged with energy, urgency and
enthusiasm as the activities I have just reviewed, the literary institution

ought to rejoice rather than complain. But it is doubtful that this will happen when such texts are hermetically sealed from history, subjected to a sterile critical formalism, piously swaddled with eternal verities and used to confirm prejudices which any moderately enlightened student can perceive to be objectionable. The liberation of Shakespeare and Proust from such controls may well entail the death of literature, but it may also be their redemption.

I shall end with an allegory. *We* know that the lion is stronger than the lion-tamer, and so does the lion-tamer. The problem is that the lion does not know it. It is not out of the question that the death of literature may help the lion to awaken.

Afterword

This book was written in 1982, at the watershed between two very different decades. If it could not anticipate what was to come after, neither could it grasp what had already happened in literary theory in the light of where it was to lead. Understanding is always in some sense retrospective, which is what Hegel meant by remarking that the owl of Minerva flies only at night. The afterlife of a phenomenon is part of its meaning, but this is a meaning opaque to those around at the time. We know more about the French revolution than Robespierre did, namely that it eventually led to a restoration of the monarchy. If history moves forward, knowledge of it travels backwards, so that in writing of our own recent past we are continually meeting ourselves coming the other way.

The 1970s, or at least the first half of them, were a decade of social hope, political militancy and high theory. This conjuncture was not accidental: theory of a grand kind tends to break out when routine social or intellectual practices have come unstuck, run into trouble, and urgently need to rethink themselves. Indeed theory is in one sense nothing more than the moment when those practices are forced for the first time to take themselves as the object of their own enquiry. There is thus always something inescapably narcissistic about it, as anyone who has run into a few literary theorists will no doubt confirm. The emergence of theory is the moment when a practice begins to curve back upon itself, so as to scrutinize its own conditions of possibility; and since this is in any fundamental way impossible, as we cannot after all pick ourselves up by our own bootstraps, or examine our life-forms with the clinical detachment of a Venusian, theory is always in some ultimate sense a self-defeating enterprise. Indeed this has been one recurrent motif of what theory has happened since this book was first published.

Even so, the late 1960s and early 1970s was a period in which new social forces were consolidating, certain global struggles (such as revolutionary nationalism) were intensifying, and a new, more heterogeneous body of students and teachers was flooding into academia from backgrounds which sometimes put them at odds with its governing consensus. Unusually, then, the campuses themselves became for a time hotbeds of political conflict; and this oubreak of militancy coincided in the late 1960s with the first emergence of literary theory. The first pathbreaking works of Jacques Derrida appeared just as French students were gearing themselves up for a confrontation with state power. It was no longer possible to take for granted what literature was, how to read it or what social functions it might serve; and neither was it quite so easy to take for granted the liberal disinterestedness of academia itself, in an era when, not least in the Vietnam adventure, the Western universities themselves seemed increasingly locked into structures of social power, ideological control and military violence. The humanities in particular depend crucially on some tacit consensus of value between teachers and taught; and this was now becoming harder to achieve.

What was perhaps most in question was the assumption that literature embodied *universal* value, and this intellectual crisis was closely linked to changes in the social composition of the universities themselves. Students had traditionally been expected, when encountering a literary text, to put their own particular histories temporarily on ice, and judge it from the vantage-point of some classless, genderless, non-ethnic, disinterested universal subject. This was an easy enough operation to pull off when those individual histories sprang from roughly the same kind of social world; but it was becoming much less apparent to those from ethnic or working-class backgrounds, or those from sexually dispossessed groups, that these supposedly universal values were in any real sense theirs. It is no wonder, then, that the Russian Formalists, French structuralists and German reception theorists were suddenly in fashion; for all of these approaches 'denaturalized' certain traditional literary assumptions in ways congenial to the academic newcomers. The Formalist doctrine of 'estrangement', invented to characterize the peculiar devices of a poem, could be extended to a critical estranging of the conventions which the academic institutions took complacently for granted. Structuralism pressed this project to even more scandalous limits, insisting that both self and society were simply constructs governed by certain deep structures which were necessarily absent from our consciousness. It thus struck a devastating blow at the humanist preoccupation with consciousness, experience, deliberated judgement, fine living, moral quality, all of which it placed boldly in brackets. The idea of a 'science of literature' was suddenly on the agenda, an enterprise which for the humanists seemed as grotesquely self-contradictory as a science of sneezing. The structuralist confidence in rigorous analysis and universal laws was appropriate to a technological age, lifting that scientific logic into the protected enclave of the human spirit itself, as Freud had done somewhat similarly with psychoanalysis. But in doing so it offered, contradictorily, to undermine one of the ruling belief systems of that society, which could be roughly characterized as liberal humanist, and so was radical and technocratic together. Reception theory took the most apparently natural and spontaneous of activities – reading a book – and showed just how many learnt operations and questionable cultural assumptions it involved.

Much of this rather brash theoretical buoyancy was soon to be dispersed. Theory of this early seventies kind – Marxist, feminist, structuralist – was of a totalizing bent, concerned to put a whole form of political life into question in the name of some desirable alternative. It went all the way down, and thus belonged in its intellectual verve and daring with the insurgent political radicalisms of the day. It was, to adapt a phrase of Louis Althusser's, political struggle at the level of theory; and its ambitiousness was reflected in the fact that what was very soon at stake was not simply different ways of dissecting literature, but the whole definition and constitution of the field of study. The children of the sixties and seventies were also the inheritors of so-called popular culture, which was part of what they were required to put in suspension when studying Jane Austen. But structuralism had apparently revealed that the same codes and conventions traversed both 'high' and 'low' culture, with scant regard for classical distinctions of value; so why not seize advantage of the fact that, methodologically speaking, nobody quite knew where *Coriolanus* ended and *Coronation Street* began and construct an entirely fresh field of enquiry ('cultural studies') which would gratify the anti-elitist iconoclasm of the sixty-eighters and yet appear wholly in line with 'scientific' theoretical findings? It was, in its academicist way, the latest version of the traditional avant-garde project of leaping the barriers between art and society, and was bound to make its appeal to those who found, rather like an apprentice chef cooking his evening meal, that it linked classroom and leisure time with wonderful economy.[1]

What happened in the event was not a defeat for this project, which has indeed been gathering institutional strength ever since, but a defeat for the political forces which originally underpinned the new evolutions in literary theory. The student movement was rolled back, finding the political system too hard to break. The momentum of national liberation movements throughout the Third World slackened in the early 1970s after the Portuguese revolution. Social democracy in the West, apparently unable to cope with the mounting problems of a capitalism in severe crisis, gave way to political regimes of a distinctly right-wing tenor, whose aim was not simply to combat radical values but to wipe them from living memory. By the close of the 1970s, Marxist criticism was rapidly falling from favour, as the world capitalist system, with its back to the economic wall since the oil crisis of the early 1970s, aggressively confronted Third World revolutionary nationalism abroad, and at home launched a series of virulent onslaughts on the labour movement and the forces of the left, along with liberal or enlightened thought in general. As if all this were not enough, the Almighty, evidently displeased with cultural theory, stepped in and picked off Roland Barthes, Michel Foucault, Louis Althusser and Jacques Lacan.

What held the fort of political criticism was feminism, which had rapidly come into its own; and it is no accident that this was also the heyday of post-structuralism. For though post-structuralism has its radical wing, its politics have been on the whole somewhat muted and oblique, and so more in keeping with a post-radical age. It preserves the dissenting energies of an earlier epoch, but combines them with a scepticism of determinate truths and meanings which blended reasonably well with a disillusioned liberal sensibility. In fact many of post-structuralism's emphases – a suspicion of semiotic closure and metaphysical foundations, a nervousness about the positive or programmatic, a distaste for notions of historical progress, a pluralist resistance to the doctrinal – merge well enough with that liberal frame of mind. Post-stucturalism is in many respects a much more subversive project than that; but it fitted well enough in other respects with a society in which dissidence was still possible, but no one had any longer much trust in the individual or collective subject who had once been the agent of it, or in the systematic theory which might guide its actions.[2]

Feminist theory, then as now, was near to the top of the intellectual agenda, and for reasons not hard to seek.[3] Of all such theoretical currents, it was the one which connected most deeply and urgently with the political needs and experience of well over half of those actually studying literature. Women could now make a unique, distinctive intervention in a subject which had always, in practice if not in theory, been largely theirs. Feminist theory provided that precious link between academia and society, as well as between problems of identity and those of political organization, which was in general harder and harder to come by in an increasingly conservative age. If it yielded a good deal of intellectual excitement, it also made room for much that a male-dominated high theory had austerely excluded: pleasure, experience, bodily life, the unconscious, the affective, autobiographical and interpersonal, questions of subjectivity and everyday practice. It was theory brought home to lived reality, which it at once challenged and respected; and as such it promised to lend a down-to-earth habitation to such apparently abstract topics as essentialism and conventionalism, the constitution of identities and the nature of political power. But it also offered a form of theoretical radicalism and political engagement in a period increasingly sceptical of the more traditional varieties of left-wing politics, as well as – not least in the case of North America – societies with only a meagre memory of socialism. As the forces of the socialist left were inexorably driven back, sexual politics began both to enrich and displace them. In the early 1970s, there was much talk of the relations between signifiers, socialism and sexuality; in the early 1980s of the relations between signifiers and sexuality; and, as the 1980s moved into the 1990s, much talk of sexuality. Theory had shifted almost overnight from Lenin to Lacan, Benveniste to the body; and if this was a salutary extension of politics into areas it had previously failed to reach, it was also, in part, the result of a deadlock in other kinds of political struggle.

Feminist theory, however, was itself by no means unaffected by the general downturn in radical politics which the late 1970s and early 1980s were to witness. As the women's movement was rebuffed by a traditionalist, family-centred, puritanical new right, it suffered a series of political setbacks which left their imprint on the theorizing itself. The heyday of feminist theory occurred in the 1970s, at a point now twenty years or so behind us. Since then, the field has been enriched by countless particular workings of the theory in terms of both general topics and specific writers; but there have been few *theoretical* breakthroughs to equal the groundbreaking work of the early pioneers Moers, Millett, Showalter, Gilbert and Gubar, Kristeva, Irigaray, Cixous, with their heady blendings of semiotics, linguistics, psychoanalysis, political theory, sociology, aesthetics and practical criticism. This is not to suggest that a good deal of impressive theoretical work has not been produced since then, not least in the fertile field of feminism and psychoanalysis;[4] but taken as a whole it hardly matches the intellectual ferment of the earlier years, an act which proved peculiarly hard to follow. Some searching 1970s debates about the compatibility or otherwise between feminism and Marxism lapsed largely into silence. By the mid-1980s, it could no longer be assumed that a feminist, especially in North America, had much more knowledge of or sympathy for the socialist project than, say, a phenomenologist. Even so, feminist criticism has established itself over the last decade or so as perhaps the most popular of all the new approaches to literature, drawing upon the theories of earlier times to revise the entire canon of literature and break open its restrictive frontiers.

The same can hardly be said of Marxist criticism, which since its apogee in the mid-1970s has languished somewhat in the doldrums.[5] It is symptomatic in this respect that the work of the West's leading Marxist literary theorist, Fredric Jameson, while still resolutely Marxist in orientation, shifted increasingly over the 1980s into the fields of film theory and postmodernism.[6] This waning of Marxism long pre-dated the momentous events of the late 1980s in Eastern Europe, when neo-Stalinism, to the relief of all democratic socialists, was finally overthrown by just the kind of popular revolutions which Western postmodernism had complacently concluded were no longer either possible or desirable. Since this event was one which mainstream currents of the Western Marxist left had been clamouring for for a good seventy years, it was hardly an abrupt disillusionment with 'actually existing socialism' in the East which caused the decline of Marxist criticism in the West. The fading popularity of Marxist criticism from the 1970s onwards was the result of developments in the so-called First World, not in the so-called Second. It stemmed in part from the crisis of global capitalism which we have glanced at already, in part from the criticisms aimed at Marxism by the various 'new' political currents – feminism, gay rights, ecology, ethnic movements and the rest – which sprang up in the wake of an earlier working-class militancy, nationalist insurrection, civil rights and student movements. Most of these earlier projects had been based on a belief in a struggle between mass political organization on the one hand and an oppressive state power on the other; most of them envisaged the radical transformation of capitalism, racism or imperialism as a whole, and so thought in ambitiously 'totalizing' terms. By about 1980, all of this had come to look distinctly *passé*. Since state power had proved too strong to dismantle, so-called micropolitics were now the order of the day. Totalizing theories and organized mass politics were increasingly associated with the dominative reason of patriarchy or Enlightenment. And if all theory was, as some suspected, inherently totalizing, then the new styles of theory had to be a species of anti-theory: local, sectoral, subjective, anecdotal, aestheticized, autobiographical, rather than objectivist and all-knowing. Theory, it seemed, having deconstructed just about everything else, had now finally succeeded in deconstructing itself. The idea of a transformative, self-determining human agent was dismissed as 'humanist', to be replaced by the fluid, mobile, decentred subject. There was no longer a coherent system or unified history to be opposed, just a discrete set of powers, discourses, practices, narratives. The age of revolution had given way to the epoch of postmodernism, and 'revolution' would henceforth be a term strictly reserved for advertising copy. A new generation of literary students and theorists was born, fascinated by sexuality but bored by social class, enthused by popular culture but ignorant of labour history, enthralled by exotic otherness but only dimly acquainted with the workings of imperialism.

As the 1980s wore on, then, Michel Foucault rapidly overtook Karl Marx as the doyen of political theory, while Freud, as cryptically re-interpreted by Jacques Lacan, was still riding high. The standing of Jacques Derrida and deconstruction proved rather more ambiguous. When this book was first published, that current was much in vogue; today, while still exerting a powerful influence here and there, it is rather less in fashion. The early, breathtakingly original works of Derrida (*Voice and Phenomenon, Of Grammatology, Writing and Difference, Dissemination, Margins of Philosophy*), are now, like the pioneering work of the early feminists, some quarter-of-a-century or more behind us. Derrida himself continued to turn out much scintillating work in the 1980s and 1990s, but nothing quite to match the ambition and profundity of these early seminal texts. His writing has become in general less programmatic and synoptic, more varied and eclectic. In the hands of some of his Anglo-Saxon disciples, deconstruction was reduced to a narrowly textual form of enquiry, lending a boost to the literary canon it offered to subvert by roaming ceaselessly over its contents, deconstructing as it went and so keeping the critical industry well supplied with sophisticated new materials. Derrida himself has always insisted on the political, historical, institutional nature of his project; but this, transplanted from Paris to Yale or Cornell, tended like the odd French wine not to travel well, and this audacious, iconoclastic thought-form proved easily assimilable to a formalist paradigm. On the whole, post-structuralism in general thrived best when it blended some broader project: feminism, post-colonialism, psychoanalysis. By the late 1980s, card-carrying deconstructionists looked like becoming an endangered species, not least after the high drama of the so-called de Man affair in 1987, when the grand master of US deconstruction, the Yale critic Paul de Man, was revealed to have contributed pro-German and anti-Semitic articles to some collaborationist Belgian journals during the Second World War.[7]

The intense feelings bred by this scandal were inevitably caught up with the fate of deconstruction itself. It is hard not to feel that some of the more doughty apologists for de Man at the time, including Derrida himself, reacted as hotly as they did because what seemed at stake was not only the reputation of a revered colleague, but the waning fortunes of deconstructive theory as a whole. The de Man affair, as though orchestrated by some hidden hand of history, curiously coincided with a downturn in those intellectual fortunes, and some at least of the ill feeling associated with the rumpus sprang from a current of theory which now felt that its back was increasingly to the wall. Rightly or wrongly, deconstruction stood accused among other sins of an unhistorical formalism; and throughout the 1980s, not least in the United States, there had been a gathering swell floating literary theory back in the direction of some brand of historicism. In changed political circumstances, however, this could no longer be the apparently discredited historicism of Marx or Hegel, with its supposed faith in grand, unitary narratives, its teleological hopes, its hierarchy of historical causes, its realist faith in determining the truth of historical events, its assured distinctions between what was central and what peripheral in history itself. What emerged on the scene in the 1980s, with the so-called new historicism, was a style of historical criticism which revolved precisely on the rejection of all of these doctrines.[8] It was a historiography appropriate for a postmodern age in which the very notions of historical truth, causality, pattern, purpose and direction were increasingly under fire.

The new historicism, which focused largely on the Renaissance period, yoked an epistemological scepticism about assured historical truth to a notable nervousness of grand narratives. History was less a determinate pattern of cause and effect than a random, contingent field of forces, in which causes and effects were to be constructed by the observer rather than taken as given. It was a tangled skein of dispersed narratives, none of which was necessarily more significant than any other; and all knowledge of the past was skewed by the interests and desires of the present. There was no firm distinction any longer between historical highways and minor footpaths, or indeed any hard-and-fast opposition between fact and fiction. Historical events were treated as 'textual' phenomena, while literary works were regarded as material events. Historiography was a form of narration conditioned by the narrator's own prejudices and preoccupations, and so itself a kind of rhetoric or fiction. There was no single determinable truth to any particular narrative or event, just a conflict of interpretations whose outcome was finally determined by power rather than truth.

The term 'power' suggests the writings of Michel Foucault; and indeed in many ways the new historicism turned out to be the application of Foucaultean themes to (in the main) Renaissance cultural history. This was itself a little odd, since if the narrational field was as genuinely open as the new historicism liked to insist, how come that the narratives which tended to get delivered were in the main so predictable? It seemed permissible to discuss sexuality, but not, by and large, social class; ethnicity, but not labour and material reproduction; political power, but not for the most part economics; culture, but not, on the whole, religion. It is only a mild exaggeration to claim that the new historicism was prepared in pluralist spirit to examine any topic at all as long as it cropped up somewhere in the work of Michel Foucault, or had some fairly direct bearing on the somewhat parlous condition of present-day American culture. In the end, much of it seemed less to do with the Elizabethan state or Jacobean court than with the fate of former radicals in contemporary California. The grand master of the school, Stephen Greenblatt, had moved from the influence of Raymond Williams, of whom he had once been a pupil, to that of Michel Foucault; and this was among other things a shift from political hope to political pessimism which well reflected the changing mood of the 1980s, not least in a Reaganite United States. The new historicism, then, certainly judged the past in the light of the present, but not necessarily in ways which always reflected credit on itself, or in ways about which it was prepared to be self-critical and self-historicizing. It is a familiar truth that the very last thing which historicisms are usually prepared to place under historical judgement is their own historical conditions. Like many a postmodern form of thought, it implicitly offered as a universal imperative – the imperative, for example, not to universalize – what could be fairly easily seen, from some way off, as the historically peculiar situation of a specific wing of the Western left intelligentisa. Perhaps it is easier in California to feel that history is random, unsystematic, directionless, than in some less privileged places in the world – just as it was easier for Virginia Woolf to feel that life was fragmentary and unstructured than it was for her servants. New historicism has produced some critical commentary of rare boldness and brilliance, and challenged many an historiographical shibboleth; but its rejection of macro-historical schemes is uncomfortably close to commonplace conservative thought, which has its own political reasons for scorning the idea of historical structures and long-term trends.

Britain's reply to the new historicism was the rather different creed of cultural materialism, which – appropriately for a society with more vigorous socialist traditions – displayed a political cutting-edge largely lacking in its transatlantic counterpart.[9] The phrase 'cultural materialism' had been coined in the 1980s by Britain's premier socialist critic, Raymond Williams, to describe a form of analysis which examined culture less as a set of isolated artistic monuments than as a material formation, complete with its own modes of production, power-effects, social relations, identifiable audiences, historically conditioned thought-forms. It was a way of bringing an unashamedly materialist analysis to bear on that realm of social existence – 'culture' – which was thought by conventional criticism to be the very antithesis of the material; and its ambition was less to relate 'culture' to 'society', in Williams's own earlier style, than to examine culture as always-already social and material to its roots. It could be seen either as an enrichment or a dilution of classical Marxism: enrichment, because it carried materialism boldly through to the 'spiritual' itself; dilution, because in doing so it blurred the distinctions, vital to orthodox Marxism, between the economic and the cultural. The method was, so Williams himself announced, 'compatible' with Marxism; but it took issue with the kind of Marxism which had relegated culture to secondary, 'superstructural' status, and resembled the new historicism in its refusal to enforce such hierarchies. It also paralleled the new historicism on taking on board a whole range of topics – notably, sexuality, feminism, ethnic and post-colonial questions – to which Marxist criticism had traditionally given short shrift. To this extent, cultural materialism formed a kind of bridge between Marxism and postmodernism, radically revising the former while wary of the more modish, uncritical, unhistorical aspects of the latter. This, indeed, might be said to be roughly the stand which most British left cultural critics nowadays take up.

Post-structuralism was not only increasingly perceived as unhistorical, whatever the justness of that charge; it was also felt, as the 1980s wore on, to have failed on the whole to deliver on its political promises. It was certainly in some general sense on the political left; but it seemed on the whole to have little of interest to say about concrete political issues, even if it had provided a whole range of social enquiries, from psychoanalysis to post-colonialism, with a set of stimulating, even revolutionary concepts. It was perhaps this need to engage the political dimension more directly which inspired Jacques Derrida to fulfil a long-deferred promise and address the question of Marxism;[10] but by then it seemed somewhat late in the day. The 1980s had been a pragmatic period of short-term views and hard-nosed material interests, of the self as consumer rather than creator, of history as commodified heritage and society (in Thatcher's infamous declaration) as non-entity. It was not an age hospitable to historical overviews, ambitious philosophical enquiry or universal concepts, and deconstruction, along with neo-pragmatism and postmodernism in general, flourished in this soil at the same time as its more leftist practitioners still sought to subvert. But it was clear also, as the 1980s moved into the 1990s, that certain embarrassingly large questions which had been put on ice by neo-pragmatism and some strands of post-structuralism, questions of human justice and freedom, truth and autonomy, had stubbornly refused to evaporate. It was hard to ignore these matters in a world where apartheid was under siege, neo–Stalinism being abruptly overturned, capitalism spreading its sway over new sectors of the globe, the inequalities of rich and poor dramatically widening, and peripheral societies coming under intensive exploitation. There were those for whom all that Enlightenment discourse of justice and autonomy was now definitively over, indeed those for whom history itself had been triumphantly consummated, and other less apocalyptic thinkers for whom those great ethical and political questions obdurately refused to disappear from theory precisely because they had not yet been effectively resolved in practice. Post-structuralism, as if aware of this, began to take a mildly ethical turn;[11] but it found it hard to compete in this region with the German tradition of philosophical enquiry from Hegel to Habermas, which in however rebarbatively abstract a fashion had clung tenaciously to these topics and produced a wealth of systematic reflection around them. It came as no surprise, then, that a group of German-oriented philosophical theorists, especially in Britain, found themselves reaching back into the very 'metaphysical' heritage of which post-structuralism was so wary, for both problems and solutions which had been perhaps rather too prematurely deconstructed.[12] At the same time, a resurgence of interest in the work of the Russian theorist Mikhail Bakhtin, around whom a heavy critical industry sprang up as the 1980s wore on, promised to unite the textual, bodily or discursive concerns of the post-structuralists with a more historical, materialist or sociological perspective.[13]

So far, we have touched on the term 'postmodernism' without pausing to unpack it. Yet it is doubtless the most widely-touted term in cultural theory today, one which, in promising to cover everything from Madonna to meta-narrative, post-Fordism to pulp fiction, threatens thereby to collapse into meaninglessness. We can, first of all, distinguish the more comprehensive, historical or philosophical term 'postmodernity' from the narrow, more cultural or aesthetic term 'postmodernism'. Postmodernity means the end of modernity, in the sense of those grand narratives of truth, reason, science, progress and universal emancipation which are taken to characterize modern thought from the Enlightenment onwards.[14] For postmodernity, these fond hopes have not only been historically discredited; they were dangerous illusions from the outset, bundling the rich contingencies of history into a conceptual straitjacket. Such tyrannical schemes ride roughshod over the complexity and multiplicity of actual history, brutally eradicate difference, reduce all otherness to the drearily selfsame, and issue often enough in a totalitarian politics. They are will-o'-the-wisps which by floating impossible ideals before our eyes distract us from what modest but effective political change we can actually achieve. They involve the dangerously absolutist faith that our varied, contingent forms of life and knowledge can be grounded in some single, ultimate, unimpeachable principle: Reason or the laws of history, technology or modes of production, political utopia or a universal human nature. For 'anti-foundationalist' postmodernity, by contrast, our forms of life are relative, ungrounded, self-sustaining, made up of mere cultural convention and tradition, without any identifiable origin or grandiose goal; and 'theory', at least for the more conservative brands of the creed, is for the most part just a high-sounding way of rationalizing these inherited habits and institutions. We cannot found our activities rationally, not only because there are different, discontinuous, perhaps incommensurable rationalities, but because any reasons we can advance will always be shaped by some pre-rational context of power, belief, interest or desire which can never itself be the subject of rational demonstration. There is no overarching totality, rationality or fixed centre to human life, no metalanguage which can capture its endless variety, just a plurality of cultures and narratives which cannot be hierarchically ordered or 'privileged', and which must consequently respect the inviolable 'otherness' of ways of doing things which are not their own. Knowledge is relative to cultural contexts, so that to claim to know the world 'as it is' is simply a chimera – not only because our understanding is always a matter of partial, partisan interpretation, but because the world itself is no way in particular. Truth is the product of interpretation, facts are constructs of discourse, objectivity is just whatever questionable interpretation of things has currently seized power, and the human subject is as much a fiction as the reality he or she contemplates, a diffuse, self-divided entity without any fixed nature or essence. In all of this, postmodernity is a kind of extended footnote to the philosophy of Friedrich Nietzsche, who anticipated almost every one of these positions in nineteenth-century Europe.

Postmodernism proper can then best be seen as the form of culture which corresponds to this world view.[15] The typical postmodernist work of art is arbitrary, eclectic, hybrid, decentred, fluid, discontinuous, pastiche-like. True to the tenets of postmodernity, it spurns metaphysical profundity for a kind of contrived depthlessness, playfulness and lack of affect, an art of pleasures, surfaces and passing intensities. Suspecting all assured truths and certainties, its form is ironic and its epistemology relativist and sceptical. Rejecting all attempts to reflect a stable reality beyond itself, it exists self-consciously at the level of form or language. Knowing its own fictions to be groundless and gratuitous, it can attain a kind of negative authenticity only by flaunting its ironic awareness of this fact, wryly pointing its own status as a constructed artifice. Nervous of all isolated identity, and wary of the notion of absolute origins, it draws attention to its own 'intertextual' nature, its parodic recyclings of other works which are themselves no more than such recyclings. Part of what it parodies is past history – a history which is no longer to be seen in linear terms as the chain of causality which produced the present, but which exists in a kind of eternal present as so much raw material torn from its own context and cobbled together with the contemporary. Finally, and perhaps most typically of all, postmodern culture turns its distaste for fixed boundaries and categories on the traditional distinction between 'high' and 'popular' art, deconstructing the borderline between them by producing artifacts which are self-consciously populist or vernacular, or which offer themselves as commodities for pleasurable consumption. Postmodernism, like Walter Benjamin's 'mechanical reproduction',[16] seeks to dismantle the intimidating aura of high-modernist culture with a more demotic, user-friendly art, suspecting all hierarchies of value as privileged and elitist. There is no better or worse, just different. In seeking to leap the barrier between art and common life, postmodernism seems to some the resurgence in our own time of the radical avant-garde, which had traditionally pursued this goal. In advertising, fashion, lifestyle, the shopping mall and the mass media, aesthetics and technology had finally interpenetrated, while political life had become transformed to a kind of aesthetic spectacle. Postmodernism's impatience with conventional aesthetic judgements took on tangible shape in so-called cultural studies, which grew apace as the 1980s unfolded, and which often enough refused to respect value-distinctions between the sonnet and the soap opera.

The debates over postmodernism and postmodernity have taken many forms. There is the question, for example, of how far down these developments go – of whether they are really, so to speak, wall-to-wall, as the dominant culture of our age, or whether they are a good deal more sectoral and specific than that. Is postmodernity the appropriate philosophy for our time, or is it the word view of a jaded bunch of erstwhile revolutionary Western intellectuals who with typical intellectual arrogance have projected it upon contemporary history as a whole? What does postmodernism mean in Mali or Mayo? What does it mean to societies which have yet to fully enter upon modernity proper? Is the word neutrally descriptive of consumerist society, or a positive recommendation of a certain style of life? Is it, as Fredric Jameson believes, the culture of late capital – the final penetration of the commodity form into culture itself – or is it, as its more radical exponents urge, a subversive strike at all elites, hierarchies, master narratives and immutable truths?

The arguments will doubtless continue, not least because postmodernism is that most robust of all theories, one rooted in a concrete set of social practices and institutions. It is possible to ignore phenomenology or semiotics or reception theory – indeed the vast majority of humankind have proved singularly successful in doing so – but not consumerism, the mass media, aestheticized politics, sexual difference. But the arguments will also continue because there are serious divergencies within postmodern theory itself. For its more politically minded proponents, such mystifying ideas as truth, identity, totality, universality, foundations, metanarrative, the collective revolutionary subject, must be cleared away precisely so that genuinely effective radical projects can get off the ground. For its more conservative apologists, the rejection of these notions goes hand-in-hand with a defence of the political status quo. There is thus all the difference in the world between Foucault and Stanley Fish, Derrida and Richard Rorty, though all four can be broadly categorized as postmodernists. For American neo-pragmatists like Rorty and Fish, the collapse of transcendental viewpoints signals, in effect, the collapse of the possibility of full-blooded political critique.[17] Such a critique, so the argument runs, could only be launched from some metaphysical vantage-point completely beyond our current life-forms; and since there is self-evidently no such place to stand – or since, even if there were, it would be irrelevant and unintelligible to us – even our most apparently revolutionary claims must always be in collusion with the discourses of the present. We are always, in short, installed firmly on the inside of the culture we hope to criticize, so thoroughly constituted by its interests and beliefs that to put them into radical question would involve leaping out of our own skins. As long as what we utter is intelligible – and any critique which is not would be merely ineffective – then we are already in complicity with the culture we seek to objectify, and so plunged in a kind of bad faith. This doctrine, which depends on an eminently deconstructable distinction between 'inside' and 'outside', is currently being deployed by some to defend the American way of life, precisely because postmodernism is uneasily aware that no *rational* critique of that way of life, or indeed of any other, is any longer possible. To pull out the foundations from under your opponent is, unavoidably, to pull them out from under oneself. In order to avoid the unwelcome conclusion that there is no rational justification for one's form of life, one must seek to disable the very idea of critique as such, branding it as necessarily 'metaphysical', 'transcendent', 'absolute' or 'foundational'. Similarly, if the idea of system or totality can be discredited, then there is really no such thing as patriarchy or the 'capitalist system' to be criticized. Since there is no totality to social life, there is no place for any overall change, since there is no overall system to be transformed. We are asked to believe, with gross implausibility, that multinational capitalism is just a random concurrence of this or that practice, technique, social relation, with no systematic logic whatsoever; and all this can then be offered as a 'radical' defence of pluralism against the terrors of totalization. This is a dogma which is perhaps rather easier to sustain in Columbia University than in the Latin American nation of that name.

If, by the mid-1990s, feminist criticism has proved the most popular of the various new literary approaches, then post-colonial theory has been pressing hard on its heels.[18] Like feminism and postmodernism, and unlike phenomenology or reception theory, post-colonial theory is directly rooted in historical developments. The collapse of the great European empires; their replacement by the world economic hegemony of the United States; the steady erosion of the nation state and of traditional geopolitical frontiers, along with mass global migrations and the creation of so-called multicultural societies; the intensifed exploitation of ethnic groups within the West and 'peripheral' societies elsewhere; the formidable power of the new transnational corporations: all of this has developed apace since the 1960s, and with it a veritable revolution in our notions of space, power, language, identity. Since culture, in the broad rather than narrow sense of the term, lies near the centre of some of these issues, it is hardly surprising that during the last two decades they should have left their imprint on those sectors of the humanities which have been traditionally concerned with culture in the narrower sense of the term. Just as the dominance of the mass media forced a rethinking of classical frontiers within the study of culture, so 'multiculturalism', which belongs to the same historical period, challenges the way the West has conceived its identity and articulated it in a canon of artistic works. Both currents – cultural sudies and post-colonialism – take a decisive step beyond the questions of theoretical *method* which held sway over an earlier phase of literary theory. What is now at stake is the problematizing of 'culture' itself, which in moving beyond the isolated work of art into the areas of language, lifestyle, social value, group identity, inevitably intersects with questions of global political power.

The result has been the breaking open of a narrowly conceived Western cultural canon, retrieving the besieged cultures of 'marginal' groups and peoples. It has also meant bringing home some issues of 'high' theory to contemporary global society. Questions of 'meta-narrative' no longer concern just literary works, but the terms in which the post-Enlightenment West has traditionally couched its own imperial project. The decentring and deconstruction of categories and identities assume fresh urgency in a context of racism, ethnic conflict, neo-colonial domination, The 'other' is no longer merely a theoretical concept but groups and peoples written out of history, subjected to slavery, insult, mystification, genocide. Psychoanalytic categories of 'splitting' and projection, denial and disavowal, have shifted from the Freudian textbooks to become ways of analysing the psycho-political relations between colonizers and colonized. Debates between 'modernity' and 'postmodernity' have special force in peripheral cultures which are increasingly dragged into the orbit of a postmodern West without, for good or ill, having fully undergone a European-style modernity themselves. And the plight of women in such societies, forced as they are to assume many of its most wretched burdens, has resulted in a peculiarly fruitful alliance between feminism and post-colonialism.

Post-colonial theory is not only the product of multiculturalism and decolonization. It also reflects an historic shift from revolutionary nationalism in the Third World, which faltered in the 1970s, to a 'post-revolutionary' condition in which the power of the transnational corporations seems unbreakable. Accordingly, much post-colonial writing fits well enough with postmodern suspicions of organized mass politics, turning instead to cultural matters. Culture is on any estimate important in a neo-colonial world; but it is hardly what is finally decisive. It is not in the end questions of language, skin colour or identity, but of commodity prices, raw materials, labour markets, military alliances and political forces, which shape the relations between rich and poor nations. In the West, especially in the United States, questions of ethnicity have at once enriched a radical politics narrowly fixated on social class, and, in their own narrow fixation on difference, helped to obscure the vital material conditions which different ethnic groups have in common. Post-colonialism, in short, has been among other things one instance of a rampant 'culturalism' which has recently swept across Western cultural theory, over-emphasizing the cultural dimension of human life in understandable overreaction to a previous biologism, humanism or economism. Such cultural relativism is for the most part simply imperial dominion stood on its head.

Like any other theory, then, post-colonial discourse has its limits and blindspots. It has sometimes involved a romantic idealization of the 'other', along with a simplistic politics which regards the reduction of the 'other' to the 'same' as the root of all political evil. This particular postmodern theme, of otherness and self-identity, is by now itself threatening to become drearily self-identical. An alternative brand of post-colonial thought, in deconstructing any too rigid opposition between colonizing self and colonized other, ends up stressing their mutual implication and so risks blunting the political cutting-edge of an anti-colonialist critique. For all its emphasis on difference, post-colonial theory has sometimes too quickly conflated very different societies under the same 'Third World' category; and its language has too often betrayed a portentous obscurantism incongruously remote from the peoples it champions. Some of the theory has been genuinely pathbreaking, while some of it has done little more than reflect the guilty self-loathing of a Western liberalism which would rather, in these hard political times, be absolutely anything but itself.

Among the more glamorous commodities which postmodern society has on offer is cultural theory itself. Postmodern theory is part of the postmodern marketplace, not just a reflection upon it. It represents, among other things, a way of amassing valuable 'cultural capital' in increasingly competitive intellectual conditions. Theory, partly because of its high-poweredness, esotericism, up-to-dateness, rarity and relative novelty, has achieved high prestige in the academic marketplace, even if it still provokes the virulent hostility of a liberal humanism which fears being ousted by it. Post-structuralism is sexier than Philip Sidney, just as quarks are more alluring than quadrilaterals. Theory has been one symptom in our time of the commodifying of the intellectual life itself, as one conceptual fashion usurps another as shortwindedly as changes in hairstyle. Just as the human body – along with a good deal else – has become aestheticized in our day, so theory has become a kind of minority art-form, playful, self-ironizing and hedonistic, one place to which the impulses behind high-modernist art have now migrated. It has been, among other things, the refuge of a disinherited Western intellect, cut loose by the sheer squalor of modern history from its traditional humanistic bearings, and so at once gullible and sophisticated, streetwise and disorientated. It has too often acted as a modish substitute for political activity, in an age when such activity has been on the whole hard to come by; and having started life as an ambitious critique of our current ways of life, it now threatens to end up as a complacent consecration of them.

There is always, however, more than one story to tell. If cultural theory has won itself some prestige, it is also because it has boldly raised some fundamental questions to which people would appreciate some answers. It has acted as a kind of dumping ground for those embarrassingly large topics nervously off-loaded by a narrowly analytical philosophy, an empiricist sociology and a positivist political science. If it has tended to displace political action, it has also provided a space in which some vital political issues could be nurtured in an inhospitable climate. It has no particular unity to it as a discipline; what, for example, do phenomenology and queer theory have in common? And none of the methods grouped under *literary* theory is peculiar to the study of literature; indeed most of them germinated in fields quite beyond it. Yet this disciplinary indeterminacy also marks a breakdown in the traditional division of intellectual labour, which the word 'theory' somehow flags. 'Theory' indicates that our classical ways of carving up knowledge are now, for hard historical reasons, in deep trouble. But it is as much a revealing symptom of this breakdown as a positive reconfiguration of the field. The emergence of theory suggests that, for good historical reasons, what had become known as the humanities could no longer carry on in their customary shape. This was all to the good, since the humanities had too often proclaimed a spurious disinterestedness, preached 'universal' values which were all too socially specific, repressed the material basis of those values, absurdly overrated the importance of 'culture' and fostered a jealously elitist conception of it. It was for the bad, since the humanities had also kept warm some decent, generous values brusquely disregarded by everyday society; fostered – in however idealist a guise – a searching critique of our current way of life; and in nurturing a spiritual elitism had at least seen through the phoney egalitarianism of the marketplace.

The task of cultural theory, broadly conceived, was to take apart the received wisdom of the traditional humanities. In this, one might claim, it has been reasonably successful, in theory if not in practice. Since this book first appeared, there have been few convincing ripostes to the various cases which literary theory has launched. Much hostility to theory has been little more than a typically Anglo-Saxon uneasiness with ideas as such – a feeling that arid abstractions are out of place when it comes to art. This edginess about ideas is characteristic of those social groups whose own historically specific ideas have for the moment won out, and who can therefore come to mistake them either for natural feelings or eternal verities. Those in command can afford to be dismissive of criticism and conceptual analysis, as those under their rule cannot. The charge that theory simply interposes a screen of obscurantist jargon between the reader and the text can be made against any kind of criticism whatsoever. Matthew Arnold and T. S. Eliot read like obscurantist jargon to the person-in-the-street unfamiliar with their critical idiom. One person's specialist discourse is another's ordinary language, as anyone familiar with paediatricians or motor mechanics will testify.

One battle which cultural theory has probably won is the contention that there is no neutral or innocent reading of a work of art. Even some quite conservative critics are these days less given to arguing that radical theorists are ideologically skew-eyed whereas they themselves see the work as it really is. A broad kind of historicism has also carried the day: there are few card-carrying formalists left around. If the author is not exactly dead, a naive biographism is no longer in fashion. The chancy nature of literary canons, their dependence on a culturally specific frame of value, is nowadays quite widely recognized, along with the truth that certain social groups have been unjustly excluded from them. And we are no longer exactly sure where high culture ends and popular culture begins.

Even so, some traditional humanist doctrines die hard, not least the assumption of universal value. If literature matters today, it is chiefly because it seems to many conventional critics one of the few remaining places where, in a divided, fragmented world, a sense of universal value may still be incarnate; and where, in a sordidly material world, a rare glimpse of transcendence can still be attained. Hence, no doubt, the otherwise inexplicably intense, even virulent passions which such a minority, academicist pursuit as literary theory tends to unleash. For if even *this* precariously surviving enclave of art can be historicized, materialized, deconstructed, then where indeed is one to find value in a degraded world? The radical would reply that to assume that social life is uniformly degraded, and only culture precious, is actually part of the problem rather than the solution. This attitude itself reflects a particular political viewpoint, rather than being a disinterested statement of fact. At the same time, the generosity of the humanist's faith in common values must be candidly acknowledged. It is just that he or she mistakes a project still to be carried through – that of a world held politically and economically in common – with the 'universal' values of a world which has not yet been thus reconstructed. The humanist is thus not wrong to trust to the possibility of such universal values; it is just that nobody can yet say exactly what they would be, since the material conditions which might allow them to flourish have not yet come into being. If they were ever to do so, the theorist could relievedly lay down his or her theorizing, which would have been made redundant precisely by being politically realized, and do something more interesting for a change.

Notes

Introduction: What is Literature?

1 See M. I. Steblin-Kamenskij, *The Saga Mind* (Odense, 1973).
2 See Lennard J. Davis, 'A Social History of Fact and Fiction: Authorial Disavowal in the Early English Novel', in Edward W. Said (ed.), *Literature and Society* (Baltimore and London, 1980).
3 *The Theory of Literary Criticism: A Logical Analysis* (Berkeley, 1974), pp. 37–42.

1 The Rise of English

1 See E. P. Thompson, *The Making of the English Working Class* (London, 1963), and E. J. Hobsbawm, *The Age of Revolution* (London, 1977).
2 See Raymond Williams, *Culture and Society 1780–1950* (London, 1958), esp. chapter 2, 'The Romantic Artist'.
3 See Jane P. Tompkins, 'The Reader in History: The Changing Shape of Literary Response', in Jane P. Tompkins (ed.), *Reader-Response Criticism* (Baltimore and London, 1980).
4 See Frank Kermode, *The Romantic Image* (London, 1957).
5 Quoted by Chris Baldick, 'The Social Mission of English Studies' (unpublished D.Phil. thesis, Oxford 1981), p. 156. I am considerably indebted to this excellent study, published as *The Social Mission of English Criticism* (Oxford, 1983).
6 'The Popular Education of France', in *Democratic Education*, ed. R. H. Super (Ann Arbor, 1962), p. 22.
7 Ibid., p. 26.

8   George Sampson, *English for the English* (1921), quoted by Baldick, 'The Social Mission of English Studies', p. 153.

9   H. G. Robinson, 'On the Use of English Classical Literature in the Work of Education', *Macmillan's Magazine* 11 (1860), quoted by Baldick, 'The Social Mission of English Studies', p. 103.

10 J. C. Collins, *The Study of English Literature* (1891), quoted by Baldick, 'The Social Mission of English Studies', p. 100.

11 See Lionel Gossman, 'Literature and Education', *New Literary History*, vol. XIII, no. 2, winter 1982, pp. 341–71. See also D. J. Palmer, *The Rise of English Studies* (London, 1965).

12 Quoted by Gossman, 'Literature and Education', pp. 341–2.

13 See Baldick, 'The Social Mission of English Studies', pp. 108–11.

14 See ibid., pp. 117–23.

15 See Francis Mulhern, *The Moment of 'Scrutiny'* (London, 1979), pp. 20–2.

16 See Iain Wright, 'F. R. Leavis, the *Scrutiny* movement and the Crisis', in Jon Clarke *et al.* (eds), *Culture and Crisis in Britain in the Thirties* (London, 1979), p. 48.

17 See *The Country and the City* (London, 1973), pp. 9–12.

18 See Gabriel Pearson, 'Eliot: An American Use of Symbolism', in Graham Martin (ed.), *Eliot in Perspective* (London, 1970), pp. 97–100.

19 Graham Martin, Introduction, ibid., p. 22.

20 See 'Tradition and the Individual Talent', in T. S. Eliot, *Selected Essays* (London, 1963).

21 'The Metaphysical Poets', ibid., p. 290.

22 'Ben Jonson', ibid., p. 155.

23 *Science and Poetry* (London, 1926), pp. 82–3.

24 *Principles of Literary Criticism* (London, 1963), p. 32.

25 Ibid., p. 62.

26 See 'The Intentional Fallacy' and 'The Affective Fallacy', in W. K. Wimsatt and Monroe Beardsley, *The Verbal Icon* (New York, 1958).

27 See Richard Ohmann, *English in America* (New York, 1976), chapter 4.

28 *The Well Wrought Urn* (London, 1949), p. 189.

29 *The New Criticism* (Norfolk, Conn., 1941), p. 54.

30 *Seven Types of Ambiguity* (Harmondsworth, 1965), p. 1.

31 See Christopher Norris, *William Empson and the Philosophy of Literary Criticism* (London, 1978), pp. 99–100.

2   Phenomenology, Hermeneutics, Reception Theory

1   There is a difference here, however: Husserl, hoping to isolate the 'pure' sign, bracketed off its phonic and graphic properties, just the material qualities on which the Formalists focused.

2 *The Idea of Phenomenology* (The Hague, 1964), p. 31.
3 See Jacques Derrida, *Speech and Phenomena* (Evanston, Ill., 1973).
4 See Richard E. Palmer, *Hermeneutics* (Evanston, Ill., 1969). Other works in the tradition of hermeneutical phenomenology are Jean-Paul Sartre. *Being and Nothingness* (New York, 1956), Maurice Merleau-Ponty, *Phenomenology of Perception* (London, 1962) and Paul Ricoeur, *Freud and Philosophy* (New Haven, Conn., and London, 1970) and *Hermeneutics and the Human Sciences* (Cambridge, 1981).
5 *Wahrheit und Methode* (Tübingen, 1960), p. 291.
6 Quoted by Frank Lentricchia, *After The New Criticism* (Chicago, 1980), p. 153.
7 See Pierre Macherey, *A Theory of Literary Production* (London, 1978), esp. Part 1.
8 See Mary Hesse, *Revolutions and Reconstructions in the Philosophy of Science* (Brighton, 1980), esp. Part 2.
9 See T. A. van Dijk, *Some Aspects of Textual Grammars: A Study in Theoretical Linguistics and Poetics* (The Hague, 1972).

3   Structuralism and Semiotics

1 *Anatomy of Criticism* (New York, 1967), p. 122.
2 *The Prison-House of Language* (Princeton, NJ, 1972), p. vii.
3 See 'Closing Statement: Linguistics and Poetics', in Thomas A. Sebeok (ed.), *Style in Language* (Cambridge, Mass., 1960).
4 Ibid., p. 358.
5 See 'Two Aspects of Language and Two Types of Aphasic Disturbances', in Roman Jakobson and Morris Halle, *Fundamentals of Language* (The Hague, 1956).
6 See Benedetto Croce, *Aesthetic* (New York, 1966); Erich Auerbach, *Mimesis* (Princeton, NJ, 1971); E. R. Curtius. *European Literature and the Latin Middle Ages* (London, 1979); Leo Spitzer, *Linguistics and Literary History* (Princeton, NJ, 1954); René Wellek, *A History of Modern Criticism* (London, 1966).
7 See his *Problems in General Linguistics* (Miami, 1971).
8 See Michael Lane (ed.), *Structuralism: A Reader* (London, 1970).
9 See Jacques Ehrmann, *Structuralism* (New York, 1970).
10 See Michel Pêcheux, *Language, Semantics and Ideology* (London, 1981); Roger Fowler, *Literature as Social Discourse* (London, 1981); Gunter Kress and Robert Hodge, *Language as Ideology* (London, 1979); M. A. K. Halliday, *Language as Social Semiotic* (London, 1978).
11 See Jacques Derrida, 'Limited Inc', *Glyph*, 2 (Baltimore and London, 1977).
12 See Richard Ohmann, 'Speech Acts and the Definition of Literature', *Philosophy and Rhetoric*, 4 (1971).

13   See Simon Clarke, *the Foundations of Structuralism* (Brighton, 1981), p. 46.
14   *The Pursuit of Signs* (London, 1981), p. 5.

4   Post-Structuralism

1   See Roland Barthes, 'The Death of the Author', in Stephen Heath (ed.), *Image-Music-Text: Roland Barthes* (London, 1977). This volume also contains Barthes's 'Introduction to the Structural Analysis of Narrative'.
2   See 'From Work in Text', in *Image-Music-Text: Roland Barthes*.
3   Something of this concern with the simultaneous urgency and 'impossibility' of meaning in literature marks the work of the French critic Maurice Blanchot, though he is not to be seen as a post-structuralist. See the selection of his essays edited by Gabriel Josipovici, *The Siren's Song* (Brighton, 1982).
4   Phillippe Lacoue-Labarthe and Jean-Luc Nancy (eds), *Les fins de l'homme* (Paris, 1981), pp. 526–9.

5   Psychoanalysis

1   See, for example, Kate Millett, *Sexual Politics* (London, 1971); but see also, for a feminist defence of Freud, Juliet Mitchell, *Psychoanalysis and Feminism* (Harmondsworth, 1975).
2   See her *Love, Guilt and Reparation and Other Works, 1921–1945* (London, 1975).
3   See the film journal *Screen*, published in London by the Society for Education in Film and Television, for some valuable analysis of this kind. See also Christian Metz, *Psychoanalysis and Cinema* (London, 1982).
4   *The Forked Flame: A Study of D. H. Lawrence* (London, 1968), p. 43.
5   See Freud's essay 'Creative Writers and Day-Dreaming', in James Strachey (ed.), *The Standard Edition of the Complete Psychological Works of Sigmund Freud* (London, 1953–73), vol. IX.
6   For a Marxist application of Freudian dream theory to the literary text, see Pierre Macherey, *A Theory of Literary Production* (London, 1978), pp. 150–1, and Terry Eagleton, *Criticism and Ideology* (London, 1976), pp. 90–2.
7   See Peter Brooks, 'Freud's Masterplot: Questions of Narrative', in Shoshana Felman (ed.), *Literature and Psychoanalysis* (Baltimore, 1982).
8   See Raymond Williams, *Drama from Ibsen to Brecht* (London, 1968), Conclusion.
9   See Colin MacCabe, *James Joyce and the Revolution of the Word* (London, 1978).
10   See my essay 'Poetry, Pleasure and Politics: Yeats's "Easter 1916"', in the journal *Formations* (1984).

11   See Wilhelm Reich, *The Mass Psychology of Fascism* (Harmondsworth, 1975); Herbert Marcuse, *Eros and Civilization* (London, 1956), and *One-Dimensional Man* (London, 1958). See also Theodor Adorno *et al.*, *The Authoritarian Personality* (New York, 1950), and for accounts of Adorno and the Frankfurt School, Martin Jay, *The Dialectical Imagination* (Boston, 1973), Gillian Rose, *The Melancholy Science: An Introduction to the Thought of Theodor Adorno* (London, 1978), and Susan Buck-Morss, *The Origin of Negative Dialectic* (Hassocks, 1977).

Conclusion: Political Criticism

1   See my *Walter Benjamin, or Towards a Revolutionary Criticism* (London, 1981), Part 2, chapter 2, 'A Small History of Rhetoric'.
2   Walter Benjamin, 'Eduard Fuchs, Collector and Historian', in *One-Way Street and Other Writings* (London, 1979), p. 359.
3   See Raymond Williams, *Communications* (London, 1962), for some interesting practical proposals in this respect.
4   See *The Republic of Letters: Working Class Writing and Local Publishing* (Comedia Publishing Group, 9 Poland Street, London W1 3DG).

Afterword

1   For useful surveys of cultural studies, see G. Turner, *British Cultural Studies: An Introduction* (London, 1990), and Antony Easthope and Kate McGowan (eds), *A Critical and Cultural Theory Reader* (Buckingham, 1992). Other works in the field include Tony Bennett *et al.* (eds), *Popular Culture and Social Relations* (Milton Keynes, 1986); R. Collins *et al.* (eds), *Media, Culture and Society: A Critical Reader* (London, 1986); Dick Hebdige, *Hiding in the Light* (London, 1988); Colin MacCabe (ed.), *High Theory/Low Culture* (Manchester, 1986); Judith Williamson, *Consuming Passions* (London, 1986); Iain Chambers, *Popular Culture: The Metropolitan Experience* (London, 1986), Morag Shiach, *Discourses on Popular Culture* (Cambridge, 1987); John Fiske, *Understanding Popular Culture* (London, 1993), Lawrence Grossberg *et al.* (eds), *Cultural Studies* (New York, 1992); Jim McGuigan, *Cultural Populism* (London, 1992); John Frow, *Cultural Studies and Cultural Value* (Oxford, 1995).
2   For a substantial collection of post-strucuralist essays of the period, see Derek Attridge *et al.* (eds), *Post-Structuralism and the Question of History* (Cambridge, 1987). The most powerful critique of post-structuralism to appear was Manfred Frank, *What is Neostructuralism?* (Minneapolis, 1984).
3   Any selection from the well-populated field of feminist criticism is inevitably somewhat arbitrary. But major works of the period include Nancy Armstrong,

Desire and Domestic Fiction (Oxford, 1987); Elaine Showalter, *The Female Malady* (London, 1987), and *Sexual Anarchy: Gender and Culture at the Fin de Siècle* (New York, 1990); Sandra M. Gilbert and Susan Gubar, *No Man's Land: vol. 1, The War of the Words* (New Haven, 1988), *vol. 2, Sexchanges* (New Haven, 1989); Patricia Parker, *Literary Fat Ladies* (London, 1987); Rita Felski, *Beyond Feminist Aesthetics* (Cambridge, Mass., 1989); Teresa de Lauretis, *Alice Doesn't: Feminism, Semiotics, Cinema* (London, 1984); Gisela Ecker (ed.), *Feminist Aesthetics* (London, 1985); Alice Jardine, *Gynesis* (Ithaca, 1985); Cora Kaplan, *Sea Changes: Culture and Feminism* (London, 1986); Nancy K. Miller, *The Poetics of Gender* (New York, 1986), Jane Spencer, *The Rise of the Woman Novelist* (Oxford, 1986). Useful anthologies include C. Belsey and J. Moore (eds), *The Feminist Reader* (Basingstoke and London, 1989); Mary Eagleton, *Feminist Literary Theory: A Reader* (Oxford, 1986), and *Feminist Literary Criticism* (London, 1991); G. Greene and C. Kahn (eds), *Making a Difference* (London, 1985); Elaine Showalter (ed.), *The New Feminist Criticism* (London, 1986); J. Newton and D. Rosenfelt (eds), *Feminist Criticism and Social Change* (London, 1988); Sara Mills *et al.* (eds), *Feminist Readings/Feminists Reading* (New York and London, 1989); Linda Kauffman (ed.), *Gender and Theory* (Oxford, 1989); Robyn Warhol and Diane Price Herndl (eds), *Feminisms: An Anthology of Literary Theory and Criticism* (New Brunswick, 1991); Susan Sellers (ed.), *Feminist Criticism: Theory and Practice* (New York and London, 1991).

4   See in particular Jacqueline Rose, *Sexuality in the Field of Vision* (London, 1986), and Teresa Brennan (ed.), *Between Feminism and Psychoanalysis* (London, 1989).

5   A valuable anthology is Francis Mulhern (ed.), *Contemporary Marxist Literary Criticism* (London and New York, 1992). Despite its relative unfashionability, Marxist criticism in the period managed to produce works such as Peter Burger's *Theory of the Avant Garde* (Manchester, 1984), Franco Moretti, *The Way of the World* (London, 1987), John Frow, *Marxism and Literary History* (Oxford, 1986), Raymond Williams, *Writing in Society* (London, 1984) and *The Politics of Modernism* (London, 1989), Fredric Jameson, *The Ideologies of Theory*, 2 vols (London, 1988) and *Late Marxism* (London, 1990), and Terry Eagleton, *The Function of Criticism* (London, 1984) and *The Ideology of the Aesthetic* (Oxford, 1991). A useful collection of Marxist criticism can be found in C. Nelson and L. Grossberg (eds), *Marxism and the Interpretation of Culture* (London, 1988).

6   See in particular his *Postmodernism, or, the Cultural Logic of Late Capitalism* (London, 1991), and *Signatures of the Visible* (London, 1992).

7   See Werner Hamacher *et al.* (eds), *Responses: On Paul de Man's Wartime Journalism* (Lincoln, Nebr., and London, 1989).

8   For typical new historicist works, see Stephen Greenblatt, *Renaissance Self-Fashioning from More to Shakespeare* (Chicago, 1980), *Representing the English*

Renaissance (Berkeley, 1988), and *Shakespearean Negotiations* (Oxford, 1988). See also Jonathan Goldberg, *James 1 and the Politics of Literature* (Baltimore, 1983), and *Voice Terminal Echo: Postmodernism and English Renaissance Texts* (New York and London, 1986). See also H. A. Veeser (ed), *The New Historicism* (New York and London, 1989). An excellent critique of the current is provided by David Norbrook, 'Life and Death of Renaissance Man', *Raritan*, vol. 8, no. 4, spring, 1989.

9 For cultural materialism, see Raymond Williams, *Marxism and Literature* (Oxford, 1977), and *Problems in Materialism and Culture* (London, 1980) and *Culture* (London, 1981). See also Jonathan Dollimore and Alan Sinfield, *Political Shakespeare: New Essays in Cultural Materialism* (Manchester, 1985), and Alan Sinfield, *Literature, Politics and Culture in Post-War Britain* (Oxford, 1989). For a general account, see Andrew Milner, *Cultural Materialism* (Melbourne, 1993).

10 See his *Specters of Marx* (New York and London, 1994).

11 See, for example, J. Hillis Miller, *The Ethics of Reading* (New York, 1987).

12 See, for example, Gillian Rose, *Dialectic of Nihilism* (Oxford, 1984); Peter Dews, *Logics of Disintegration* (London, 1987); Howard Caygill, *Art of Judgement* (Oxford, 1989); Andrew Bowie, *Aesthetics and Subjectivity: From Kant to Nietzsche* (Manchester, 1990); J. M. Bernstein, *The Fate of Art* (Oxford, 1992); Peter Osborne, *The Politics of Time* (London, 1995).

13 For Bakhtin, see Katerina Clark and Michael Holquist, *Mikhail Bakhtin* (Cambridge, Mass., 1984), Tzvetan Todorov, *Mikhail Bakhtin: The Dialogical Principle* (Manchester, 1984), and Ken Hirschkop, *Bakhtin and Democracy* (forthcoming).

14 For the general theory of postmodernity, see Hal Foster (ed.), *The Anti-aesthetic: Essays on Postmodern Culture* (Washington, 1983); Jean-François Lyotard, *The Postmodern Condition* (Manchester, 1984); David Harvey, *The Condition of Postmodernity* (Oxford, 1989); Jameson, *Postmodernism, or, The Cultural Logic of Late Capitalism*. Other general accounts include Christopher Norris, *The Contest of Faculties* (London, 1985), A. Kroker and D. Cook, *The Postmodern Scene* (New York, 1986), Ihab Hassan, *The Postmodern Turn* (Columbus, 1987), Jonathan Arac (ed.), *Postmodernism and Politics* (Manchester, 1986), John Fekete (ed.), *Life after Postmodernism* (London, 1988), and Alex Callinicos, *Against Postmodernism* (Cambridge, 1989).

15 For some general surveys, see Robert Venturi *et al.*, *Learning from Las Vegas* (Cambridge, Mass., 1977), Christopher Butler, *After the Wake* (Oxford, 1980), Ihab Hassan, *The Dismemberment of Orpheus* (New York, 1982), Linda Hutcheon, *Narcissistic Narrative* (Waterloo, Ontario, 1980) and *A Poetics of Postmodernism* (New York and London, 1988), Brian McHale, *Postmodernist Fiction* (New York and London, 1987), Patricia Waugh, *Metafiction* (London and New York, 1984), Lisa Appignanesi (ed.), *Postmodernism: ICA Documents 5* (London, 1986).

16 See Walter Benjamin, 'The Work of Art in the Age of Mechanical Reproduction', in Hannah Arendt (ed.), *Illuminations* (New York, 1969).

17 See Stanley Fish, *Doing What Comes Naturally* (Oxford, 1989), and Richard Rorty, *Contingency, Irony, and Solidarity* (Cambridge, 1989).

18 Edward Said's *Orientalism* (New York, 1979), is commonly regarded as the founding work of post-colonial theory; see also his *Culture and Imperialism* (London, 1993). Other influential texts are Benedict Anderson, *Imagined Communities* (London, 1983), Gayatri Chakravorty Spivak, *In Other Worlds* (New York and London, 1987), Robert Young, *White Mythologies* (London, 1990), Homi Bhabha (ed.), *Nation and Narration* (London and New York, 1990) and *The Location of Culture* (London, 1994). For an abrasive critique of post-colonial theory, see Aijaz Ahmad, *In Theory: Classes, Nations, Literatures* (London, 1992).

Bibliography

This bibliography is designed for readers who wish to follow up all or any of the various fields of literary theory dealt with in the book. Works under each heading are listed not alphabetically, but in an order in which they might best be tackled by a beginner. All the works discussed in the book are given, as well as some extra items, but I have kept the list as selective and so as manageable as possible. With a few exceptions, all of the works listed are in English.

Russian Formalism

Lee T. Lemon and Marion J. Reis (eds), *Russian Formalist Criticism: Four Essays*, Lincoln, Nebr., 1965

L. Matejka and K. Pomorska (eds), *Readings in Russian Poetics*, Cambridge, Mass., 1971

Stephen Bann and John E. Bowlt (eds), *Russian Formalism*, Edinburgh, 1973

Victor Erlich, *Russian Formalism: History–Doctrine*, The Hague, 1955

Fredric Jameson, *The Prison-House of Language*, Princeton, NJ, 1972

Tony Bennett, *Formalism and Marxism*, London, 1979

Ann Jefferson, 'Russian Formalism', in Ann Jefferson and David Robey (eds), *Modern Literary Theory: A Comparative Introduction*, London, 1982

P. N. Medvedev and M. M. Bakhtin, *The Formal Method in Literary Scholarship*, Baltimore, 1978

Christopher Pike (ed.), *The Futurists, the Formalists and the Marxist Critique*, London, 1979

English Criticism

Matthew Arnold, *Culture and Anarchy*, Cambridge, 1963
Literature and Dogma, London, 1873

T. S. Eliot, *Selected Essays*, London, 1963
  The Idea of a Christian Society, London, 1939; 2nd edn. London, 1982
  Notes Towards the Definition of Culture, London, 1948
F. R. Leavis, *New Bearings in English Poetry*, London, 1932
  and Denys Thompson, *Culture and Environment*, London, 1933
  Revaluation: Tradition and Development in English Poetry, London, 1936
  The Great Tradition, London, 1948
  The Common Pursuit, London, 1952
  D. H. Lawrence, Novelist, London, 1955
  The Living Principle, London, 1975
Q. D. Leavis, *Fiction and the Reading Public*, London, 1932
Francis Mulhern, *The Moment of 'Scrutiny'*, London, 1979
I. A. Richards, *Science and Poetry*, London, 1926
  Principles of Literary Criticism, London, 1924
  Practical Criticism, London, 1929
William Empson, *Seven Types of Ambiguity*, London, 1930
  Some Versions of Pastoral, London, 1935
  The Structure of Complex Words, London, 1951
  Milton's God, London, 1961
Christopher Norris, *William Empson and the Philosophy of Literary Criticism*,
    London, 1978
D. J. Palmer, *The Rise of English Studies*, London, 1965
C. K. Stead, *The New Poetic*, London, 1964
Chris Baldick, *The Social Mission of English Criticism*, Oxford, 1983

American New Criticism

John Crowe Ransom, *The World's Body*, New York, 1938
  The New Criticism, Norfolk, Conn., 1941
Cleanth Brooks, *The Well Wrought Urn*, London, 1949
W. K. Wimsatt and Monroe Beardsley, *The Verbal Icon*, New York, 1958
  and Cleanth Brooks, *Literary Criticism: A Short History*, New York, 1957
Allen Tate, *Collected Essays*, Denver, Col., 1959
Northrop Frye, *Anatomy of Criticism*, Princeton, NJ, 1957
David Robey, 'Anglo-American New Criticism', in Ann Jefferson and David
    Robey (eds), *Modern Literary Theory: A Comparative Introduction*, London,
    1982
John Fekete, *The Critical Twilight*, London, 1977
E. M. Thompson, *Russian Formalism and Anglo-American New Criticism*, The
    Hague, 1971

Frank Lentricchia, *After the New Criticism*, Chicago, 1980

Phenomenology and Hermeneutics

Edmund Husserl, *The Idea of Phenomenology*, The Hague, 1964
Philip Pettit, *On the Idea of Phenomenology*, Dublin, 1969
Martin Heidegger, *Being and Time*, London, 1962
   Introduction to Metaphysics, New Haven, Conn., 1959
   Poetry, Language, Thought, New York, 1971
William J. Richardson, *Heidegger: Through Phenomenology to Thought*, The Hague, 1963
H. J. Blackham, 'Martin Heidegger', in *Six Existentialist Thinkers*, London, 1961
Hans-Georg Gadamer, *Truth and Method*, London, 1975
Richard E. Palmer, *Hermeneutics*, Evanston, Ill., 1969
E. D. Hirsch, *Validity in Interpretation*, New Haven, Conn., 1976
Georges Poulet, *The Interior Distance*, Ann Arbor, 1964
Jean-Pierre Richard, *Poésie et profondeur*, Paris, 1955
   L'Univers imaginaire de Mallarmé, Paris, 1961
Jean Rousset, *Forme et signification*, Paris, 1962
Jean Starobinski, *L'Oeil vivant*, Paris, 1961
   La relation critique, Paris, 1972
J. Hillis Miller, *Charles Dickens: The World of his Novels*, Cambridge, Mass., 1959
   The Disappearance of God, Cambridge, Mass., 1963
   Poets of Reality, Cambridge, Mass., 1965
Robert R. Magliola, *Phenomenology and Literature*, West Lafayette, Ind., 1977
Sarah Lawall, *Critics of Consciousness*, Cambridge, Mass., 1968

Reception Theory

Roman Ingarden, *The Literary Work of Art*, Evanston, Ill., 1973
Wolfgang Iser, *The Implied Reader*, Baltimore, 1974
   The Act of Reading, London, 1978
Hans Robert Jauss, 'Literary History as a Challenge to Literary Theory', in Ralph Cohen (ed.), *New Directions in Literary Theory*, London, 1974
Jean-Paul Sartre, *What is Literature?*, London, 1978
Stanley Fish, *Is There a Text In This Class? The Authority of Interpretive Communities*, Cambridge, Mass., 1980
Umberto Eco, *The Role of the Reader*, Bloomington, Ill., 1979
Susan R. Suleiman and Inge Crosman (eds), *The Reader in the Text*, Princeton, NJ, 1980

Jane P. Tompkins (ed.), *Reader-Response Criticism*, Baltimore, 1980

Structuralism and Semiotics

Ferdinand de Saussure, *Course in General Linguistics*, London, 1978
Jonathan Culler, *Saussure*, London, 1976
Roman Jakobson, *Selected Writings* (4 vols.), The Hague, 1962
   and Morris Halle, *Fundamentals of Language*, The Hague, 1956
   Main Trends in the Science of Language, London, 1973
Paul Garvin (ed.), *A Prague School Reader on Esthetics, Literary Structure and Style*,
   Washington, DC, 1964
J. Vachek, *A Prague School Reader in Linguistics*, Bloomington, Ill., 1964
Jan Mukařovský, *Aesthetic Function, Norm and Value as Social Facts*, Ann Arbor,
   1970
Claude Lévi-Strauss, *The Savage Mind*, London, 1966
Edmund Leach, *Lévi-Strauss*, London, 1970
Vladimir Propp, *The Morphology of the Folktale*, Austin, Texas, 1968
A. J. Greimas, *Sémantique structurale*, Paris, 1966
   Du Sens, Paris, 1970
Claude Bremond, *Logique du récit*, Paris, 1973
Tzvetan Todorov, *Grammaire du Décaméron*, The Hague, 1969
Gérard Genette, *Narrative Discourse*, Oxford, 1980
   Figures of Literary Discourse, Oxford, 1982
Yury Lotman, *The Structure of the Artistic Text*, Ann Arbor, 1977
   Analysis of the Poetic Text, Ann Arbor, 1976
Umberto Eco, *A Theory of Semiotics*, London, 1977
Michael Riffaterre, *Semiotics of Poetry*, London, 1980
Mary Louise Pratt, *Towards a Speech Act Theory of Literary Discourse*, Bloomington,
   Ill., 1977
Terence Hawkes, *Structuralism and Semiotics*, London, 1977
Jacques Ehrmann (ed.), *Structuralism*, New York, 1970
Jonathan Culler, *Structuralist Poetics*, London, 1975
   The Pursuit of Signs, London, 1981
Fredric Jameson, *The Prison-House of Language*, Princeton, NJ, 1972
Michael Lane (ed.), *Structuralism: A Reader*, London, 1970
David Robey (ed.), *Structuralism: An Introduction*, Oxford, 1973
Richard Macksey and Eugenio Donato (eds), *The Structuralist Controversy: The
   Languages of Criticism and the Sciences of Man*, Baltimore, 1972

Post-Structuralism

Jacques Derrida, *Speech and Phenomena*, Evanston, Ill., 1973
   Of Grammatology, Baltimore, 1976

Writing and Difference, London, 1978
Positions, London, 1981
Ann Jefferson, 'Structuralism and Post-Structuralism', in Ann Jefferson and David
 Robey, *Modern Literary Theory: A Comparative Introduction*. London, 1982
Roland Barthes, *Writing Degree Zero*, London, 1967
 Elements of Semiology, London, 1967
 Mythologies, London, 1972
 S/Z, London, 1975
 The Pleasure of the Text, London, 1976
Michel Foucault, *Madness and Civilization*, London, 1967
 The Order of Things, London, 1970
 The Archaeology of Knowledge, London, 1972
 Discipline and Punish, London, 1977
 The History of Sexuality (vol. 1), London, 1979
Hayden White, 'Michel Foucault', in John Sturrock (ed.), *Structuralism and Since*,
 Oxford, 1979
Colin Gordon, *Michel Foucault: The Will to Truth*, London, 1980
Julia Kristeva, *La révolution du langage poétique*, Paris, 1974
 Desire in Language, Oxford, 1980
Paul de Man, *Allegories of Reading*, New Haven, Conn., 1979
Geoffrey Hartman (ed.), *Deconstruction and Criticism*, London, 1979
 Criticism in the Wilderness, Baltimore, 1980
J. Hillis Miller, *Fiction and Repetition*, Oxford, 1982
Rosalind Coward and John Ellis, *Language and Materialism*, London, 1977
Catherine Belsey, *Critical Practice*, London, 1980
Christopher Norris, *Deconstruction: Theory and Practice*, London, 1982
Josué V. Harari (ed.), *Textual Strategies*, Ithaca, NY, 1979
Jonathan Culler, *On Deconstruction*, London, 1982

Psychoanalysis

Sigmund Freud: see the volumes in the Pelican Freud Library (Harmondsworth,
 1973–86), esp. *Introductory Lectures on Psychoanalysis, The Interpretation of
 Dreams, On Sexuality* and the *Case Histories* (2 vols.)
Richard Wollheim, *Freud*, London, 1971
J. Laplanche and J.-B. Pontalis, *The Language of Psycho-Analysis*, London, 1980·
Herbert Marcuse, *Eros and Civilization*, London, 1956
Paul Ricoeur, *Freud and Philosophy*, New Haven, 1970
Jacques Lacan, *Ecrits: A Selection*, London, 1977
 The Four Fundamental Concepts of Psycho-Analysis, London, 1977
A. G. Wilden, *The Language of the Self*, Baltimore, 1968
Anika Lemaire, *Jacques Lacan*, London, 1977

Elizabeth Wright, 'Modern Psychoanalytic Criticism', in Ann Jefferson and David Robey, *Modern Literary Theory: A Comparative Introduction*, London, 1982
Simon Lesser, *Fiction and the Unconscious*, Boston, 1957
Norman N. Holland, *The Dynamics of Literary Response*, Oxford, 1968
  Five Readers Reading, New Haven, Conn., 1975
Ernst Kris, *Psychoanalytic Explorations in Art*, New York, 1952
Kenneth Burke, *Philosophy of Literary Form*, Baton Rouge, 1941
Harold Bloom, *The Anxiety of Influence*, London, 1975
  A Map of Misreading, London, 1975
  Poetry and Repression, New Haven, Conn., 1976
Colin MacCabe, *James Joyce and the Revolution of the Word*, London, 1978
Shoshana Felman (ed.), *Literature and Psychoanalysis*, Baltimore, 1982
Geoffrey Hartman (ed.), *Psychoanalysis and the Question of the Text*, Baltimore, 1978·

Feminism

Michèle Barrett, *Women's Oppression Today*, London, 1980
Mary Ellmann, *Thinking About Women*, New York, 1968
Juliet Mitchell, *Women's Estate*, Harmondsworth, 1977
M. Z. Rosaldo and L. Lamphere (eds), *Women, Culture and Society*, Stanford, 1974
S. McConnell-Ginet, R. Borker and N. Furman (eds), *Women and Language in Literature and Society*, New York, 1980
Kate Millett, *Sexual Politics*, London, 1971
Nancy Chodorow, *The Reproduction of Mothering: Psychoanalysis and the Sociology of Gender*, Berkeley, 1978
Juliet Mitchell, *Psychoanalysis and Feminism*, Harmondsworth, 1976
Annette Kuhn and AnnMarie Wolpe (eds), *Feminism and Materialism*, London, 1978
Jane Gallop, *Feminism and Psychoanalysis: The Daughter's Seduction*, London, 1982
Janine Chasseguet-Smirgel (ed.), *Female Sexuality*, Ann Arbor, 1970
Elaine Showalter, *A Literature of Their Own: British Women Novelists from Brontë to Lessing*, Princeton, NJ, 1977
Josephine Donovan, *Feminist Literary Criticism*, Lexington, Ky., 1975
Sandra Gilbert and Susan Gubar, *The Madwoman in the Attic*, London, 1979
Patricia Stubbs, *Women and Fiction: Feminism and the Novel 1880–1920*, London, 1979
Ellen Moers, *Literary Women*, London, 1980
Mary Jacobus (ed.), *Women Writing and Writing about Women*, London, 1979
Tillie Olsen, *Silences*, London, 1980
Elaine Marks and Isabelle de Courtivron (eds), *New French Feminisms*, Amherst, Mass., 1979

Julia Kristeva, *About Chinese Women*, New York, 1977
Hélène Cixous and Catherine Clément, *La jeune née*, Paris, 1975
Hélène Cixous, Madeleine Gagnon and Annie Leclerc, *La venue à l'écriture*, Paris, 1977
Hélène Cixous, 'The Laugh of the Medusa', in *Signs*, vol. 1, no. 4, 1976
Luce Iragaray, *Spéculum de l'autre femme*, Paris, 1974
    Ce sexe qui n'en est pas un, Paris, 1977
Sarah Kofman, *L'énigme de la femme*, Paris, 1980

Marxism

Terry Eagleton, *Marxism and Literary Criticism*, London, 1976
Raymond Williams, *Marxism and Literature*, Oxford, 1977
Pierre Macherey, *A Theory of Literary Production*, London, 1978
Terry Eagleton, *Criticism and Ideology*, London, 1976
Cliff Slaughter, *Marxism, Ideology and Literature*, London, 1980
Tony Bennett, *Formalism and Marxism*, London, 1979
Terry Lovell, *Pictures of Reality*, London, 1980
Lee Baxandall and Stefan Morowski (eds), *Marx and Engels on Literature and Art*, New York, 1973
Leon Trotsky, *Literature and Revolution*, Ann Arbor, 1971
Mikhail Bakhtin, *Rabelais and his World*, Cambridge, Mass., 1968
V. N. Voloshinov, *Marxism and the Philosophy of Language*, New York, 1973
Georg Lukács, *The Historical Novel*, London, 1974
    Studies in European Realism, London, 1975
Lucien Goldmann, *The Hidden God*, London, 1964
Christopher Caudwell, *Illusion and Reality*, London, 1973
John Willett (trans.), *Brecht on Theatre*, London, 1973
Walter Benjamin, *Understanding Brecht*, London, 1973
    Illuminations, London, 1973
    Charles Baudelaire, London, 1973
    One-Way Street and Other Writings, London, 1979
Terry Eagleton, *Walter Benjamin, or Towards a Revolutionary Criticism*, London, 1981
Pierre Macherey and Etienne Balibar, 'On Literature as an Ideological Form', in Robert Young (ed.), *Untying the Text*, London, 1981
Ernst Bloch *et al.*, *Aesthetics and Politics*, London, 1977
Fredric Jameson, *Marxism and Form*, Princeton, NJ, 1971
    The Political Unconscious, London, 1981
Martin Jay, *The Dialectical Imagination*, London, 1973
Raymond Williams, *Politics and Letters*, London, 1979
    Problems in Culture and Materialism, London, 1980

Index

Terry Eagleton is John Edward Taylor Professor of English Literature at the University of Manchester. His numerous books include *The Rape of Clarissa* and *Nationalism, Colonialism, and Literature* (with Fredric Jameson and Edward W. Said), both published by the University of Minnesota Press.